DEAD PETS

𝕰at them † 𝕾tuff them † 𝕷ove them

For Silky.
And for Henry,
who never met him.

DEAD PETS

Eat them † Stuff them † Love them

SAM LEITH

CANONGATE
Edinburgh · New York · Melbourne

First published in Great Britain in 2005 by
Canongate Books Ltd, 14 High Street,
Edinburgh EH1 1TE

1

British Library Cataloguing-in-Publication Data.
A catalogue record for this book is available on.
request from the British Library.

ISBN 1 84195 648 1

Designed and typeset by Estuary English.

Printed and bound by GGP Media, GmbH, Poessneck, Germany.

www.canongate.net

All photographs of Henry and Jay Jay © Alex Leith.

There is no final enough of wisdom,
experience — any fucking thing. No
Holy Grail, No Final Satori, no
solution. Just conflict.

Only thing that can resolve conflict is
love, like I felt for Fletch and Ruski,
Spooner, and Calico. Pure love. What
I feel for my cats past and present.
Love? What is it?

Most natural painkiller what there is.
LOVE.

WILLIAM S BURROUGHS' last written words

D E A D P E T S

INTRODUCTION

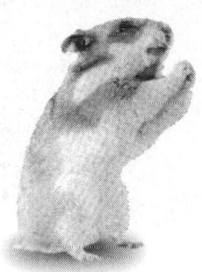

I REMEMBER SILKY. I remember him, or her, as if it were yesterday.

Silky was my truculent, unimaginatively named hamster. The apple of my six-year-old eye. All day long he would sleep, buried invisibly in the middle of a nest of paper which closely resembled the shredded white radish they give you in sushi restaurants. Sometimes, if his cage was shaken violently enough, his little golden nose would quest twitching from his bed to investigate a finger poked through the bars of his cage. Into this, he would sink his needle-sharp, caramel-coloured teeth. And every night, while I slept, Silky would spend his hours of wakefulness trying to escape.

It was not seldom that, around the time I was getting on the outside of my second bowl of pre-school Shreddies, the alarm would be raised. The door of the cage would be noticed swinging open, or one of the cleats fastening it to its plastic base would have popped mysteriously loose, or the furry Houdini would have found some way, with or without the collaboration of our several cats – who had their own reasons for being accomplices – to squeeze his tiny form through a wide place between two bars and head out, fearless or oblivious, into the wider world.

Stalag Luft Hamster had, again, been broached, and every human in the house would be conscripted to return my brave adventurer to protective custody. The cats, with their mysterious and shifting allegiances, would silently volunteer their help.

On one such occasion, Silky looked to have made it clean away. All the usual

procedures had been followed. Pipes had been knocked. Curtains had been drawn back and the indoor woodpile dismantled log by careful log onto the sitting-room carpet. Moments of silence – hands and knees shagged with downed cobwebs, ears cocked at the skirting boards – had been enjoined, in the hopes an unguarded, inquisitive squeak would give him away.

The long game, as the fugitive entered his seventh or eighth hour at large, had been tried. Forlorn trails of sunflower seeds had been sown, and ignored. Slippery jam-jars had been baited with little corners of cheese, and poised, uptilted invitingly, on opened books on the floor. Behind the sofa in the sitting room, I lay propped on my arms, as still as a Khe San sniper for ten or fifteen minutes, attention zeroed in on the length of string I had in my arms. A few feet away, in the middle of the room, the other end of the string was tethered to a stick; which in turn propped up one end of an upturned Tupperware dish, precariously, over a small pile of Shreddies.

Nothing doing. Evening was drawing on and, even given Silky's exceptional resourcefulness and aggression, my reserves of optimism were on the ebb. In my memory of this, it was late summer, and the light of the setting sun falling through the west-facing sash window of my bedroom and across my bed was mellow and golden. I had climbed the stairs, my face hot with unshed tears, and flopped in despair onto the coverlet. And on that instant I heard a single rising squeak, shrill as an unattended kettle, and heard, or perhaps felt, a crackle of fragile bones.

Silky had escaped the kitchen. Silky had negotiated the stairs. Silky had evaded the cats. And Silky had settled down for a nice kip somewhere warm and dark and safe – between my mattress and my bedstead. And my careless six-year-old bottom had crushed him to death.

When I lifted the mattress, what I saw was pitiful. His small body was perpendicular to the side of the bed, just halfway up. Just where I had sat down to mourn him. And his nose, so often dabbed with my blood, was now soggy with his own. The whole front half of his body was scarlet; the back still pale and furry. The image that strikes me now, though I doubt it would have then, is of a partially used tampon. No end for a hamster.

And presently, I was making a high shrill noise of my own.

Silky, then, was my introduction to dramatic irony. But he was also my introduction to death. And nearly everyone's first encounter with death, if they are lucky, comes in the form of the death of a pet; everyone's first preparation for the lifelong task of grief.

All those tiny extinctions.

I think of the sickly goldfish jouncing back from the fairground in a miraculously bulging clear polythene bag of water – and extravagantly mourned three days later in an earthed matchbox, or in a Viking funeral attended by the smell of bleach and a roar of water. And oh. All those doomed terrapins.

I think of my swimming, looping colony of tiny sea-monkeys, tenderly hatched from seeds – my only companions in a lonely Tribeca apartment, boiled to death in their plastic aquarium when I left it, carelessly, in the direct sunlight of a New York summer.

I think of my own gerbils: robust, cobweb-coloured Eurydice and her companion, a smaller, trembling albino I named Persephone (I was a pretentious and, perhaps even then, morbid child). I doted on Eurydice just as I once had on Silky. I remember watching in astonishment, one night, when a moth blundered into her cage and she plucked it, one-handed, from the air, folded its wings primly down against its flanks and ate it head first as if it were a sunflower seed.

When Eurydice succumbed to cancer, or starvation, or whatever, and returned to the underworld, my parents would not let me see the body. I finally winkled out of them why. It was because Persephone – in for a few pomegranate seeds, in for the full *menu dégustation* – had taken the opportunity to chew all the meat off her fallen companion's hindleg. Pale fur, again stained with blood.

I think of the colonnades of lollystick gravestones, or gravestones pressed with childish thumbs from clay, which rise and fall in the quiet corners of suburban gardens.

I think of the countless cats and dogs which "went to sleep" or "were in a lot of pain" or "are with Grandma in Heaven" – cats and dogs the watchful child saw grow thin, stalking the margins of corridors, defecating eccentrically, dripping from ears or nose, unwashed knots of fur clotting their coats …

Pets teach us about loss, and about the nature of the world. But they also teach us about responsibility. Think of the first time a child dimly intuits, in the screech of brakes and the whomp of an impact on the other side of the hedge, the connection between letting Buster slip the lead and Buster going to visit Grandma in Heaven.

And these lessons are often learned, too, among other children.

Remember the one child who would return to school after having had the school gerbils to look after over the holiday? (Measles and Mumps, or Bubble and Squeak, school gerbils always seemed to be called.) And remember the child's downcast eyes; its unconvincing insouciance. Remember the looks of mistrust and suspicion from his or her classmates; unwhispered the observation that Measles had come back looking thinner, or a different colour than you remembered, or female.

I think of my friend Rebekah, one of whose two giant African land snails (Triptych and Coriander) actually did, whimsically, change sex, and start breeding with its companion. All of one long summer the ice compartment in her fridge was a mollusc Auschwitz, as tray after tray of their legions of offspring was slid in for extermination by freezing.

I never knew till then that freezing was the best way of killing baby snails. Animals seldom excite the stirrings of scientific curiosity in children more than in the manner of their deaths – though the chain of cause and effect is equally often, if we are honest, the other way round.

Witness an incident I have no personal memory of, but which my mother has often told me about over the years. I was no more than seven or eight; my brother Alex, two and a half years younger. She came upon us both lying companionably side by side on the floor one day, propped on our elbows, scrutinising something just out of her sight on the carpet in front of us.

She tiptoed up, feeling fond and maternal, to eavesdrop on our conversation. Yikes. What we were studying was the messy corpse of a squirrel, thoroughly cat-chewed from the waist down. "What do you think it died of?" my little brother was asking in a reverential whisper. I replied with an air of great sagacity, "A brain haemorrhage. Definitely."

We owe these creatures furred and feathered, faithful fallen companions, our thanks.

But it was Silky, of all of them, that stayed with me. The last squeak. I sometimes

think that, having had a childhood of otherwise exemplary happiness, it is to that moment – to the squeak of a dying hamster – that I owe all my subsequent personality problems. The drinking, the inexplicable objectless rages, the crushing paranoia and anxiety, the suicidal ideation, the low thrum of depression that underscores what should by all accounts be one big episode of *Tiswas*.

In his poem "As I Walked Out One Evening", W H Auden wrote:

> *In the burrows of the Nightmare*
> *Where Justice naked is*
> *Time watches from the shadow*
> *And coughs when you would kiss.*

It's like that for me, too. It's Silky. Silky squeaks when I would smile.

I need to settle some sort of account. I need to write this book: a sort of garden of remembrance, with digressions, for all those loved creatures who have gone, and whose archetype, for me, is that little golden hamster I squashed so many years ago. Then, perhaps, as I lie in that place between waking and sleep, I will at last hear it: the silence of the hamsters.

Very few of the pets you will read about here are alive. But the silent majority rest in memory, in the bosom of the Almighty or in the belly of next door's mastiff, in legend, in visited and unvisited graves. *Requiescant in pace.*

A NOTE ON the methodology: there isn't one. There are nearly as many dead pets as there are dead human beings, so I have been selective, and have followed my natural inclinations. I have jumbled real historical dead pets with mythic ones and, for the home enthusiast, included some pointers as to how to stuff them or to stuff yourself with them, as you prefer. Any eccentricities of choice are mine, and the many factual errors and omissions likewise.

Finally, this not being a work of academic scholarship, I make no apologies for stretching the definition of the word 'pet' from time to time. Also the word "dead".

WESSEX TAILS

THOMAS HARDY'S DOG WESSEX WAS, TO HEAR MOST PEOPLE TELL IT, AS VICIOUS A LITTLE BRUTE AS EVER WALKED GOD'S GREEN EARTH AT THE HEIGHT OF A SHIN. A WIRE-HAIRED TERRIER "OF SORTS WITH A PEDIGREE UNKNOWN TO THE KENNEL CLUB", ACCORDING TO THE HARDY ENTHUSIAST RICHARD CURLE, WESSEX BOTH BARKED AT AND BIT THOSE AROUND HIM MORE OR LESS INDISCRIMINATELY: POSTMEN, STOATS, YOU NAME IT.

IN ONE OF THE few surviving portraits of him, a black and white photograph, he looks like a heap of mops. Hardy doted on him.

Wessex arrived in the Hardy household at the age of four months, in September 1913. Florence Hardy, the poet's widow, was as kind as she was able to Wessex in the biography she wrote of her husband.

"This dog," she wrote, "a wire-haired terrier, was of great intelligence and very friendly to many who visited Max Gate,[1] though he had defects of temper, due perhaps to want of thorough training." That is to say, he used fiercely to attack unwanted visitors, and other visitors also. The only person Wessex ever let pick him up was Lawrence of Arabia.

According to Hardy's perhaps more clear-eyed modern biographer, Michael Millgate, Wessex was "quarrelsome, snappish and generally ill-behaved, a perpetual cause of trouble and anxiety, but Hardy treated him with a tenderness and indulgence even greater than Florence's".

Hardy was a notorious old skinflint – even wondering, in a gloomy and paranoid moment in 1917[2] whether it was possible to feed a wife and dog on a diet entirely consisting of cow-parsley (a bountiful natural resource in the Max Gate area). He never carried this plan through – quite the reverse, in fact, at least as regarded the dog.

Wessex was not only issued with his own fluffy eiderdown to lie on in Hardy's study, but was given goose and plum pudding to eat at Christmas. Millgate charges Hardy, furthermore, with "making no offer to clear up the mess when he was, predictably, sick". There, we must assume, went poor old Florence after Christmas lunch, on hands and knees with shovel and newspaper, paper hat skew-whiff, and still perhaps tasting her festive cow-parsley lunch.

Florence Hardy credited Wessex with psychic powers. "Among those to whom he showed partiality," she recalled, "was Mr William Watkins, the honorary secretary to the Society of Dorset Men in London."

On the evening of April 18th, 1925, Watkins dropped by Max Gate to visit. Wessex rushed into the hallway at the sound of his arrival and "as was his wont ... greeted his friend with vociferous barks.[3] Suddenly these gave way to a piteous whine." Wessex followed Watkins around, prodding him from time to time with a paw, but then withdrawing it with "a sharp cry of distress".

Watkins, ignoring the dog, left an hour later, around ten o' clock, looking cheery and full of beans. Early the next morning Watkins's son called to announce that his

---

[1] Max Gate was Hardy's house near Dorchester.

[2] He was in a particularly stinky mood at the ruinous cost of the injections his wife was receiving for her pharyngitis.

[3] We must take Florence's word, I suppose, over the exampled evidence of Wessex's character, as to the friendliness of these barks.

father had dropped abruptly dead only an hour after returning from Max Gate.

It was the habit of Wessex to bark vociferously whenever the phone rang. On this occasion, Florence tells us however, he "remained silent, his nose between his paws". It is, obviously, possible to conjecture that the signs Florence was reading as a prodigy of empathy were nothing other than the tokens of guilt, and that Wessex had, by some unspecified contrivance, killed his so-called friend, Mr Watkins. But where would be the sense in that? We must give Wessex the benefit of the doubt.

Wessex was the subject of a rather twee fictional *jeu d'esprit* published in 1964 by J Stevens Cox at the Toucan Press, Beaminster, Dorset. *The Return of Wessex* affected to be written, postmortem, by the dog, under the name Wessex Redivivus.

Wessex – the "fiery, faithful little dog" of Richard Curle's introduction – announces that "I've come back from the shady lanes and groves where dogs go when nobody has any more use for them and they're forgotten", and makes a complaint at his unflattering portrayal on the front cover of *The Domestic Life of Thomas Hardy* "with my back turned to the Missus's bath-tub ... it's a positive scandal". Well.

The reminiscences in *The Return of Wessex* are said to have been based, at least tenuously, on the historical evidence, so it's fair to set down what we learn from them. Wessex confirms his affection for T E Lawrence, who used to visit as "Mr Shaw". He makes no mention of the Watkins incident, though he seems to hint at a possible explanation for his habitual bad temper, alluding darkly to "brimstone in my water pot".

Wessex was responsible for one minor archaeological discovery, unearthing a Samian potsherd depicting long dogs chasing a hare. Wessex himself would have been lucky to get hold of a hare, though walking with Hardy in Came Wood one fine June day, Wessex met a hedgehog. Wessex showed every sign of wishing to eat the hedgehog, so the hedgehog rolled itself up into a ball.

HARDY: "Can't you manage him, Wessie?"
(Turns hedgehog over with stick. Hedgehog looks unappetising even this way up.)

HARDY: "Well, no, you're very wise, really."

Wessex did, on another occasion, eat a number of flying ants.

HARDY: "No, no, Wessex. Not dog-food."

And so on.

By the time Hardy was 80, Wessex's viciousness was in full flower. Millgate alludes, in the same paragraph as a mention of Wessex, to an "acute … servant problem" in the household. Were they related? We can speculate. Wessex, he says, "not only bit postmen and terrorised servants but had once killed a stoat after a long and bloody battle".

The steady eclipse of Wessex's wellbeing coincided closely with the drawing of shadows over his master's own life. In 1926, Hardy himself was very old and knackered, and in November said good-bye to his, and Wessex's, dear friend Lawrence of Arabia, who was starting for India.

Lawrence called by Max Gate. The way Florence records it, Hardy knew that he was seeing him off for the last time.

"Hardy was much affected by this parting, as T E Lawrence was one of his most valued friends. He went into the little porch and stood at the front door to see the departure of Lawrence on his motor-bicycle. This machine was difficult to start, and, thinking he might have to wait some time, Hardy turned into the house to fetch a shawl to wrap round him. In the meantime, fearing that Hardy might take a chill, Lawrence started the motor-bicycle and hurried away."

One imagines the old poet shuddering back out onto the porch, in a cold November wind, shawl wrapped round him, watching the motorcycle round a corner and pass out of sight, grieving all the more for the botched good-bye.

By Christmas, Wessex, now thirteen years old, was ill and obviously near his end. He had developed a tumour. The festive season was passed cheerlessly, and two days after Christmas, he passed. Hardy wrote in his journal:

27 December. Our famous dog Wessex died at half past six in the evening, thirteen years of age.

28. Wessex buried.

28. *Night.* Wessex sleeps outside the house the first time for thirteen years.

Wessex was buried in a small turfed grave, in the shrubbery on the west side of Max Gate, where he remains to this day, alongside several pet cats and one other dog, called Moss.

Hardy designed Wessex's headstone himself. It looks like this:

THE
FAMOUS DOG
WESSEX
August 1913 – 27 Dec 1926
Faithful. Unflinching.

From Florence: "There were those among Hardy's friends who thought that his life was definitely saddened by the loss of Wessex, the dog having been the companion of himself and his wife during twelve years of married life. Upon summer evenings or winter afternoons Wessex would walk with them up the grassy slope in the field in front of their house, to the stile that led into Came Plantation, and while Hardy rested on the stile the dog would sit on the ground and survey the view as his master was doing. On Frome Hill when his companions sat on the green bank by the roadside, or on the barrow that crowns the hill, he would lie in the grass at their feet and gaze at the landscape, 'as if', to quote Hardy's oft-repeated comment on this, 'it were the right thing to do'."

The day after Wessex was buried, Florence wrote to a friend: "Of course he was merely a dog, & not a good dog always, but *thousands* (actually thousands) of afternoons & evenings I would have been alone but for him, & had always him to speak to. But I mustn't write about him, & I hope no one will ask me about him or mention his name."

The keenness with which both felt Wessex's death is evidenced elsewhere. When Virginia Woolf visited Max Gate the following summer, she described – sour old cow that she was – Florence as having "the large sad lack lustre eyes of a childless woman".

Maybe there's something in that. Moss, the first dog buried in the Max Gate cemetery, belonged to Hardy and his first wife, Emma. He had been beaten

to death by a tramp in the autumn of 1890, and Millgate speculates that the reason he was not immediately replaced was that "to this childless couple who increasingly and almost pathologically made children of their pets, the experience of losing Moss was too painful to bear repetition". Instead, they had cats, who were also buried in the pet cemetery. One of them was called "Kiddleywinkempoops".[4]

†4 Mercifully, known as "Trot" for short. Those of us who prefer to keep pristine our image of Hardy as a bleakly noble tragedian may choose to assume Emma named the moggy.

Perhaps Florence's affection for Wessex – she, like Emma, was childless – was maternal in character. Hardy himself, at times, seemed to love the dog more than he loved his wife. When in the autumn of 1924 Florence underwent a life-threatening operation to remove a cancerous tumour from her neck, Hardy decided to stay in the country rather than go down to London to be with her. Florence, poignantly, explained her husband's absence to Sydney Cockerell[5] as being out of concern for the dog's well-being: it would have "broken his heart (literally) if we had both gone away".

†5 Director of the Fitzwilliam Museum in Cambridge. He went on to be, along with Florence, Hardy's joint literary executor.

It was a peculiar affectation of Hardy, as far as I can tell, that the dog should have been described as "famous". During his life Wessex – psychic powers, vociferous barking and occasional interest in the life contemplative notwithstanding – does not seem to have enjoyed any especial celebrity. In fact, though Florence encouraged Hardy to write a poem about Wessex, the poet insisted he would not do so until the dog was good and dead. So, duly, he wrote the following elegy:

DEAD "WESSEX" THE DOG TO THE HOUSEHOLD

Do you think of me at all,
Wistful ones?
Do you think of me at all
As if nigh?
Do you think of me at all
At the creep of evenfall,
As when the sky-birds call
As they fly?

Do you look for me at times,
Wistful ones?
Do you look for me at times
Strained and still?
Do you look for me at times,
When the hour for walking chimes,
On that grassy path that climbs
Up the hill?

You may hear a jump or trot,
Wistful ones,
You may hear a jump or trot –
Mine, as 'twere –
You may hear a jump or trot
On the stair or path or plot;
But I shall cause it not,
Be not there.

Should you call as when I knew you,
Wistful ones,
Should you call as when I knew you,
Shared your home;
Should you call as when I knew you,
I shall not turn to view you,
I shall not listen to you,
Shall not come.

I found this poem almost unbearably moving until I realised that it can be sung, with some jollity, to the tune of "She'll Be Coming Round The Mountain When She Comes".

CHAPTER 1

HENRY I

AS I SIT writing this, there is a black cat sitting, patiently, between me and my story. He positions himself dead centre on the scuffed red leather of my dead grandfather's old desk, tail curled round himself, aspect upright, face intent on the screen. My hands are forced to reach round either side of him to get at the keyboard. From time to time, a swift movement of the cursor triggers some sort of hard-wired hunting instinct, and he bats at the screen with a paw.

I occasionally try to move him. But, in the way of cats – which know, for example, unerringly which particular story you are reading in a newspaper, and will unfailingly sit on it, purring – he will be determined to return to exactly where he was. This will involve slithering out of my hands, hopping painfully from floor to lap – he's still too young to be able to jump the whole way, but has learned that ten front claws speared firmly into layers of first denim and then human flesh are sufficient to bear his weight – hopping from lap to keyboard, and wandering round on the keyboard before settling where he was.

My mother once lost two months' work to a cat strolling across her keyboard. Cats know where the delete key sits. You don't want to piss them off.

If you shut Henry outside the study, he cries and scrabbles at the door. It's not

pretty, but it's effective. Easiest to leave him here. Besides, I'm soft. Henry is my first cat, and Henry is eight weeks old.

I was writing a book about dead pets before I owned a live one. When I got him, I thought: "Good. This is a win-win situation. If he stays alive I have a cat. If some terrible accident befalls him, I have some more material for my book."

Cats are good things. I grew up with cats. Among my earliest memories are memories of cats.

Here are some examples:

1) Sitting on the end of my parents' bed on the morning of my mother's thirtieth birthday, when I was six or seven, and Mum announcing with pride that there was a new member of our family called Ferdie. Bursting into tears.

2) Slowly appreciating, when he emerged from under the bedclothes, that Ferdie was not – as I had instantly imagined, and the image persists to this day – a hairy grown-up stranger resembling a thinner and more Turkish-looking version of Tom Selleck in *Magnum PI*, who would henceforth be sharing my parents' life and affection in a bizarre but altruistic ménage à trois, from which I would be excluded.

3) Realising that Ferdie was, in fact, a Siamese red-point kitten, and that things were going to be just fine.

4) Realising, more than twenty years later, that I was a more anxious child than, given my happy circumstances, I strictly needed to be.

5) Growing familiar with the sudden, hair-raising yowling and spitting many-limbed cartoon furball that would irrupt horizontally into the kitchen at head height when Ferdie and our other cats, for reasons yet unfathomable to human science, would decide to have a fight.

6) Discovering areas of carpet unexpectedly swampy with cat pee, disgusting to the careless foot of the sock-wearing child.

7) Becoming a connoisseur of the glue-sniffing pungency of cat pee; of the strange caterpillar-arching backwards boogie of the about-to-be-sick cat, and of the horrible chunkiness of what it invariably then produced just seconds before you could hurl it out of the window.

8) Checking my shoes for dead mice, and parts of dead mice.

9) Watching with disgust as my infant brother soothed himself by sucking the ears of our most senile cat, Jen (who dribbled incessantly, incidentally, from the nose and ears alike) in the last years of her life.

10) Watching with profound suspicion as my no-longer-infant brother, now 28 and still living with me, eyes our new kitten with something like hunger.

Which brings me back to Henry. It being lunchtime, there I was, in the pub, when my colleague Ulrike dropped by for a drink on her way back from the other pub. The tale she told was full of woe. She had just bought her gorgeous six-year-old son Cameron a kitten for his birthday. Tears sprang to his little eyes; in fact, his eyes streamed. Instead of swelling up with pride and excitement, little Cameron swelled up with galloping all-over eczema. Instead of choking up with emotion, he choked up with a profound, throat-closing allergy.

So, Ulrike was faced with the realisation that however much Cameron loved Bagheera, whom he had named after a favourite character in *The Jungle Book*, she was going to have to donate Bagheera to a good home or, failing that, a bad home, before her son, literally, expired.

This is where I came in. For as she said, "Do you know anyone who wants a kitten?", and I took another gulp of my delicious beer, a thought entered my brain. This was unexpected. However, it was not, for all the reasons numbered above, the first time that such a thought had formed in my brain; rather, it was the first time that the stimulus and response loop (that is to say, me) had been so tight.

"Me," was the thought.

"M—" was what I said, before thinking better of it.

"Me me me! I want a kitten!" the thought repeated. I sat, smoking sagely and ignoring it. Something nagged away at me. It was to do with the essential futility and directionlessness of my life. I lived in a miserable state of arrested adolescence, incapable of hanging onto a girlfriend, and having survived three decades without taking personal responsibility for more than making sure there was enough to drink in the house by closing time, and that I had paid the cable bill recently enough so I didn't miss *South Park* . . .

Why would I want to ruin all that by getting a kitten?

"Me!" I emailed Ulrike after lunch. "Me! I want a kitten ..."

Within 48 hours, my brother and I were sitting in our Brixton flat at breakfast time making googly eyes at a bewildered, shorthaired black moggy. The mog in question was a shade smaller than one of my eight-hole Dr Marten boots, and approximately the same shape.

We were daddies. The *pride*.

We had that very morning got up unprecedentedly early – something like 7.30. It was after a night of very uneven sleep for me. Dreams had run into dreams, all of them infested with cats. I woke, went back to sleep, woke, hovered on the threshold of sleep. Cats cats cats. Terrible dread. Horrible anxiety. Cats neglected; cats forgotten; cats multiplying till the house was full of them; cats suffering deaths in the mouths of three-legged dogs; cuts from broken wineglasses ... malevolence, failure ...

We had driven in our crappy little car – an ancient Suzuki Swift with one wing mirror held on by gaffer tape, and bodywork so flimsy that the last time crackheads broke in to nick the stereo, they didn't bother breaking the glass but just bent the top of the door back – to Forest Hill, and found Ulrike getting ready for work with a towel on her head.

Her son was looking mournful. Ulrike was looking mournful. Ulrike's boyfriend was looking mournful. In the middle of the wooden floor was a small white wire cage lined with a blue foam pad, and beside it was a ridiculously tiny kitten. That was Bagheera.

We spent a few slightly awkward minutes. We watched Cameron's tearful, wheezy goodbye. Then, half-apologetic, half-greedy, we scooped up all the cat's goodies – litter tray, spare food, flea treatment – as if we were looting a pet shop at a time of national tragedy. We felt like murderers. The cat cried all the way home.

"The Naming of Cats is a difficult matter," T S Eliot warned. "It isn't just one of your holiday games." Nor it is. The fact that this cat had arrived pre-named was a source of anguish to me. Not least because it was called Bagheera. I couldn't own a cat called Bagheera.

Yet why did I feel guilty about changing its name? It wasn't as if this vagrant collection of fur and bone – which had just been given its third home and third

name in fewer months than it had been alive – was going to notice, let alone care. Nevertheless, it needed to be called Henry, for reasons which made sense to me but will seem risibly pretentious to the world at large.

The point is that there was a prearranged slot in my head for a cat called Henry, because of my loyalty[6] to the American poet John Berryman. Berryman was a gloomy, bearded, bespectacled drunk who looked, in at least one author photograph, transfixingly like Ricky Tomlinson in *The Royle Family*. He ended his life, silly bugger, by throwing himself off a bridge in Minneapolis in 1972.

Before he did that, though, he wrote a long, wonderful,

†6 Can you owe loyalty to someone who is dead and you have never met? Christians think so.

riddlingly strange sequence of poems called the *Dream Songs*, starring a character called Henry, who acts as a rough proxy for Berryman himself. Berryman's friend Robert Lowell called the *Songs* "poignant, abrasive, anguished, humorous", and they are. But what's great about the *Songs*, is that as well as being sad, they are really, actually funny – funny ha-ha – in a way that very little serious poetry is. They often read like a set of ruefully comical suicide notes. They banter with you, they cajole, they turn cartwheels, they sympathise. Henry, who often addresses you as "friend" or "pal", and whose voice is as utterly distinctive as any in poetry, does become a sort of friend. And at times over the years that I've been addicted to him, Henry's voice has been a real comfort.

And because they are dream songs, Henry – like any figure in a dream – changes shape. Sometimes he's a middle-aged man in a bar. Sometimes he's a crazed veteran holed up in the mountains with a gun. A good few times he is in the process of being dismantled. Often he's blacked-up as an old-style minstrel. Once he's even a wee boat, chugging away with an outboard motor. But a lot of the time, he's a cat:

I am Henry Pussy-cat! My whiskers fly.

(From 'Dream Song 22')

So I wanted a real Henry Pussy-cat. And now I had one.

We plonked his cage in the middle of the sitting-room rug, and opened the door, and shuffled arse-backwards away from him on knees or tiptoes, and watched him start to wander out. He left the cage with his head low, sniffing. One paw would advance, pat the carpet, retreat, advance again, take a little weight, retreat, advance again. He sniffed in tiny circles, widening them steadily, testing his claws on the rough rug. It took him maybe ten minutes to conquer the rug and start moving out into the kitchen, the bathroom, the foot of the stairs.

But it didn't take him long to get brave. Once he was satisfied the rug wasn't going to bushwhack him when he wasn't looking, he began a long and highly aerobatic battle with a host of imaginary enemies. He was, like all kittens, easily distracted by bits of string.

Twenty minutes later, my friend Sophia, who was living in my spare room at the time, came down the stairs wrapped in her towel, heading for the bathroom. She paused, and squinted down at her feet. "Is that a … *cat?*"

HENRY HAD BEEN in my home for approximately two hours when the following thought hit me:

If he dies, nobody will ever believe that it was an accident.

✦✦✦ FIVE INTERESTING THINGS TO DO WITH YOUR DEAD PET ✦✦✦

1 : [OF 5] TURN IT INTO AN ETERNAL DIAMOND OF REMEMBRANCE

A SWISS FIRM called Algordanza, which previously specialised in turning human remains into artificial diamonds, is now accepting animal corpses. The diamonds can be laser-inscribed with the animal's names and dates – legible by magnifying glass – and displayed on a tasteful ornamental base, or even set into a ring or pendant. The process of turning the ashes into a diamond takes between two and three weeks and costs an absolute fortune.

DEADPETS
Case Study No. 2

BLONDI:
HAIRY ARYAN

BY 1944, HITLER WAS FUCKED.

AND DIDN'T THE fun-sized genocidal maniac know it? As the German war effort crumbled around his ears, Hitler told anyone who would listen – according to Hugh Trevor-Roper,[7] in his *The Last Days of Hitler* (Macmillan, 1947) – that there were only two people on earth he could trust. One was Eva Braun, his blonde-haired, blue-eyed doxie. The other was Blondi, his blonde-haired, brown-eyed dog. He added, ominously and quite in defiance of common sense, that at the final hour and in the last ditch, he knew that the

[7] Later Lord Dacre. Distinguished historian. Not to be confused with Paul Dacre, editor of the *Daily Mail*. Lord Dacre's reputation was damaged in the autumn of his career by his vouching for the authenticity of the 'Hitler Diaries', a funny hoax which was to have

continued overleaf

been one of the few true stories ever to appear in the news pages of the *Sunday Times*, but then wasn't. Not really Hugh's fault. Though he initially held the diaries to be genuine, he changed his mind at the eleventh hour, and told the newspaper so. He was overruled by the distinguished historian Rupert Murdoch, with the words "Fuck Dacre".

†8
Indeed, Hitler's love of dogs ignited a minor historical debate in 1995 when a Labour MP, John Battle, joined battle in the pages of the *Catholic Herald*: "Walking back to the House of Commons from Pall Mall a friend urged me to have a glance at the dog's grave next to a monument to Frederick, the Duke of York, at the top of the steps at the end of Waterloo Place," he wrote. "It's a small gravestone, dated 1934, marking the grave of 'Ciro', Hitler's dog, opposite what was formerly the German Embassy. My friend commented that only in England could be found a monument commemorating Hitler's pet dog. Does English sentimentality know no bounds?" What? Interrogated by an enterprising *Evening Standard* journalist, Mr Battle insisted: "I've seen it myself. It's behind some railings and under a bush. It's written in German." The headstone, marked "London, February 1934", bore the legend "Ein Treuer Begleiter": "a true companion". The German

continued right

only one who would stick by him was Eva.

Did he expect Blondi to betray him? If so, that might go some way to explaining what happened afterwards. But for a time, at least, there was an uneasy détente. In 1945, while he directed the dying throes of the war from his final redoubt – his reinforced concrete bunker beneath the Reich Chancellery in Berlin – Hitler had Blondi, and her puppy Wolf, by his side. His few excursions from the bunker (air-raid warnings tended to serve as an alarm clock) were to give Blondi a breath of fresh air.

"Woof," we can imagine her saying, as she watched the master developing a series of Herbert-Lom-in-the-*Pink-Panther*-style tics. We can't know what was in her head. Living in an underground bunker, what was in her head was probably: "Walkies."

Hitler's fondness for Blondi followed a familiar pattern. He liked dogs disproportionately.[8] When he was fighting in the First World War, he adopted a dog that had crossed the lines, and named her Foxl. Towards the end of the war, Foxl went missing. "Whoever stole her," he said, "will never understand what the loss meant to me."

Hitler's butler, Heinz Linge, was captured by Russians towards the end of the Second World War and interrogated on Stalin's orders. It was only in early 2005 that the transcripts of those interrogations finally emerged. Stalin's men had done their work. Herr Linge cracked under the pressure and confessed that when Blondi fell ill, Hitler insisted she be provided with a special ration of eggs, lean meat and dripping. He was given regular updates on her progress, and woe betide the bearer of bad news: "It was easier for him to sign a death warrant for an officer on the front than to swallow bad news about the health of his dog."

In happier times, Hitler even tried to give Blondi the sexual satisfaction that he seemed to find so elusive himself. He commanded a breeder to produce a pedigree[9] male dog, and introduce it to Blondi. Emerging from a briefing on the progress of the war on the Eastern Front, Hitler asked Herr Linge whether Blondi and her mate had got it on. "Yes, my Führer, the Act of State has been completed." "How did Blondi take it?" "They both behaved like beginners." "How do you mean?" "They both fell down."

Hitler, according to Herr Linge, burst into laughter at this exchange. I confess to finding it baffling. Let us ascribe it to the differing national sensibilities reflected in the celebrated German sense of humour.

By April 29th, 1945, however, the game was well and truly up. On the afternoon of that day, Hitler summoned his former surgeon, Professor Werner Haase, to the bunker, and introduced him to Blondi.

She was born a dog but she died a guinea-pig: as Hitler's paranoia reached its apex, he started to fret that the ampoules of prussic acid prepared[10] as suicide pills for himself and the staff might not work. Blondi had to go first.

Hitler did not attend her murder. With the help of the dog-handler, Sgt Fritz Tornow, Professor Haase forced open Blondi's jaws and crushed a capsule in her mouth with a pair of pliers. She died instantly. Hitler came in afterwards, looked at her body, and left without a word to lock himself into his room. Did he cry?

Later, Hitler, looking glazed, shook a number of his bunkermates' hands, and presented his secretaries with a poison capsule each as a farewell present. The two other dogs in Hitler's household – more kindly, some will think – were shot.

The last man to leave the *Führerbunker* was Hitler's Luftwaffe adjutant, Col Nicolaus von Below. At midnight, von Below went above. Hitler remained below. The rest is history.

embassy, at the time, sought to defuse the potential diplomatic row. They insisted that the dog was actually called Giro, not Ciro, and that it had been an Alsatian belonging to Leopold von Hoesch, last ambassador of the Weimar Republic to the Court of St James's.

†9
Obviously.

†10
According to Ian Kershaw in his magisterial *Hitler 1936–1945: Nemesis*, these were created by an SS surgeon with the magnificent name of Dr Ludwig Stumpfegger.

CHAPTER 2

WHERE THE DEAD LIVE

PART ONE
CALIFORNIA

"SKIPPY", THE LITTLE peeling wooden grave marker said. "He loved life."

I don't think you ever really forget your first pet cemetery – the first marker that catches the eye and tweaks the heart.

I certainly won't forget mine. I was in California on a job. It was high summer.

†11
Among the Pixies' best songs is one that may be considered relevant: 'Monkey Gone To Heaven'.

I was due to report on a burlesque striptease competition in the Mojave desert a couple of days later. I had a big red Chevrolet and a brand new CD of the Pixies album *Trompe Le Monde* to help me get there,[11] and for the moment I was in San Francisco, killing time and looking for dead pets.

Why California? Evelyn Waugh's brilliant short novel *The Loved One*, probably the literary locus classicus for animal interment, is set in California. (Actually, it's set in LA, but LA is – as Waugh, to give him his due, more than hinted – a town simply too hostile to human life to sustain extensive journalistic research.) *The Loved One* contains two parallel cemeteries – or, rather, two businesses offering full-service packages of embalming, interment, ritual and commemoration. Whispering Glades is for humans. The Happier Hunting Ground is for pets. The novel's hero starts out working in the latter, and is, as it were, promoted to the former. The suggestion is that they are not substantially different. They are both kind of cheesy. Waugh's novel has a certain blackness of heart.

Waugh's description of the lurid awfulness of Whispering Glades was based almost exactly on a real cemetery in LA, Forest Lawn. When the typescript of *The Loved One* was presented to a legal adviser for Waugh's publisher, Chapman and Hall, the gentleman in question went bananas. He was firmly of the opinion that they could be sued for libel, and therefore refused to sanction its publication.

Crafty old Evelyn had an idea. He gave a copy of the typescript to his friend Ed Stanley – Lord Stanley of Alderley – and cooked up a plot with him. Soon after, Lord Stanley's lawyers received a letter from him informing them that he would like to add a codicil to his will. It stipulated that on his death, he wished to be transported to LA and buried in Forest Lawn, because he understood it bore a close resemblance to the haven of peace and beauty so movingly described in Mr Waugh's novel.

Chapman and Hall's lawyers were presented with a copy of the codicil, and decided that Stanley's apparently earnest decision would be a cracking opening defence should any libel proceedings arise, not least because he was a member of the House of Lords. They rolled over and Chapman and Hall published.

Lord Stanley, just to be on the safe side, kept the codicil in his will for ten years. After that, he revoked it. A favour is one thing, but he didn't want to impose the bad taste and ruinous expense of Forest Lawn on his heir.

Waugh's biographers don't seem to have found any evidence of there being a direct original for the Happier Hunting Ground – and if any of the age's West Coast cat-embalmers did recognise themselves, they kept schtum. But the West Coast seemed to me to be a good place, in his spirit, to look for dead pets. But it was, oddly, more or less by accident – a single paragraph; an aside in the guidebook – that I discovered the pet cemetery in the Praesidio.

At the top left hand side of the big fat thumb-shape of San Francisco sticking up into the bay, is a big stretch of coastal parkland, criss-crossed by approach roads to the Golden Gate Bridge, and skirted, as the sun goes down, by the joggers and rollerbladers of the smart breeder area next door. This is the Praesidio. It used to be a garrison, and the legacy of that is the very big military cemetery at the dead centre of it. The military cemetery is a landmark, but less well known is the little pet cemetery tucked away to the west of it.

Paths and roads – without sidewalks; tricky for pedestrians – wind steeply down from the approach to the Golden Gate Bridge, through the park. I was picking my way round the curve of one such, wearily, when I rounded a corner and found myself looking down, across a patch of open ground, towards a scrappy shack.

Between me and the shack (a side road passed by its front), tucked in to the left, was the cemetery: a roughly rectangular area of land maybe half the size of a football pitch, enclosed by a knee-high pale – a peeling white picket fence more ornament than use. Sunlight slanted down through the trees and past the girders onto it. Gosh it was lovely. I picked my way down and went round to the break in the fence.

The sign that was posted at the entrance to the little cemetery was, like most of the grave markers, made of whitewashed wood. It was peeling now, badly, and the stick-on lettering was all but gone. You could make out where the letters had gone by the thin rime of greenish rain sediment, or lichen, that had formed around their outlines. This is what it said:

KEEP GRAVES
IN LINE. PLACE
MARKER, [*illegible*]
NAME   STOP
STEALING &
DIGGING FLOWER
S UP. HEAPT
STONS & PLAIN
STONES ARE

GRAVES
PLEASE
SHOW   RESPECT
WHATEVER
REASON HERE
YOU MAY BE.
THANK U!

This, too, is a military cemetery of sorts. Not military in the sense that the animals saw active service – those cemeteries exist as well. Rather, it was where the pets of the soldiers garrisoned here, and their families, were put to rest.

On the other side of the break in the fence from that sign, there was what, I guess, might be called the grave of the unknown lapdog. It was another whitewashed plywood marker, rounded on top. At a slant across it was stencilled simply the word, UNKNOWN – and underneath that, taking up most of the face of the marker, was a big red heart.

From between these two, a path ran forward between the rows of graves. Some sort of purple flowers were rioting across the right hand side of the cemetery, under where the overpass ran, with the thunkety-thunk of the cars passing overhead, and further down, to the left, the path curved left towards a beleaguered low palm tree. The grass between the graves was yellowing in the dust.

I walked from grave to grave, taking photographs.

1971
Mr Bird
A Canary
And
Bilbo Baggins
White Mouse
Loved Pets
Of the De Young
Children

…was one. "Tweek and Buffy The Hamsters (both 1999–2000)" was another.

And what, I wondered, was Ken's status in the US military? Ken's name appeared encircled in a heart on the smart headstone commemorating his two bassett hounds, Mr Twister and Raspberry. Mr Twister's specific inscription was: "MY # ONE-DERFUL LITTLE MAN IN BASSETT CLOTHES".

Skippy stuck in my head because it wasn't clear what sort of animal Skippy was. The meanings of these markers, even more perhaps than human gravestones, was private. The owners of Skippy the kangaroo, or the caterpillar for all I know, who loved life and lost it, knew what he was. I picked up, from beside Skippy's grave, a section of branch, attached to a couple of pine cones, that was lying in the path. I moved it just in front of Skippy's grave marker, for the photograph. Skippy, or one of his ethereal associates, took against this: the invasion of his privacy, or the falsification, my first. My disposable camera jammed. I lost the whole roll.

Skippy – in his indefiniteness – seemed to stand as a reproach. Silky went unburied. It would be too much to say that he – or she – went unmourned, but I don't, in honesty, even know what happened to his, or her, body. Did Mum or Dad, as I wailed and ululated on the bed, or the floor, or wherever, quietly take his broken body and slip it into a black plastic binliner alongside a cardboard pizza box and wilted, sodden shreds of last night's salad? Did they fling it, like the nameless rodent victims of the cats – mangled or decapitated shrews, mostly – into a hedge? Or did they bury it with full ceremony, inside the garden walls. Perhaps they did, and I stood in solemn attendance. If so, why have I forgotten?

Skippy loved life. I don't even know whether Silky loved life. I would like to think that, however fleetingly, he, or she, did. Perhaps I didn't care enough. If Silky was Polynices, I was no Antigone. Now Skippy was, at some level in my mind, and after all these years, standing in for Silky.

As I walked through the graveyard, I noticed something I hadn't expected. The same feeling of quietness you experience in a human cemetery had, unexpectedly, stolen upon me. Even the mirth Skippy's epitaph provoked was, somehow, inward. The hyena laughter, the cynicism, the prophylaxis against empathy and against grief, had died in my throat.

As I moved through the graveyard, I noticed I was going sideways down the rows, watching my feet. I was making sure not to step on any graves.

PART TWO
KENT

TO GET FROM Brixton to Tonbridge I leave nearly two hours, and need every last minute of it. I find my tiny car lurching in a panic up improbably steep Tunbridge Wells cul-de-sacs, and barrelling down unlabelled country roads. I try all at the same time to drive, and smoke, and read a map, and read my impenetrable notes of the lucid directions Celia Preston gave me over the phone a few days previously. I am, in short, a mess.

It isn't, totally, an accident that Orchard Pet Cemetery is so hard to find. Mrs Preston deliberately doesn't plaster the surrounding countryside with signs. Among the many concerns that beset those in her line of work is that of vandalism. If the local hooligans can't find this place, they can't bash or dig it up.

"I have to pay monthly insurance premiums by law, but it covers you for practically nothing," she says. "It covers you in case somebody walking through the plot trips on a plaque and twists their ankle and decides to sue you. But if someone comes in and smashes up all the graves, I'm not covered at all."

Celia is the sort of woman you instantly warm to. She is in, I guess, her 50s, with short dark hair, tinted glasses, a sensible warm jacket and a big barrel-like black Labrador. She is friendly, pragmatic, and takes the line of work she is in seriously without being immune to laughter at its occasional absurdities.

From the little carpark – really, a flat bit of grass to the right hand side of the drive, with room for about ten cars – she walks me up a pretty path, lined colonnade-style with fruit trees. Over a fence to the left you can see some feral-looking pale-brown sheep romping through a field – remainder of a herd of a special ancient breed of non-shearable sheep that Celia and her husband kept during the 30 years they farmed this land. They gave up the farm a few years ago, but have kept the pet cemetery on. At the head of the path, the path jinks left and into the Garden of Remembrance.

If you read Stephen King's celebrated novel, *Pet Sematary*,[12] or see the gruesomely riveting film of the same name based on it, you would be led to believe that places of animal burial are, basically, spooky. The premise of *Pet Sematary* is that an animal graveyard is set up on an Ancient Indian Burial Site. Strange bad magic means that when something is buried there, it will return infallibly to life and claw its way out of the ground in ugly, mangled, clotted with earth and fiercely carnivorous zombie form. This poses no trouble with goldfish or stick insects, but is pretty scary when a good-sized tomcat or, as in the film, a human child, undergoes this process.[13] This sort of thing is mostly fictional.

[12] Curiously, there is as a result of the Stephen King thing an unexamined assumption among Brits that all Americans spell cemetery (particularly in the context of "pet") in this strange "sematary" way. It ain't so – Americans spell cemetery the same way we do. (An exception is the Ramones. The reason for this, it emerges, is that the Ramones wrote their song – which appears, no less transfigured than the inmates of the sematary, in an appendix to this book – for the film.) What a testament to the cultural impact of that movie.

Orchard Pet Cemetery is – on this crisp November morning – as pretty and peaceful a resting place for a dead cat as you could hope for. It sits in the low part of a wide roll of open farmland. You can see far up to hills, and as you stand among the grave markers, there's no road immediately apparent. The ground is well tended; the graves mostly dignified. A loop of pathway circles through the graves, and a handful of the dwarf apple trees that give this place its name punctuate the rows of marble plaques, or "memorial tablets", as the literature has it.

†13
I saw this film, and read the book. The scene where the evil dead child hides under the bed and uses a straight razor to slice through the Achilles tendon of a passing adult is, God help us, really frightening.

Orchard, which is about to celebrate its tenth year, is a small operation. Most pet cemeteries are. Celia ran it, more or less, as a hobby rather than a profit-making enterprise. At its best, it would produce a couple of thousand pounds profit a year – "enough for a holiday" – but she can't quite explain what it was that made her want to do it in the first place.

The closest she gets is to explain that Orchard was started when she was approached by a friend, a highly successful Tunbridge Wells solicitor, who, she said, had been trying for years and years without success to get planning permission for a pet cemetery.[14] She realised that this patch of land – on the edge of the farm, set away from the road, and far enough from water courses to satisfy the planners – was ideal. So they went into business.

†14
Why? Who knows. Guvd on him, in any case.

Initially, Celia confesses, she had little or no idea what she was doing. The first client – a dog – she really couldn't figure out what to do with. It was that in-at-the-deep-end experience that she learned from. Over time it became clear one needed a place to take the animals; a method for separating them, discreetly and kindly, from their grieving owners; a room to fill in the paperwork; a ceremony lined up.

So this is what they do now. Celia, sometimes with a helper when it comes to dealing with, say, a particularly big dog, will come and collect your dead animal. For this, there will be a small fee. Alternatively, you can deliver it to her. Her car, in any case, contains a number of dog and cat beds, into which the creature's body can be loaded and removed with care and dignity.

Sometimes these creatures are stiff. Generally, they will be not in lifelike poses but, say, stretched straight out, or mangled by a car bumper, or in some other way physically confused. Celia will prepare the animal for burial, curling it up as if it were sleeping. Many owners bring in measurements, guessing from the extent of their elongated, squashed Great Dane that its coffin will need to be enormous. Celia will quietly insist on taking her own measurements. Even some big dogs curl up smaller than you would expect.

Once the creature is posed as if sleeping, Celia pops it in the deep freeze so it will keep its shape. She takes them out, she says, 24 hours before the burial. It occurs to me that the odd one of her larger clients, therefore, might be still frozen in the middle at the time of their funerals. I do not have the courage to raise the matter, however.

The posing of the body, again, she takes seriously. She recalls one night a couple of years ago, trying to put into good decorative order a Persian cat that had been horribly damaged in an encounter with a car. She sat up all night washing its long fur and drying it with a hairdryer. "It took hours and hours sitting with this cat and the hairdryer. I thought it would be quite easy at first, but it took ages. But it came out beautifully. It looked wonderful."

"Just before the burial," says Celia, "when you open the coffin and say, 'Would you like one last look?' or 'Would you like to say goodbye?', and they go, 'Oh ... He looks just like he's sleeping ...' That's when" – and she makes a thumbs-up gesture of pride and satisfaction – "you know you've done it right."

We walk around the plots. There's a row of three little dog graves, near the front, the plaques set in patches of artificial lilac gravel a couple of feet square. They are decorated with little plastic models of dogs, and the odd fake flower. They look very camp.

Celia has no trouble, when confronted with this sort of kitschy stuff, keeping a straight face. These camp little dead dogs, too, are loved. "Sometimes, afterwards, you have to explode," she says. "But it's not hard to be solemn when they are here. The thing is, they really are so upset. It's always very moving. For a lot of these people, they don't have children, and it is like losing a child."

She points to a column of four well-appointed plots with black memorial tablets, each bearing flowers. The nearest two, whose names are visible from the path, are

Dex and Sammy. They are four Samoyeds – yappy little dogs. The owners are a couple who, Celia says, had a series of Samoyeds but then, in among them, had a child. Every year, the family visits on the dogs' birthdays.

She points out another grave, near the entrance to the cemetery. "Rocky – A Dear Friend." Rocky was an enormous boxer dog. Celia and a colleague went to collect Rocky from a London council estate, and found the owner, a taxi-driver, who had been drinking, unhinged by grief. Two of them had barely been able to haul Rocky into the lift to take him out to the street, and, Celia said, what with the condition of the owner, she was wondering what her chances were of recovering her fee. He paid up good as gold.

"He comes to visit Rocky constantly," she says. "That dog means so much to him."

Until very recently, Orchard's coffins were made by an elderly local artisan whose main line of work was making coffins for children. Celia shows me a photograph – a handsome, dark, velvet-lined box that looks equally as suitable for burying a human child as the most beloved of dachshunds. The old gentleman has since retired and sold his business, however. The new people insist on making coffins only for children.

How much is a pet coffin? It depends, obviously, on the size. One suitable for a cat or small dog is £80, rising to £150 for a big dog. Really huge dogs – Japanese tozers, or Pyrenean mountain dogs[15] – or larger animals (Celia has never buried a pony) require individual quotation.[16] The marble memorial tablets, too, are offcuts from human gravestones. They therefore come in a bit cheaper.

When it comes to the burial, Orchard works to

†15 One of Orchard's clients was a Pyrenean mountain dog of such staggering proportions that there was no way it would fit in a coffin. Celia determined that it would have to be lowered into its grave, just curled in its dog-basket. One of her neighbours, she recalls, was shocked to drive up past the cemetery and see Celia's 11-year-old son struggling up with a laden wheelbarrow, covered in a tarpaulin. Protruding from the tarpaulin and swinging down to brush the grass on the ground was an enormous furry tail.

†16 The impecunious might want to consult Forget-Me-Not, a company in the pretty Norfolk town of Hunstanton (pronounced "Hunston") which offers, as its brochure puts it, "the alternative to the plastic sack". Forget-Me-Not are, as far as they know, the only company specialising in flat-pack coffins for pets. Under the motto "Care, Comfort, Dignity, Choice", they offer four sizes of environmentally friendly coffin made from mostly recycled board in mottled white. The sizes range from 130 x 60 x 55 mm (budgies, hamsters) at £8, to large dogs at 920 x 585 x 245 mm, which will set you back £55. All coffins are biodegradable, easy-to-assemble, and come with an adhesive label "to record your pet's name and any last message, waterproof liner, and a white, lace-trimmed taffeta liner".

accommodate exactly the wishes of the bereaved. They do, however, also offer a standard service, at which they read a text by the American playwright Eugene O'Neill, written after the death of his own dog.[17] (O'Neill was uncommonly fond of the Dalmation he knew as "Blemie". Blemie, who joined the O'Neill household in the late 1920s, slept in a canopied miniature four-poster, wore a bespoke raincoat from Hermes of Paris, and was described by the O'Neills as "the only one of our children who never disappointed us".)

†17
See Appendix I, p. 231.

Sometimes families bring their living pets along to the ceremonies: it is "especially nice and touching when they bring them to say goodbye". The casket would be lowered into the grave, frequently with a family member helping hold it, and earth would be scattered.

The ceremonies are not religious in character. Indeed, Celia surprises and intrigues me by saying that "again and again people specifically say to me that they don't want anything religious involved". Is this, I wonder, a specific reaction against the so signal failure of most western religious traditions to make accommodation for dead pets? Or theological fastidiousness? In pet cemeteries in the States, you can often see crosses, and even plaster Jesuses or Virgins atop graves. Here, not so. Plaster or plastic models of animals, on both sides of the Atlantic, are standard. But Christian iconography is more prevalent over there.

The largest single outgoing for the cemetery, says Celia, is maintenance. Each owner pays £24 a year for the upkeep of their plot. Celia pays to have the grass regularly mown and the paths weeded. As we pass one grave, we notice that water has puddled up above the level of the gravel surrounding the tablet. Not much more than a metre down here, you hit claggy blue clay so the drainage is sometimes tricky. You need to keep an eye on the groundwater. This grave will have to be sorted out.

Orchard is kept in very good shape; as it needs to be. Almost all the people who take the trouble to give their pet a decent burial also take the trouble to visit the grave. In summer, says Celia, they come with sandwiches to picnic in the garden of remembrance; in winter, around Christmas time, they come to lay wreaths.

Orchard, like most pet cemeteries, is dominated by dogs and cats. Like Precious the cat, whose tablet reads "Forever Precious To All Who Knew Her". Or "Yuri

Bear", who is not a bear but a dog.

But there are others. There's the tortoise – a life cut short at only 50 (tortoises have been recorded living to 188).[18] There are little trios of guinea pigs, with names like Dino and Coco and Holly, with each name and death date solemnly limned in marble.

Most of Celia's own dead pets are buried, she says, in her garden at home. But up towards the top of the Garden of Remembrance, she points out the marble tablet marking the grave of one of hers. "Our Faithful Ferret 'Tick'," it says. "1984–1994." Celia has a sticker in her estate car's back window, I notice as I leave, that says "I ♥ ferrets". Ferrets, too, can be faithful after their fashion.

This, then, seems like the very model of what a pet cemetery should be. So why, when she talks about it, do I get a sense of something winding down? In the pet cemetery business, red tape is, like some hypertrophic convolvulus, steadily suffocating the black crepe. "It would probably be easier," says Celia crisply, "if I wanted to bury nuclear waste."

To the taxidermist, the principal founts of red tape are DEFRA and the protected species mob. To the pet undertaker, it's Health and Safety. Celia's little plot – containing no more than a hundred or so graves – is subject to levels of bureaucratic interference that are making planting cats look less and less like a going proposition.

There are already regulations about the depth at which bodies have to be buried, and regulations about the height of the headstones. In her case, planning permission requires that no grave marker be more than half a metre high – so she generally insists on graves being marked by the flat plaques, or "tablets of remembrance".

She used to have to submit monthly returns detailing what she had buried that month, not animal by animal, but in tonnes. So on a quiet month, a cat, say, and a couple of guinea pigs, she would be sending in returns saying, "0.000 …".

Every month, she says, inspectors turn up and look at the cemetery and tick a

† 18
Timothy, the Powderham Castle tortoise, and the subject of an excellent biography by the journalist Rory Knight-Bruce, lived through the Irish potato famine, the Crimean War, the assassination of Abraham Lincoln, Beatlemania and the deaths of Kurt Cobain and Mother Teresa. He finally turned up his scaly chelonian toes in the spring of 2004. (The approaching end had been signalled a few weeks before with the words, from Lord and Lady Devon's daughter Nell: "Timothy's looking a bit dead, Mum.") He was more than 160: the oldest living creature in the British Isles.

box and go away again. And now, she has just been told that to continue interring whole animals, under new EU regulations, the forms she will have to fill in alone will cost (and cost her) £1,000 to process.

She has just received, too, an ominous pamphlet. It is dark green, and its front cover is marked with an enormous yellow question mark; an accusatory, Big Brotherish question mark. "Have you heard" says the yellow text nestling in the armpit of the question mark. Below and beside are some red block capitals, in a box, designed to look as if they have been spray-painted on through a stencil, or thumped down with a rubber stamp. "BY LAW", they advise.

The content is little more attractive than the advertisements on the London Underground intended to strike fear into those who watch television without a licence. A mixture, tonally, of the smug and the totalitarian.

†19
"Unless the equivalent leaflet has been issued to your employees," says the tiny writing in the footnote on the leaflet. Had there not been a footnote on the leaflet, I would have wanted to add my own footnote at the exact same point – a meta-footnote – pointing out that this grotty piece of scaremongering parasitic tat was, perhaps, shooting itself in the foot by pointing out in the fag-end of 2004 that poster-shirkers had been liable to prosecution since early 2001 – and that Nothing Had Happened.

"From 1st March 2002 … health and safety enforcing authorities will have had 11 months to take action against you for failing to display this poster", it warned.[19] "Why is the poster so important?" it asked. "… because it conveys information requiring action from you BY LAW", it responded.

Gist: the poster is something you're supposed to stick up, as an employer, in the workplace, informing employees about your duties towards them in the health and safety department. To those employers who are, by now, terrified of being prosecuted for failing to display a poster, or more terrified of the can of worms that poster will open for them, the kindly leaflet suggests a solution. Buy a Chancellor© Starter Pack … "the simple, cost-effective route to the implementation of mainstream health and safety law".

If you employ five or more people, the starter pack (because the law requires you to draw up a "health and safety policy statement") will cost you £124.95. If you employ fewer than 5, it's a snip at £99.95. Basically, the Chancellor© Starter Pack is a bunch of leaflets. I leave it to others to decide whether or not it is what might be called a profiteering direct-marketing rip-off.

This leaflet is not the problem. But this leaflet is a symptom of the problem. Celia is feeling cornered by this, and by what it represents; by the tedious, grindingly annoying official hoop-jumping that makes work for inspectors and filing clerks and yet makes it next to impossible for someone like Celia to get on with doing what she wants to do: that is, to alleviate the suffering of the unhappy bereaved by sticking their pets underground, in a nice box.

Celia has had to be pragmatic. Orchard no longer buries whole animals. Instead, owners – many of whom really want their pet buried whole – make do with caskets of ashes, cremated at a local furnace. "He's a local guy," she says. "He burns all sorts of things. But he doesn't let the public in."

Orchard still provides an admirable service. But it's sad, isn't it, and perhaps symptomatic, that small, loved local concerns like this are being stifled by regulation? Up and down the country, little pet cemeteries like Orchard will struggle in just the same way, and many of them will be forced to give up the fight.

And in a thousand little pretty plots, set back from little-travelled by-roads, the grass will grow long and lush over the graves.

PART THREE

CYBERSPACE

"I KNOW IF you could speak to me you'd say please don't cry," croons the voice over a gentle synthesiser and the plinking of – is it? – a xylophone. "I'm no longer in pain … Free am I. If only I could see you now … On the pathway beyond life's gateway …" My eyes mist. "On the pathway," repeats the voice, "beyo-o-o-nd life's gateway …"

The song is issuing from the tinny speakers of my computer on a permanent loop. Henry, who had been sitting next to the speakers, has flattened his ears. For the fifth or sixth time now it moves through candlelight and roses to the eternal

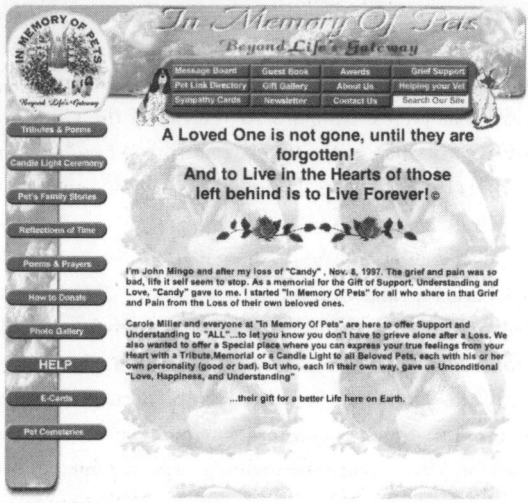

flame that "forever shines and shines – sweet as candy! – shines and shines".

The screen is white, with rows of blue navigation buttons on two sides. Over a background image of four angels curled in sleep, there is a motto printed, underscored by a pair of twined red roses.

It says:

> *A Loved One is not gone, until they are forgotten!*
> *And to Live in the Hearts of those left behind is to Live Forever!*

After it, there is printed a small round ©.

Above, bookending the site, are drawings of a King Charles spaniel and a Siamese cat, each sporting animated, perma-flapping pink angel wings.

In Memory of Pets – www.in-memory-of-pets.com – is as far as I can tell the oldest and best pet cemetery on the world wide web. In the last three years, the site has hosted memorials to 689,000 departed pets. While theologians continue to struggle with the question of where pets go when they die, hundreds of thousands of bereaved owners have furnished their own answer: pets go to the Internet when they die.

In Memory of Pets is special, though. Unlike the increasing number of sites that came after, it still makes a principle of not charging, and its continued existence is the result of the sheer devotion, finally, of one remarkable man.

It was in 1997 that John E Mingo Sr, a veteran of the US Marine Corps and former Coca-Cola salesman, now in his mid-fifties, reached one of the very darkest times in his own life. A pet rescued him. And then, when that pet was gone, he returned the favour.

The pet was called Candy, and she can be seen on the very front page of the site. She's the King Charles spaniel with the wings.

The story begins in 1990, when John was 41. He was living then with his wife and kids, and three spaniels called Toby, Buffy and Candy. He says he wasn't, at that time, particularly close to the dogs; but Candy would nevertheless curl up on his pillow to sleep every night, just beside his head.

Around New Year, 1991, things started to fall apart. John was taken to hospital with chest pains, and had to have a triple bypass. The following four years saw him suffer eight heart attacks. He was able, each time, to return to his job with Coca-Cola. But then in 1996 he underwent a further heart operation and Coke called time on him.

He found himself deeply depressed, and with a family unable, quite, to cope with the pressure of his unhappiness. Then, one day after everyone else left for work and John was surfing the Internet on his computer, Candy came and sat by him – laying her paw on his leg, as if in a sort of compact.

For seventeen months she never left his side.

"My family didn't really pull through for me," says John when I speak to him on the phone, in an accent gently inflected with the New England vowels of his Maine childhood. "They just thought I should get over it. But nobody wants to retire at 47. Candy helped me. She showed me a lot about how life should really be, through an animal's eyes. Why can't humans be like that?"

But in October of the following year, Candy fell ill. She was diagnosed with cancer and given a year or two to live. Even that time was stolen from her. She went downhill fast. Her two-year lease of life ended up being only a week. She went in for surgery and, writes John, "never left the recovery room": "What was left of my heart, on Nov 8th 1997, went with her."

When John first started looking on the Internet, the only site he could find that addressed pet loss was the Rainbow Bridge[20] – which refers to a prose poem of unknown origin which appears in the appendix to this volume. It seems to act as a sort of rough theological consolation: pets wait for their masters – like Kipling's Dinah – in a sort of halfway house where there is no pain or predation. When master and pet are reunited, they cross the bridge together.

†20
See www.petloss.com;
a site with 90,000
listings for dead pets.

John put up his own site for Candy. It was the first incarnation of In Memory of Pets, and was intended, as he put it, "to pay her back for what she did for me". After a while, something odd started to happen. He received emails from others who were, like him, grieving for an animal loss. They asked whether he'd let them include their pets on his site. The decision was not, knowing what Candy had given him, a hard one. He opened In Memory of Pets to the world.

"When I first started," John says, "I had to do everything by hand. I was doing this seven days a week, seven hours a day. People would send me things by mail or email, and I'd have to put them up on the site myself. It's more automated now – but when the forms come in, we still review them personally; for spelling errors and that sort of thing. But we make sure it's as they want it. The younger kids – I try to leave it alone the way they put it.

"And once your posting is up, if you want to change it, we don't have the mechanism to do that so we have to go in and change it ourselves.

"In Memory of Pets receives around two hundred new postings every day. Ninety-nine per cent are dogs and cats," he says, "but we've had everything from guinea pigs and bunnies to frogs, fish and snakes. Some kids did ants. There's a tiger, and there's an elephant on there, too, from some zoo.

"There are a lot of people in the closet, still, though. They grieve, but they don't feel comfortable sharing that with people, and so there's a lot of anonymous stuff … Pet loss … People have nervous breakdowns. I talked to one lady and her daughter wanted to commit suicide.

"Some of these sites now charge $25 a year per pet. There are a lot of poor people out there, so I leave it free. I think it's the best thing to do."

The site – with its unconditional promise of a permanent memorial – provides consolation. It also helps gather a community of the bereaved. One of the features that In Memory of Pets has adopted is the Candle Ceremony.[21]

†21
See Appendix II.

This was an idea that originated in the early months of 1993, on the Prodigy Internet server. On the Dogs Bulletin Board, there went up a thread called All Pets To Heaven, and one of the participants, Lisa Singer, said that she lit candles every Monday night in memory of those waiting at the Rainbow Bridge: her "Bridge Babies".

Others started to join her, and soon a loosely codified, non-denominational ceremony – to be conducted simultaneously wherever those who wanted to join in were – was established.

Within months, through the Internet, the ceremony had become a phenomenon; co-ordinated through chat-rooms but practised on- and off-line all over the world.

As the writer Marion Hale puts it, in a brief report on the history of the ceremony posted at www.petloss.com: "When a human loved one dies a prescribed ritual provides a cushion between the loss and the return to 'normal' life. When the loved one is a furbeing[22] society provides no means of closure. For many of us the Candle Ceremony has brought peace, acceptance and the hope of eternal reunion."

†22
Not a word you'll find in many dictionaries, but one widely used by the online pet bereavement community.

If you have no candles, or are allergic to them, you can simply light another lamp: "The idea is to send out light to our furbabies who have gone to the Bridge, and whatever is available to you is perfectly fine."

The ceremony was originally conducted simultaneously – at 10 p.m. EST on a Monday evening – but with its globalisation, and the mobile communities in chat-rooms, what began as a brief candle has become more of an eternal flame.

As John Mingo shrugs of the ceremony on his own site: "I ran into a big problem with time zones." The candle ceremony online, therefore, has become a moveable feast: an idea rather than a practice. But it has helped to produce a pet bereavement community like none, surely, that has ever existed before.

"People have become friends," says John. "Over the years, they submit things … we keep in touch. I visited one family in Switzerland two years ago. They invited me, and even paid for my tickets, so I went.

"There was another girl from Switzerland, actually, who called me this morning asking about her dog's eyes, that she thought were looking funny; and I tried to help her, but I had to tell her I'm not a vet. Often, you know, at two or three in the morning, some young child has lost his bunny, and the parents don't understand. I get those calls."

The theme tune that loops over the site was written by Libby Benson, another bereaved pet owner who became a friend. She lost two pets over time, and she offered to write a song for John. "I asked if she could put Candy in it ... 'Sweet Candy' – that's my pet."

One of the key contacts John has had, however, is with a couple named Ken and Carole Miller, who got in touch from Hershey, Pennsylvania. Carole is retired; Ken is director of the town's medical centre. At first, they were just people posting their own stories of loss on the site – they lost two dogs within a week of each-other – but they became, over email and the telephone, friends. They offered to help him with the site.

"When Ken and Carole came in," says John, "I was on my twelfth heart attack. It matters a lot to me to keep this site going, and it can't be permanent if I die! I was living in New Hampshire then, and I flew down to meet them ..."

In Memory of Pets now own their own server in Texas, and they have a maintenance man who does work for them from Hershey. But the costs of a successful hack can be devastating, and John sounds wearily bewildered at the thoughtlessness of those who would choose to mess with such a site.

"Hackers are a real problem for us," he says. "The last one knocked us down for a month – some hacker from Russia got a programme going that was sending messages about Citibank."[23] The site, which is registered with the IRS, receives no more than $850 a month in donations.

†23
This is a common cyber-con called 'phishing'.

That doesn't come close to covering the costs. Every time it breaks down, it costs John, Ken and Carole $175 an hour to get fixed. They muddle through.

Since then, that friendship has provided a refuge. In the autumn of 2004, while he was still living in New Hampshire, John's marriage finally broke up. He speaks with sadness but without rancour about it. "I got a divorce. She couldn't cope with my illness any more. I was given six months to live, and I went beyond that ... then I was

given three months to live, and I went beyond that … I gave her what she wanted and I left. I moved down here to Hershey. It's hard, but I don't blame her."

John, a Protestant, says he tries "not to get involved in church". But he firmly believes that animals will go to heaven. "I'm 54 years old," he says, "and I have had twelve heart attacks. I did die. And I had a vision that I was in heaven – with animals. I can't prove it's true. But I stick with it."

Candy, then, is waiting for John on the other side of life's gateway. At the time of writing, however, he has a companion on this side too. "For a long time, my idea was I just wanted to help others," he says. "But then … I got a puppy."

John called his puppy: "Angel."

DEADPETS

Case Study No. 3

Duty was my Lobster, my Lobster was she,
And when I walked with my Lobster
I was happy.

STEVIE SMITH
"DUTY WAS HIS LODESTAR"

GÉRARD DE NERVAL'S
LOBSTER

THE LOBSTER IS NOT NORMALLY HELD TO BE A PET. GAZE INTO THE EYES OF A
LOBSTER. DO YOU SEE COMPASSION THERE? AFFECTION? NO. TRY GIVING A LOBSTER
A CUDDLE. EXACTLY. IF YOU CAN CURL UP IN FRONT OF THE TV WITH A CUP OF HOT
COCOA AND A LOBSTER ON YOUR LAP, YOU ARE A BRAVER MAN THAN I.

TWO DOCUMENTED HISTORICAL instances of lobster–human bonding exist. (I
omit Salvador Dali, who – by using his lobster as a telephone – demonstrated an
instrumental, functionalist view of the creature quite alien to that of the animal
lover. Also, his lobster was plastic.)

The French Romantic poet Gérard De Nerval (1808–1855) is the pioneer of domestic lobster ownership. A gloomy dreamer, the young Gérard Labruine made a name for himself by translating Goethe's *Faust* into French before he was out of his teens. He also made a name for himself by conceiving the notion that he was descended from the Roman emperor Nerva, and so calling himself "De Nerval".

He was hopeless with girls.

Little is known of Gérard's lobster. It does not seem to have had a name, and even Nerval scholars have declined to hazard a guess about its sex. What we do know is that Gérard used to walk his lobster on a pale blue ribbon in the gardens of the Palais-Royal in Paris. Did he do this in the rain? Or were there fountains? Lobsters don't do too well out of water for any length of time.[24] History, again, does not relate.

†24
This nagging zoological anomaly has led some scholars to conclude that the lobster did not, in fact, exist. They contend that the lobster was invented by Théophile Gautier, as a joke to liven up his history of Romanticism. They further contend that the story was swallowed whole by subsequent literary historians, on the grounds that they are easily impressed by eccentric gestures and don't know much about lobster biology.

When asked about his lobster, Gérard said this: "Why should a lobster be any more ridiculous than a dog ... or any other animal that one chooses to take for a walk? I have a liking for lobsters. They are peaceful, serious creatures. They know the secrets of the sea, they don't bark, and they don't gnaw upon one's monadic privacy like dogs do."

He added: "Goethe had an aversion to dogs, and he wasn't mad."

Perhaps so. Gérard De Nerval, on the other hand, may have been mad. When not walking his lobster, he used to try – armed with a "French–Nightingale Dictionary" written by a certain Dupont de Nemours – to draw the caged birds on the quai de la Mégisserie into conversation.

He was probably lonely.

Gérard's lobster was not with him on his final promenade in the rue de la Vieille-Lanterne – a street or two away from where he was born, at 96 rue Saint-Martin. It was January 25th, 1855, and the mercury stood at eighteen degrees below zero. Brass monkeys weather. Gérard had sold his hat to the pawnbroker.

The rue de la Vieille-Lanterne no longer exists. It was shadowed by the bell-tower of Saint-Jacques-de-la-Boucherie, an ancient landmark surmounted by four mythical animals carved in stone. One shop window had an Egyptian mummy on permanent display. Off one side of the street an enormous yellow-painted key hung, advertising a locksmith's shop. According to Alexandre Dumas, who retraced Gérard's last steps, there was a crow hanging around. It did not caw, but emitted the occasional shrill whistle. French biographers suggest these details may have symbolic significance.

Gérard was found at precisely 9:30 the next morning, hanged from the bars of a low window by an apron-string. He never redeemed his hat.

POSTSCRIPT

THE ONLY OTHER man to love a lobster was Homer Simpson. In Season 10 of *The Simpsons* one 'Mr Pinchy', briefly, supplants Santa's Little Helper in Homer's affections.

Canny viewers are alerted to the end of their relationship when Homer announces: "Pinchy got all dirty in the yard chasing birds. But don't worry! I put him in a nice, hot bath." Bart sniffs the air: "Hey! What smells so good?"

BOUNCE

FANCY CALLING A GUARD DOG BOUNCE. ALEXANDER POPE WAS BRAVE IN PRINT BUT – IT SEEMS – A DEVOUT PHYSICAL COWARD IN PERSON. HAVING ONCE PUBLISHED HIS EPIC RASPBERRY AT THE LITERARY ESTABLISHMENT, *THE DUNCIAD*, HE WENT THROUGH A LONG PERIOD, ACCORDING TO HIS SISTER, OF LIVING IN MORTAL TERROR OF BEING GIVEN A CAULIFLOWER EAR BY AN ANGRY POETASTER.

ODDER STILL, HE had very good reason for this. Crowds of authors had made their feelings known to booksellers: "a crowd of authors besieged the shop; entreaties, advices, threats of law and battery, nay, cries of treason, were all employed to hinder the coming out of The Dunciad". One Dunce had written to Sir Robert Walpole denouncing Pope as public enemy number one; another made a clay effigy of Pope and did terrible violence on it. Pope didn't give a hoot. But he kept a weather eye open.

In fact, once the *Dunciad* came out, the set-up of this Augustan poet's life started to look a good deal like an East End caper movie. The Dunces, it turned out, did not like it up 'em.

In the summer of 1728, barely two weeks after the poem was published, Pope was strolling in parkland across the Thames from his house when a pair of likely lads recognised him (having been crippled by tubercular disease, he wasn't hard to spot), and decided to give smarty-pants a good shoeing. One of them hoisted him aloft, pulled the Papal trousers around his ankles, and beat him on the bare backside with a broom handle until the blood flowed – according to report – yellow with gall.

Pope was found abandoned, with his trews still at half mast, by his friend Martha Blount, who hoisted him in her apron, restored his trousers, and packed him onto the ferry home. This story was publicly denounced as fiction by Pope, but he had a 'rep' to keep up. I'd like to think that there's at least a dribble of truth in it.

Thereafter for a long time Pope made sure never to leave the house without being, as they say now, thoroughly tooled up.[25] As well as a pair of pistols, he brought "a great faithful Danish dog": Bounce.

†25
Pope's view: "with pistols the least man in England was above a match for the largest".

We can get a sense of Bounce's bearing and dimensions from his appearance in a 1718 portrait of the poet by Jonathan Richardson. He is handsome, rather short-eared, and dark tan in colour with a very narrow blaze running from forehead to nose. His master's name is inscribed on his collar, and he is looking up at Pope faithfully. Pope himself, in keeping with his curmudgeonly reputation, is looking out at the painter tetchily – as if he's been distracted from the book he's holding.

Bounce seems to have been boisterous, but near in Pope's affections. George Lyttleton presaged a visit by writing to Pope: "You need not be told that the Desire of seeing you is one great cause of that impatience, but to show you how much I am Master of my passions, I will be quiet here for a week or ten days longer, and then come to you in the most outrageous Spirits, and Overset you like Bounce when you let her loose after a regimen of Physick, and Confinement."

Pope regarded Bounce favourably, when compared to his human friends: "If it be the chief point of friendship to comply with a friend's notions and inclinations, he possesses this in an eminent degree; he lies down when I sit, and walks when I walk, which is more than many good friends would pretend to."[26]

At a low time, Pope even wrote of "having kiss'd Bounce (my only friend there [Twickenham] now)". Certainly, Bounce entered the affections of Pope's friend the Prince of Wales. Pope gave him one of Bounce's puppies as a present, wearing a collar engraved as follows:

> I am His Highness' Dog at Kew;
> Pray tell me Sir, whose Dog are you?

Bounce also had a place in Pope's literary career, being the author, in May 1736, of a charming verse letter contrasting her own robust Twickenham-dwelling qualities with the nonciness of court dogs. It was called "Bounce To Fop. An Heroick Epistle from a Dog at Twickenham to a Dog at Court", and was initially attributed to "Dr Sw[if]t".[27] Some scholars imagine it to have been a coded attack on Lord Hervey;[28] I prefer to take the straightforward view that it is an uncoded attack on a dog called Fop.

During the course of his life, Pope owned several dogs, gave several away, and seems to have called them all Bounce. (This accounts, I guess, for the occasional confusion in the documents over Bounce's sex.)

When the last recorded Bounce finally snuffed it,[29] Pope was himself pretty much on finals too. He was very ill throughout the last three years of his life, and hearing of the dog's death in 1744, though not the manner of it, he was as worried for his own health. On April 10th, he wrote from his sickbed to his friend Lord Orrery in Somerset. Bounce had, in fact, been bitten by a mad dog and put down:

> I dread to enquire into the particulars of the Fate of Bounce. Perhaps you conceald them, as Heav'n often does Unhappy Events, in pity to the Survivors, or not to hasten on my End by Sorrow. I doubt not how much

†26
What would it be like, mind, if our human friends lay down when we sat in a chair, or followed us around everywhere on foot?

†27
Dean Swift was a pal of Pope and may have had a hand in the poem's composition

†28
Described in Peter Quennell's biography of Pope as "one of the handsomest men in London ... a fascinating effeminate personage".

†29
This one was another puppy of the original Bounce, given by Pope to Lord and Lady Orrery as a present in 1742.

Bounce was lamented: They might say as the Athenians did to Arcite, in Chaucer:

> *Ah Arcite! gentle Knight! Why would'st thou die,*
> *When thou had'st Gold enough, and Emilye?*

> *Ah Bounce! Ah gentle Beast! Why wouldst thou dye*
> *When thou hadst Meat enough, and Orrery?*

For what in nature could Bounce want, at Marston? What should any one, Man or Beast, want there, but to live always under the benigne Influence of Lady Orrery? I could dye more resign'd any those people here, who are less hurt by anothers Suffering, & before whom therfore I make no conscience to complain, nay to roar, or be as peevish as the devil.

Poor old Pope. But with Bounce's descendants at court, thanks to his gift to the Prince, the consolatory promise in the epistle can perhaps be said to have come true:

> *Then Bounce ('tis all that Bounce can crave)*
> *Shall wag her Tail within the Grave.*

✦✦✦ FIVE INTERESTING THINGS TO DO WITH YOUR DEAD PET ✦✦✦

2 : |OF 5| PLASTINATION

THIS IS THE process invented by the sinisterly-hatted anatomist Dr Gunther Von Hagens, and so spectacularly on display in the human corpses shown in his Body Worlds exhibition. A complicated process is used to replace the perishable materials of the body with plastics – so you end up with something that does not smell or decay, but that is substantially identical to the living animal at even quite microscopic levels of detail. At least one private company – VisDocta Research in Italy – is prepared to do this for domestic pets.

CHAPTER 3

HENRY II

I WROTE ABOUT Henry's arrival at home in the column I do for the *Daily Telegraph*. This was in part a desperate effort to fill space during a week in which I hadn't the first idea what to write about and, in part, a blatant plea for attention. It is an axiom of my profession that, other than the Palestinian Question and abortion,[30] the only thing you can write about in newspapers that absolutely guarantees a torrent of correspondence from readers is pet animals.

†30
Or, but only if you are writing in the *Daily Telegraph*, anything to do with the armed forces – particularly if you get the precedence of two ranks, the founding date of a regiment, or the capital letters in the name of a medal wrong.

My friend Alexander Chancellor was forced to stop writing about his Jack Russell puppy Polly because the sheer volume of correspondence it generated – utterly swamping the postbag excited, in general, by his wise and humane commentary on world affairs – started to make him feel jealous of it. A similar thing happened when Peter McKay of the *Daily Mail* started to write about his puppy.

The RSPCA is and always has been a charity that, compared to those dealing with the welfare of the merely human, attracts an obscene number of bequests.

If you carpet bomb the blameless natives of a third-world country, rob them of their natural resources, profiteer shamelessly on the back of their desperate pharmaceutical needs, or force their children into sweat shops to manufacture shoddy designer trainers for the spoilt brats of the metropolitan west, you can expect a few hippies to picket your offices with placards.

But chase a fox, crate a calf, or squirt shampoo into a baby rabbit's eyes, and you can expect to have your home burned to the ground, your relatives threatened with death or mutilation, and the corpse of your recently dead mother dug up from the cold earth and held hostage.

I got four letters. That's not very many, I admit. But by my standards, it was something of a record.

One was from a kindly 80-year-old woman, who wished me every happiness with the kitten, and regretted that she was no longer able to look after an animal companion herself. She added a plea that, whatever I did, I should get Henry neutered. She had nothing to worry about on that count. The last thing I wanted was a flat reeking of the pungent ankle-high territorial sprayings of a sexually thwarted tomcat.

Another was from some sharp public relations person at Felix, the catfood wing of the terrifying global megacorporation Nestlé. They enclosed – perhaps out of goodwill, but possibly in the hopes of a mention in the column – a kitten starter pack, which consisted of three one-serving pouches of luxury kitten food, a short introductory handbook to cat ownership, and a fluffy white nylon mouse. To my immense annoyance, this mouse supplanted in the cat's affections all the expensive toys I had hitherto bought him.

The third was addressed to "Sam Leith, Pretend Columnist, The Daily Telegraph etc …" I get a few of these. There was no return address. Inside was a cut-out section of my column, scrawled over with a greeting in biro that hailed me as a "childish wanker".

The fourth was from a member of the Wirral Branch of the Cat Protection League. I think it was addressed to me, because the verso side of the very small piece of paper on which it was written contained a letter, dated two days previously and apparently to another department in the paper, complaining about the use of offensive language ("sh-t") and political correctness ("Ms" and "gone for") in the paper.[31] Anyway, she had been concerned to read that I had acquired a cat.

"I hope nothing has happened to him – I trust Henry is alive & well, and being well looked-after. As a member of Cats Protection Wirral I am very concerned about this, & hope he hasn't been ill-treated."

Why would she think it would have been ill-treated? Did she assume, just from my byline photograph, that I was such a person as tortures cats for fun? Had I dropped – apart from the line about taxidermy – a hint in the column?

In short: did they all, somehow, *know?* This was getting worse.

What's more, Ulrike had in the meantime learned from a mutual friend that I was halfway through writing a book about dead pets, and it had made her uneasy. I kept getting these text messages that said, in capital letters: "GIVE HIM BACK!" Also, she knows where I live and I am very cowardly about fighting, and did not fancy my chances against her boyfriend or, for that matter, Ulrike herself, who looks like she knows how to handle herself.

I went out in search of a cat manual of some sort. I knew how to reduce it, and I had discovered certain of its enthusiasms, but I still found it hard to even try to figure out what was going on in its head. These were its enthusiasms:

1) Dr Marten boots, laces of. When I brought my boots down into the sitting room of a morning, and sat on the big chair in my socks, Henry stationed himself opposite, and pounced aggressively on any lace I twitched by way of trying to do up my shoes. Putting shoes on could take up to ten minutes.
2) Receipts, crumpled. Better than mice.
3) Socks, clean. These were fished off the drying rack – the top of the drying rack – at great personal risk (you have not truly laughed until you have seen a small cat lose its footing on the top of a collapsible drying rack, and fall down through the middle of it, crashing into every single bar on the way down). They were redistributed through the house, and filed away in stashes. There is

† 31
It is a curious quirk of the particular type of angry person who likes to write to newspapers that they see no contradiction between their anger at offensive language, and their anger at "PC" usages designed to minimise, um, the possibility of giving offence.

a peculiar look of deliberate dignity that appears on the face of a cat who pads round a corner with a single sock dangling from its mouth and encounters the owner of the sock.

4) Thin bits of insulated wire, chewing of. Two sets of earphones went that way.
5) Lengths of wicker, four inches long, with a gently obtuse angle in the middle. Great for juggling, for some reason.
6) Dr Marten boots, trajectories of. Favourite game: hide behind door. Cross direction of travel to ambush forward boot just as rear boot is coming forward to join it. Enjoy sound of swearing and mild concussion as you fly across room and thump into skirting board.

Henry's disposition, as far as I could tell, was alert, curious and rather brave. His eyes were clear, green-brown, very large and with spookily rounded pupils. There were twin patches of very sparsely furred skin running from above his eyes to his large bat-like ears. On his throat was his principal distinguishing mark: a white blaze that gave him, in repose, a faintly clerical air.

The cat manual I bought was from Dorling Kindersley and was, like many of that publisher's productions, lavishly illustrated in full colour, very thoughtfully designed, pretty expensive and close to useless. I now knew what a Sphynx looked like from two angles, but not much more about cat psychology. I did know, however, that Henry would need to get vaccinated if he were not to peg out at first contact with another cat; and that he would need to get his nuts cut if he were not – when puberty hit – to turn my sitting room into a temple of musk and rutting cat.

Two sexually hopeless males in one household were quite enough to be going on with.

PETERING OUT:
THE NATION'S DEAD DARLINGS

CHILDREN WHO GREW UP IN THE FIRST WORLD IN THE LAST HALF CENTURY WERE, IN ONE PRETTY PROFOUND WAY, DIFFERENT TO THE COUNTLESS GENERATIONS OF CHILDREN WHO LIVED BEFORE. WE LIVED IN TWO WORLDS AT ONCE: ONE OF THEM INFINITELY MORE VIVID AND POPULOUS AND COMFORTING THAN THE GREY QUOTIDIAN IN WHICH WE ATE AND CRIED AND FILLED OUR NAPPIES.

WE HAD TV. This is not to be underestimated.

Your grandfather, between sips of his mashed apple, will of course tell you different. He will tell you that before the arrival of the electric childminder, children had infinitely richer lives. They had their imaginations. Something as

simple as a ration book, or an earlouse, or a green-shield stamp could open a world of magical adventure. They built carties and scrumped apples and made catapults. All you needed was a hoop and a stick and a grubby old hanky, and you could be the captain of your very own pirate ship…

Your grandfather is full of it. TV rules. Did Fox Media set out ruthlessly to corner the global hoop-and-stick market? I don't think so.

As well as keeping us entertained and freeing up our parents for drink and adultery, TV was the place where children – in my case, of the late 70s – met. It was a consensual hallucination.

I had little or no idea what the insides of my schoolmates' houses looked like, or what happened there on the weekends (I believe they invited each other round to play). But I knew what the insides of their heads looked like, and what went on there every afternoon during *Heads and Tails*. We all inhabited a common imaginative landscape: one peopled by Fingerbobs and Pugwash, by Bod and Ludwig, by Johnny Morris and Zippy and Mr Ben and Morph's sinister sidekick Chas, and the Marvellous Mouse Organ, and Derek Griffiths' moustache.

Animals featured heavily in children's programming. These animals fell into two categories. There were the first sort, heavily represented, and very unlike the sorts of animals we were used to seeing around us. These were a) weird, and b) though many of them got into scrapes, immortal.

I'm referring, for example, to Fingermouse: a conical bit of paper plainly attached to a human finger. I'm referring to Parsley, who did not resemble a lion as we understood it. I'm referring to George the hippo, who unlike most other hippos was pink and furry. And gay, probably. I'm referring to Custard, who was somehow *wobblier* than the cats we were used to; or Bagpuss, who was full of pyjamas. And so on.

The second category of kids' TV animal was considerably more accident-prone. These were the real animals: from Johnny Morris's cockney iguanas to Dapple, the rocking horse on *Play School* which, if not exactly real, did at least seem to exist in the real world. These were, like Bernie Winters and Schnorbitz, mortal.[32]

Far and away the most important TV animals in this category were the *Blue*

Peter pets. These animals were the nation's pets. Petless children could turn on the telly in the afternoon and feel as if the *Blue Peter* animals were, somehow, held in trust for them. That was the idea.

Similarly, the *Blue Peter* garden was at once a source of help and hints for those children lucky enough to have a set-aside corner of their Dad's allotment to dig in, and a little patch of imaginary green for urban children who hadn't so much as a window box to liven their bleak afternoons.

When the former died, into the latter they went; and a nation of children snivelled into their jammy dodgers. *Blue Peter* meant well, but *Blue Peter* has, frequently, had bad luck with pets. The garden has, over the years, become something of a pet cemetery itself. Still, bone meal is the gardener's friend.

At the time of writing, *Blue Peter*'s score in a little over three decades of pet ownership is as follows:

> DOGS: 9 (three surviving)
> CATS: 6 (three surviving)
> TORTOISES: 5 (one surviving)
> PARROTS: 2 (both dead)

The auguries weren't – if we are honest – good to start with. The first *Blue Peter* pet, Petra – "a puppy ... for children who were not allowed to have animals of their own" – arrived in 1962 and snuffed it after a single episode.

Born November 4th, 1962, the plucky little black mongrel appeared on the last show before Christmas that year. She arrived in a huge cardboard box, done up to look like a Christmas present and presented to Valerie Singleton and Christopher Trace by no less a personage than the Head of Children's Television. Singleton cut the ribbon, and lo! it was a dog. Viewers – in the first instance of a tradition that was to give the show's animals their many interesting names[33]– voted to call her Petra.

What you won't read in Biddy Baxter's revisionist history

†32
Both Bernie Winters and Schnorbitz were mortal. In point of fact, however, they cheated by replacing the canine half of the pocket-faced comedy duo several times over. When Bernie Winters died, he was not replaced. The fourth Schnorbitz continues a low-key solo career, and is available for dinner parties. He can be contacted through www.supperwiththestars.co.uk.

†33
Two stick out. Viewers voted to name one of those moribund parrots Joey. In the

Continued overleaf

63

early 1980s, *Blue Peter*
adopted as a good cause
an adult human cerebral
palsy victim named Joey
Deacon, assuming that
his plight would kindle
human fellow-feeling
in its pre-teen viewers.
Many milk-bottle tops
later, it became clear
that what the show
had kindled in the
hearts of its pre-teen
viewers – and was it
ever, honestly, going to
be otherwise? – one of
the most enduring and
offensive playground
impersonations in
modern history. 'Joey'
and 'Deacon' became
classroom shorthand
for a simpleton. The
other interesting name
was given to one of the
six surviving puppies
(the runt didn't make
it) of *Blue Peter* golden
retriever Bonnie's
seven-strong 1991 litter.
Viewers voted to call one
of the bitches Biddy. The
tough-minded founding
producer of Blue Peter
was Biddy Baxter. The
dog's name was later
changed to Millie.

†34
The deal with the BBC,
in some cases – as with
Noakes – was that the
pet would be put in the
charge of the presenter,
who would collect an
allowance for the animal's
food, lodging and vet's
bills. There's no reason
to suppose the high
mortality rate among *Blue
Peter* pets had anything
to do with expenses fraud.

Petra: A Dog For Everyone (Pelham, 1978) is that Petra died almost immediately afterwards. She was just for Christmas.

There was a cover-up. Innocences were at stake. The producers scoured the country for a lookalike, and it was the lookalike that appeared as "Petra" on the show. What was the phoney Petra like? She detested blue trousers, and had good taste in music, once biting a hole in the pants of the bassist for the pop band The Hollies. She was sexually discriminating, too. In a move of spectacular pimpishness, the producers of the show invited viewers to vote on which of five male dogs would be allowed to mate with her. She ended up being shagged by a beagle, but – thwarting the hopes of the show – refused to conceive. She was finally knocked up on her own terms, by a Shetland sheepdog to whom she had taken a fancy.

Petra was joined on the *Blue Peter* set by her daughter Patch, one of a litter from the autumn of 1965. She joined the show as John Noakes's first pet,[34] in 1966. Patch was not to live long, however. In May 1971 she contracted E Coli Septicaemia and died.

Noakes – the dog-loving *Blue Peter* presenter to top them all – had to go on air to break the news of Patch's death to the viewers. Noakes broke down. "During the rehearsals," Baxter was to write later, "whilst John was reading out some of those letters, that tough little Yorkshireman – who is afraid of nothing and nobody – suddenly stopped. He couldn't see the writing through his tears."

Yet for John Noakes and the viewers of *Blue Peter*, the death of Patch closed one door and opened another. For into all of our lives[35] there was to bound a shaggy, boisterous black-and-white Border collie called Shep.

Noakes and Shep hit it off immediately, and such was

Shep's enthusiasm that "Get Down, Shep!" became a national catchphrase. In 1977, Shep was accorded the unusual canine distinction of appearing in effigy in Madame Tussauds. A model of John Noakes appeared beside her.

†35
This is a figure of speech. I wasn't born for another two and a half years or so.

Petra, showing no apparent jealousy at being upstaged by the chemistry between Noakes and her younger rival, carried on into old age. She did well to get that far. Though good-natured, she was something of a weakling and, for reasons that are unclear, had lost all her front teeth by the age of five.

Increasing wonkiness – she was rheumatic, diabetic, deaf, and all but toothless – forced her retirement in early 1977. Her retirement was pre-announced, causing a flurry of panic. Young viewers told to expect "important news" about Petra assumed the worst, and wrote in begging that she not be put down. They were reassured that she was simply retiring to live with a kindly, bespectacled lady called Edith Menezes – and, at the end of June, she did.

As with many stars who leave the limelight, the decline was swift. In the second week of September, Edith reported that Petra had lost the use of her back legs. By September 13th, she was peeing where she lay. It was time to call it a day. Petra was put down the following morning. The BBC received 20,000 letters of condolence, 40,000 requests for photographs, 5 offers of free plots in pet cemeteries, and 1 phone call from an enterprising taxidermist wondering whether they would be interested in having the mutt stuffed. They decided against. With the help of subscriptions from grieving viewers, a large bronze bust of her by the sculptor William Timym was erected in the *Blue Peter* garden.

With Petra out of the picture, Shep was top dog. He pressed the advantage. In 1978 the Barron Knights released a tribute song to Shep. It was called: "Get Down Shep!" The chorus should give you the general idea:

> *Get down Shep! Keep still, boy –*
> *Do as you're told, come 'ere*
> *Get down Shep! Behave yourself*
> *Or I'll cuff you round the ear ...*

Shep was at the height of his fame. He left *Blue Peter*, and in a highly unusual deal

– the show's producers fearing a national outcry if they were seen to split up a beloved double-act – was allowed to keep his presenter. The two went on to star in several series of *Go With Noakes!* before Shep tired of stardom and – perhaps – his excitable co-star, and retired in 1980.

Shep spent his retirement with Edith Menezes, the largely unsung saint who, for 27 years, was in charge of looking after the *Blue Peter* cats.[36] Reconciled at last with Shep, John Noakes went on live television – on a now-forgotten programme called *Fax* – to announce Shep's death. Again, he wept.

†36
Menezes died in 1994.

†37
Historians of prime ministerial pets will note that fun-loving Mr Major adopted a stray black and white cat called Humphrey in 1989. The cat lived in Downing Street until Mr Major's ruthless successor as prime minister, cat-hating Cherie Booth QC, had Humphrey DELETED ON LEGAL ADVICE. A public outcry forced Ms Booth to issue photographs of herself cuddling a Humphrey lookalike. The pictures, though transparently DELETED ON LEGAL ADVICE, were swallowed whole by the same supine press corps that waved through the 45 minute claim, and the whole thing blew over.

Somehow, the dogs that were to come after never seemed quite to reach the high water mark set by Shep and the phoney Petra. I wondered, for a moment, whether it was simply that I saw through the distorting lens of having outgrown the show; but since I was only four in 1978, when Goldie the golden retriever showed up, that seems unlikely. More likely it's that golden retrievers are, simply, curiously characterless hounds. Goldie, donated by Guide Dogs For the Blind, joined the show along with Simon Groom – also a rather colourless character. Goldie was fecund – giving birth to thirteen young in two litters. The first litter contained a bitch called Lady Diana; it was 1981. Goldie retired from the show – like Shep, taking her pet presenter with her – in 1986, and spent a happy retirement in Derbyshire. She pegged out in 1992.

Goldie's daughter Bonnie succeeded her on the show, and did much the same as her mum. Her offspring – and by now, the whole vote-for-a-name thing had got completely out of hand, with 40,000 democracy-crazed pre-teens writing in with suggestions – included Biddy (see footnote 33), Major, named for the new prime minister,[37] and Margot, named for the dancer Margot Fonteyn, who had herself just handed in her dinner pail. Tragic Margot the dog died at the age of five.

Anthea Turner and Bonnie won prizes two years running at the Olympia dog show. Bonnie died in 2001 at the ripe old age of fifteen. Anthea is still going strong.

Blue Peter currently has three dogs: rescue mutt Mabel, wonky-hipped childless pedigree Lucy, and sheepdog Meg – who has made a cameo on *The Archers* and, sinisterly, dabbled with being a sniffer dog. All are, as far as I know, alive, so they need not detain us here.

Blue Peter had bad luck with parrots. Some parrots last a century or more.[38] Not so *Blue Peter* parrots. Joey, a Brazilian Blue-Fronted parrot arrived in 1967, shortly after the second *Blue Peter* book, but died of an infection in 1968. He was succeeded by a parrot called Barney, who died in short order of a rare lung disease. After that, they gave up.

The longest-lived *Blue Peter* pet was their first tortoise. Fred, a hardy tortoise of Greek extraction and indeterminate age, arrived on the show in the autumn of 1963, and promptly went to sleep. He was hibernating, apparently. This was, as viewers were to discover yearly until Fred's death in 1979, the most exciting weapon in the average tortoise's televisual entertainment armoury.

Actually, hibernation was technically the second most exciting trick Fred played. The most exciting was changing sex. As a viewer with a high definition telly and a sharp eye for tortoise pudenda wrote in to point out early in his career, Fred was a girl tortoise. She was duly renamed Freda, and showed no signs of minding.

It was safety first with Freda. *Blue Peter* was generally keen on helping its viewers keep their tortoises alive and well, and so liked to remind them when it was hibernation time each year, and show them how to make a nice tortoise nest in a straw-lined cardboard box. She made an annual pre-hibernation appearance – like Her Majesty attending the Christmas service at Balmoral – before nodding off.

A further precaution was taken with Freda that, while compromising her dignity, may have contributed to her longevity. Her name was painted down the left flank of her shell in block capitals. As the *Blue Peter Book of Pets* (BBC, 1969) admonished young tortoise owners: "many tortoises that have crawled into a pile of autumn leaves or garden rubbish have been saved from the bonfire because of the conspicuous paint on their shells". (Would it were the same story

†38
A parrot said to have belonged to Winston Churchill is reported by newspapers to have reached the age of 100 once every year or so, when news is thin on the ground. There is no evidence I know of that Winston Churchill ever owned a parrot.

†39
One occasionally seems to see, as with the cats, a pattern of executives not losing their nerve, exactly, but thinking twice, after the event, about the wisdom of having all these pets.

†40
A diverting but ultimately irrelevant place in the history of tortoise death is occupied by Pat, the tortoise in Tom Stoppard's brilliant play *Jumpers*. George, a moral philosopher who happens to share his name with the *Blue Peter* tortoise, is carrying Pat around the place trying to find his pet hare, Thumper. Pat and Thumper are important to George's investigation into Zeno's Paradox. In an earlier experiment into the same paradox – did St Sebastian, killed by all those arrows, actually die of fright? – George has negligently discharged an arrow off-stage. He notices, with horror, that blood is coming from the top of the wardrobe. He puts Pat on the ground, stands on a chair, and peers onto the top of the wardrobe. From the wardrobe, he retrieves the body of Thumper, stuck through by the earlier arrow. Distracted by grief, George steps off the chair and – crunch! – onto poor old Pat. Curtain. Moral philosophers aren't always safe around pets.

for winos.) *Blue Peter* advised its viewers to use "non-lead" paint.

Freda's successors, Maggie and Jim, joined the show in 1979, while viewers were still grieving for Freda. Tortoise-loving viewers were to learn how bitter grief could get. Still babies – they appeared in a cameo on the show when they hatched in the late summer of 1974 – Maggie and Jim lasted only the blink of an eye in chelonian terms, before the cold snap of January 1982 claimed both their lives.

Their deaths were nearly too much to bear. *Blue Peter* wondered: should they give up on tortoises altogether?[39]

The years since Freda's arrival on the show had seen a considerable rise in awareness, both here and in other European countries, of tortoise welfare issues. Mass tortoise importation had begun at the very end of the 19th century, and it wasn't pretty. Only around one tortoise in ten sold into captivity and trafficked in cramped, unsanitary conditions from North Africa to the pet shops of the affluent West – was estimated to have survived. It was like Amistad for tortoises. It gives one new respect for Freda's hardihood and stoicism. She never lived to see the historic decision, in 1984, to extend Category One protection to spur-thighed, Hermann's, and marginated tortoises under the Convention for the International Trade in endangered species. The trade in death was over.[40]

Blue Peter, meanwhile, decided they needed another tortoise – albeit one carefully provenanced. The sainted Edith Menezes came up trumps, donating her tortoise Pork Pie to showbusiness. Pork Pie – thought to be around eight – burst onto *Blue Peter* in 1982, and was promptly renamed George.[41]

George built on the achievements of his predecessors. He

was trodden on by one of his co-stars,[42] took the opportunity of a live broadcast to piss on an Olympic hurdler,[43] and in 1988 went on a thrilling two-week, one-hundredth-of-a-mile per hour[44] road trip. On the latter occasion, burglars had made the mistake of letting George out of his pen in the garden during a robbery at Edith Menezes' house. George bolted after them. Edith, finding him missing, assumed the worst. After he failed to return for several days, he was assumed dead, and a solemn tribute to his life and achievements was broadcast on the show. The following day he was found, still in pursuit, by a woman walking her dog.

George lived on to celebrate his 21st birthday[45] with a party live on *Blue Peter* in 2003. The following year he dropped dead. Old age. Edith had been wrong. At the time he was blowing out the candles on his cake, George was actually around 80.

He knew only fleetingly, and in the December of his years, the love of a lady tortoise. Shelley – an Anna Nicole Smith among chelonians – joined the programme "to be a friend for George" only the month before his death. Did she tire him out?

George was buried with full honours in the *Blue Peter* garden. His place there is marked with a plaque and a rhododendron. Shelley is still, at the time of writing, thriving. Perhaps she yearns, sometimes, for those rhododendrons.

The first *Blue Peter* cat, a seal point Siamese named – again, by viewers – Jason, arrived in 1964. By not moving much, Jason lived until 1976.[46] He was not unmourned: the Oxford Union passed a motion, "This house regrets the passing of Jason the *Blue Peter* cat", and stood for two minutes in solemn silence.

His successors, Jack and Jill, born around the time of Jason's death, were feistier. Twin silver tabbies, they didn't like being on TV much, and frequently ran away. Jason's Sphynx-like imperturbability turned out to be the path to long life. Jill dropped dead of a heart attack in May 1983 – not a good innings by any means. Jack followed "very unexpectedly" three years after. Most cats make it past ten.

Edith Menezes, the cat lady and seemingly bottomless fount of replacement

†41
The viewers again.

†42
Mark Curry

†43
Kriss Akabusi

†44
Roughly. He burned up something like three miles in the fortnight he was on the run.

†45
He was held, presumably, to have been born again when he joined the cast of *Blue Peter*.

†46
He caught a chill, and his kidneys failed.

pets, supplied another kitten, called Willow. Willow's principal distinctions were wailing off camera and, in 1989, getting spayed. *Blue Peter* had decided that there were too many kittens coming unwanted into this wicked world, and that the responsible thing to do would be to prevent Willow's children from ever being born.[47] Was this why she cried? By 1991, the noise had become intolerable, and she was fired. She now lives in Sussex. She was succeeded by a pair of rescue cats called – the pits, this – Kari and Oke. They retired in 2004, aged thirteen, to live with Willow. They were succeeded by an orange and white rescue mog called Smudge. At the time of writing, he lives on.

†47
Jill had two kittens in 1980.

†48
Presumably Lewisham was unable to furnish a double.

Since the *Blue Peter* garden is where so many of these animals ended up, it is perhaps worth a note. In 1974 it was created ex nihilo in a patch of scrubby wasteland next to the canteen in TV Centre by the *Gardener's World* veteran Percy Thrower – a green-thumbed digger of the old school with fixed views on the use of DDT to control greenflies. Its highlight was a sunken ornamental pond, with all fish in it, and some trees. As every child who learned about the turning of the seasons through the progress of Mr Thrower's cyclical battle against the greenfly menace knows, its darkest hour came in 1983, when an enterprising gang of hoodlums hopped over the wall in the middle of the night, trampled the flowerbeds, pulled out the trees, shattered the ornamental urn, laid waste to the sundial and did something very very nasty – the exact nature of which is still earnestly disputed to this day – to the fishpond. Whatever it was, it killed the fish. Thrower teared up on live TV when, on the next *Blue Peter*, they broke the news to the children.[48]

Responsibility, or partial responsibility, was apparently admitted in the year 2000, when the footballer Les Ferdinand – at the time a pupil at Hammersmith Comprehensive – copped to the crime. "We got into a bit of bother," he told the obscure cable football show *45 Minutes*, adding in a way that his footie-playing old pal won't find helpful: "What I will say is I helped a few people over the wall, but I'm not at liberty to say whether Dennis Wise was one of them." Mr Ferdinand, however, subsequently recanted his confession, using an interview in the organ of record, the *Daily Star*, to insist that he had been "joking" about the vandalism, and Dennis Wise denied ever having had anything to do with it. The vandals are unshriven.

Since Thrower's death in 1988 – hastened, some still think, by the activities of the vandals – the garden has not been quite as it was. The sunflower competitions continue, but there has been talk of "sexing up" the format for a child market now more interested in Sony PlayStations than slug pellets. The BBC, not long ago, had to go so far as to deny that the garden was for the chop.

Certainly, its place as the home of nothing more than a green thought in a green shade is gone. The darkness of the outside world leaked in when Thrower's sanctuary became the most unlikely part of the BBC to become entwined in the vicious row over the death of Dr David Kelly. It emerged that the garden – because he assumed it to be the one part of Television Centre not to be bugged by the security services – had become the favoured place for the reporter Andrew Gilligan to hold clandestine meetings.[49] *Et in Arcadia ego.*

†49
He was the reporter who first broadcast Dr Kelly's view that the "45 minute claim" made by the Government to encourage us into war with Iraq was a lie.

Did old Gilligan, I wonder, during these meetings sometimes glance over at the bust of Petra, and wish he were lying once again on his front in a deep 70s shagpile, kicking his sandalled feet in the air, watching *Blue Peter* on the telly and waiting for his mum to bring him some Um Bongo, a Club biscuit and a packet of crisps? The shadows lengthen ...

CHAPTER 4

DADDY, IS TIMMY IN HEAVEN NOW?

The fate of the sons of men and the fate of beasts is the same; as one dies, so dies the other. They all have the same breath, and man has no advantage over the beasts; for all is vanity. All go to one place; all are from the dust, and all may turn to dust again. Who knows whether the spirit of man goes upward and the spirit of the beast goes down to earth?
Ecclesiastes 3:19–22

Be comforted, little dog. Thou too in the Resurrection, shall have a little golden tail.
Martin Luther

IN THE LATE SUMMER OF 2004, I DISPATCHED A NUMBER OF LETTERS. THEY READ AS FOLLOWS...

Dear Your Holiness [or Dalai / Rabbi / Mr Hubbard / Osama etc.]

I do hope you will forgive me for troubling you out of the blue.

I am in the process of writing a book for the British publisher Canongate about how people experience and cope with the deaths of their pet animals. Among the chapters I think very important to include is one about the teachings of different religious traditions on this subject: there seems to be very little readily available to the general reader.

I was wondering whether you might be able to find time, between now and the beginning of next year, to talk to me about Catholic [or Muslim / Hindu / Scientological etc] teaching on this issue. Put very starkly, the big question would be: do animals go to heaven? I appreciate, however, that the theological position will be rather more complicated than that. I'd be interested in touching on such issues as whether it's acceptable to use, say, the sign of the cross in an animal's memorial, and on theodicy,[50] how best parents might frame, in Christian terms, an answer to a child's sense of injustice at the loss of a cat, or hamster.

> †50
> Theodicy is the business of justifying the ways of God to man. Milton: once studied, never forgotten.

Thank you for your time. I look forward to hearing from you.

There were variations for presumed and actual local sensibilities. The one to the secretary of the Pagan Federation of Great Britain had to be tweaked substantially, and the choice of "cat, or hamster" for my examples was insouciant, but not accidental. I wanted to leave the issues of dogs and Vietnamese pot-bellied pigs out of the picture until I'd had the chance to get in a room with a senior Muslim sheik or, inshallah, the Chief Rabbi.

At least in the short term, unfortunately, the letters I sent told me much less about the comparative theology of animal posterity than they did about how rude you can get away with being if you have a deity on your side.[51] Running these down was a long story. But here, roughly, is how it all breaks down.

ANGLICANS

THE ANGLICAN CHURCH has no official line on the subject. Opinions on animal immortality – like those on many other subjects within the Anglican Communion – seem to vary pretty widely. Especially helpful to me, however, were the former Archbishop of York, Lord Habgood,[52] and the former Bishop of Salisbury, John Baker.

†51 (from previous page) I make an exception for the excellent Dr Rowan Williams, the Archbishop of Canterbury. I received, practically by return, a polite note from a member of Dr Williams's staff. The Scientologists and the Baha'i were equally obliging, though neither had much to say at all about animal theology.
†52 Who wrote me a long, thoughtful letter, and forbore even to mention that I had misspelled his name.

Both men take a liberal view of the theology of pet posterity, suggesting we approach the question by asking what it is about humans that makes them able to relate to God, and to what extent animals share the same capacities. Lord Habgood thinks that what's important here – what makes us human and, by implication, gives us a soul – is the ability to form relationships, "with all that this implies in terms of insight, sympathy and love, and the possibilities of community formation arising out of this". This ability depends heavily on language, but not exclusively so. Animals can, therefore, manifestly go some way towards this kind of "soul-forming relationship":

Thinking along these lines leads me to expect that pets, by virtue of their close relationships with human beings, may to some extent share whatever relationship we have with God in the hereafter. If what I am, and the loving relationships I have forged, are essentially dependent on one another, it can be argued that I would not be myself in heaven without them.

If I understand him rightly, he is implying Timmy's claim on a place in heaven is argued on two grounds: the extent to which his non-linguistic, sub-human capacity for affection goes some way to giving him a doggy soul; and his importance to the integrity of the souls of those who loved him. That is, heaven wouldn't be heavenly if you were missing your dog; and you wouldn't be you if you didn't remember you had a dog to miss.

In any case, he says he thinks it therefore reasonable to commemorate pets with "some kind of religious ceremony", but not extending that to cover all animals. There must be, he says, some kind of "gradation in value" down the scale of creation

– whereby humans are higher than dogs, and that while God loves a flatworm, he loves the Jews more (I paraphrase).

Basic to any theism, argued Bishop Baker, is the conviction that everything in existence is brought into existence and owes its continuing existence to God. So the question to consider is "which creatures God might continue to sustain in existence after physical death in eternal life. What, for example, would be the point of giving eternal existence to all the krill there have ever been, not to mention bacteria?"

There are two arguments that Bishop Baker suggests might be considered in trying to figure out whether animals get through the pearly gates: what he calls the "representational" and the "relational".

The first criterion is based on the conjecture, pretty common through history, that we might expect to see in heaven a perfect consummation of what we see here below – and that every aspect of the created order would therefore be represented, albeit in a format that would offer no harm to any other. The lion would lie down with the lamb. The tapeworm would roam free in the meadow.

Then there's the relational argument. There are higher-order categories of creatures – pets among them – that are capable of being involved in relationships with each other, and with us. "These relationships are an integral part of what they and we are, what we have become in our lifetime, and it is therefore perfectly reasonable to believe that God would keep those relationships in being as part and parcel of our reality to which God gives eternal life. Can we eg imagine St Francis in heaven without animals?"

Quite so. Bishop Baker signed his letter off with a modest disclaimer. "The C of E does not, as far as I know, have any official statement of teaching on these things, and what I have said here is purely my own thoughts."

BUDDHISTS

I REGRET TO say that Buddhism has little obvious to offer Timmy, though its admirable peace-loving proponents are far less likely to shoot him for "worrying their sheep". The Buddhist Society of the UK directed me to the Four Noble truths as the main point of reference.

These are as follows:

1) Suffering and unsatisfactoriness exist.
2) The cause of suffering and unsatisfactoriness exists.
3) The cause may be brought to an end.
4) The means whereby this may be achieved: the Noble Eightfold Path.

The Noble Eightfold path looks to the outsider like a step-by-step guide to getting your shit together and being nice:

1) Right Seeing.   2) Right Thought.
3) Right Speech.   4) Right Action.
5) Right Livelihood.   6) Right Effort.
7) Right Mindfulness.   8) Right Contemplation.

The last two of these steps, which are towards a final freedom from desire and, hence, the suffering that proceeds from attachment to the world, involve meditation – something dogs are presumably not good at. But nor do Buddhists believe that we have special individual "souls", as most Western traditions seem to: in fact, No-I (realising that you aren't, as you thought, you) is kind of the point. We may have to acknowledge that whether Timmy goes to heaven is the wrong question to ask a Buddhist.

"It would be towards an acceptance of the fact of death as part of life that Buddhism would direct anyone adult or child," was the concise but friendly observation of their registrar, presumably in response to the question of where Timmy's death fits into the pattern of things. She added: "I know of no special teachings for pets."

That is not to say that dead pets are ignored. When "Jack Benny", a cat belonging to The Venerable Khyongla Rato Rinpoche of New York's Tibet Centre, suffered from kidney problems, The Venerable Khyongla Rato Rinpoche took measures to ease his passing. He told Wallace Sife, author of *The Loss of a Pet*, that he bought a cassette recorder and "played tapes of the teachings of His Holiness, the Dalai Lama, so the cat could hear them repeatedly over several days". The cat did not recover.

There is, incidentally, a misconception that orthodox Buddhist teaching includes promises of reincarnation – or, to give it its smart name, the transmigration of souls – as an option. Perhaps, some will think, you will be reunited with Timmy the dog if – before being shot for worrying Christian sheep – he lived the canine life contemplative, and you were a bit of a bad 'un. He might be promoted to a horse or something, and you'd be demoted, and for the next life you'd happily share a paddock.

Apparently it doesn't work like that.

CATHOLICS

SOME SUPPORT FOR the view of animals as being "souled" comes from church fathers. Origen believed that all creatures were originally endowed with free will and souls   and that the order of fallen nature reflected whether those souls had been naughty or nice. They were "clothed with the body of this or that irrational animal" according to the degree of their fall into evil.

On the other side, you have the inheritors of a hard-nosed scholastic tradition. St Thomas Aquinas, under the influence of ancient Greek philosophy, divides animate creation in three. In club class, there are humans, who have "rational" souls – directed towards God and capable of a conscious relationship with the divine. Back in steerage, there are animals, who have "sensitive" souls. And then, stowed in the luggage hold, are algae, cauliflowers and such like, who have "vegetative" souls". Only club class ticket holders get to heaven. Stick insects and triffids, and microbiological oddities like giant viruses, are unclassified, except for stick insects, which are – just – in coach.

"Intellectual creatures are ruled by God as though he cared for them for their own sake," wrote Aquinas, "while other creatures are ruled as being directed to rational creatures." That's as much as to say that animals are there to serve us: to eat or draw a plough or fetch the paper. "By divine providence they are intended for man's use in the natural order," he wrote, "hence it is not wrong for man to make use of them either by killing or in any other way whatever." (Does that last clause mean man in general, and St Thomas Aquinas in particular, is entitled to have sex with chickens?)

The Cartesian view, and it has persisted in being influential, was that animals are basically automata that run "just like a clock" and "have no reason at all". Descartes wondered even whether animals were capable of feeling pain. He never trod, evidently, on a sleeping dog's foot in the dark.

Where, then, does the Catholic Church now stand?

The Pope did not write back. It is possible I had his address wrong. It is also possible that he had bigger fish to fry. Between my non-correspondence with him in 2004, and the preparation of this manuscript for publication, something not altogether unexpected, but sad, happened: Pope John Paul II died. We can assume, then, that he by now knows exactly whether Timmy will go to heaven, but is not in a position to enlighten us.

Before he went, however, he did take an interest in the matter. In fact he set the cat among the pigeons – arguably, that is, he set the stage for cat and pigeons to be reunited in the hereafter – in January 1990. He said: "The animals possess a soul and men must love and feel solidarity with our smaller brethren." This is a big step. Yikes, thought a number of people. If animals have souls, what's so special about humans?

More practically, the odd one will have doubtless wondered, does that mean we will be sharing the hereafter with a million billion stray dogs, every mosquito that has ever been swatted, and whatever it is that causes strep throat? Why not give up on salvation and go on holiday to Bangladesh instead?

A cunning piece of theological footwork solved the problem. Carlo Molari, who was Professor of Theology and Dogma at the University of Urbino, welcomed the announcement as: "very important and significant [...] a 'sign of the times' because it demonstrates the Church's desire and deep concern to clarify present confused thinking and attitudes towards the animal kingdom. There should be no need, but the Pontiff, in reiterating that animals came into being because of the direct action of the 'breath' of God, wanted to say that also these creatures, as well as man, are possessed of the divine spark of life and that living quality that is the soul. And are therefore not inferior beings or only of a purely material reality."

So Catholic dogma, as it stands, looks a bit like this. Animals have souls. They are definitely one step up from stocks and stones. But they do not have *immortal* souls. You can bless them all you like, but you cannot perform the rites of the church on them, and they will not be accompanying you into the hereafter.

JEWS

THE REV ALAN GREENBAT, Honorary Consultant to the Chief Rabbi, says that there are differing views on the relationships between humans and animals in Jewish thought. But, bottom line, it looks like Jewish gerbils don't make it to the afterlife, either.

The theological position doesn't seem dissimilar to the Catholic one – that is, mainstream thought accords two levels to the soul. "Soul" is a generic term. Within Jewish theology you have subdivisions. There is "nefesh", which is a life-soul possessed by all living creatures. Only humans, however, have a "neshama", which is a higher-level soul.

All of us go to the "Olam Haba" (the world to come) before returning to the creator, and it's the duty of us humans – being gifted not only with neshama but with "bechirah", that is, free will and the capacity to make moral judgments – to prepare ourselves for this. Those with only a nefesh aren't expected to make preparations for the afterlife. They won't be there.

There are no canonical pet burial rites in Judaism.

There are, incidentally, certain exceptional animals in Jewish theology, created for specific purposes – Balaam's ass, Noah's dove, the serpent in Eden, and the Shamir in the construction of the Temple.

The Rev Greenbat says, however: "these were created for miraculous purposes and should not be confused with the normal order of things".

HINDUS

THE OUTLOOK IS bright for the terminally ill Hindu animal companion. There's no Hindu heaven, but there's a future for Timmy in this world, and the prospect of a pleasant postmortem interlude, too.

Hindus credit animals with souls, believing ourselves – with a humility rare beside the generally anthropocentric traditions of other religions – to be a continuation of animals. Hindus, I might add, will tend to disapprove of the recipe section of this book. "Animals are not put on earth for the consumption of mankind," writes Jay Lakhani of the Vivekananda Centre for Hindu Education. "Unfortunately human beings can only survive on other life forms, but then the best way to survive would be on vegetables than the more evolved beings like animals." Sorry.

The idea of life after death, he says, is very different in Hinduism than in the Abrahamic religions, because of the issue of reincarnation. Dogs and cats and hamsters, too, will be reincarnated, and if you are attached to an animal in this life, there is a strong likelihood, writes Mr Lakhani, that you will be reborn in close proximity to it in the next. Between births, moreover, there is a sort of intermission in which we may create our own "mental heaven and hell" for a short period and re-create people or other beings we like.

"The way we can console a child about the loss of a pet," he adds, "would be to say that the pet has gone to a better world: as that pet was exhibiting almost human characteristics like loyalty and love, it is highly likely for that pet to be reborn as a human child. So would that not be preferable to living an animal life?"

MUSLIMS

FOR THIS SECTION I am indebted to Dr A Majid Katme, to whom I was directed by the Muslim Council of Britain. He sent me a bullet-pointed brief on Islamic attitudes to animals that did not prevaricate.

"God Almighty has created man, animals and all the universe," he wrote. "Animals were created separately from man ... Darwin theory is a myth, a theory and is not accepted in Islam! There is no evolution: man from animal/monkey!"

Man, he explained, occupies a privileged position in the order of the creation as a "viceregent of God", and is "in charge" of all creation, including animals, but owes them a duty of care.

"The holy book *Al Qur'an* and the sayings *Ahadith* of the final prophet Muhammad (peace be upon him) contain a lot of datas on animals. In the *Qur'an*, there is the biggest chapter/Surah titled 'The Cow'. Other titles in the *Qur'an*: The Cattle, Ant, Bees, Spider, Elephant ... These are mentioned in the Qur'an too: sheep, goat, camel, horse, donkey, fish, birds ..."

Every species of animal, he explained, is a community like us; each having unique ways of eating, sleeping, reproduction, language, recreation, social life, feelings and needs which should be respected. And every animal praises the

Creator – though we may not be able to understand it – with a prayer unique to its species or type.

Animals, he says, have souls – and will be raised on the Day of Judgment. "Many animals go to Heaven like sheeps … some go to hell like the snake, not as punishment but to torture the guilty/persistent cruel sinful man!"

Likewise, human behaviour towards animals will be questioned by God. Islam orders animal rights: natural food; no animal protein to the animals we eat; no GM food; water; natural reproduction; motherhood; shelter; natural environment, recreation, socialisation; open air; sun; light; space; protection from extreme weather; cold; heat; rain etc …This goes double for both domestic and edible animals. Cruelty – from foxhunting to vivisection – is forbidden and "punishable".

"A person can go to paradise for facilitating food or drink to an animal," writes Dr Katme. He adds, conversely, that it really is a good idea to make arrangements for the neighbours to feed the cat if you are going away for the weekend. "A person can go to hell … because of depriving an animal from food or drink (as stated by the prophet Muhammad, peace be upon him)."

As far as pets go, they are all for it. Indeed, Abu Hourayrah – a companion of the prophet Muhammad (peace be upon him) – used to look after a kitten, or hourah. Hence his name: Abu Hourayrah – the father of kittens.

"Cat is a recommended pet at home, but after taking all hygienic precautions. It is not allowed to keep dog at home as a domestic animal as it is unclean, a source of diseases, bodily injury, attacks and problems … But one could go to Heaven for getting water to a thirsty dog!"

Horses, sheep and some birds are "highly respected". Feeding a cat is "a charitable act, to be rewarded".

I rest easy in my bed.

SCIENTOLOGISTS

IN ALL THE many millions of words of his published writings, L Ron Hubbard seems to have had nothing to say about the posterity of dogs. This, at least, according to a very nice Scientologist I shared a cup of coffee with in the Starbucks at Victoria Station.

A cat did come into it, however.

"Close your eyes," she said. I did. "Now think of a cat. Create a picture in your mind's eye of a cat. Got it?"

I could see a slightly self-satisfied looking long-haired Persian; fur blueish, nose snub. "Yup," I said.

"Right," she said. "Who's looking at the cat?"

"Me?"

"Exactly."

This is a demonstration of the Scientological idea of the soul. The imaginary cat – for Hubbard, as for Schrödinger – is a teaching aid.

As far as the psychology of pet loss goes, Scientology has some things to say. Scientologists, like Freudians, spend a lot of time trying to get rid of negative associations with past events. In Dianetics (which really covers Hubbard's theory of mind; Scientology is the spiritual end of it) we have two sides to our mind. The analytical mind processes day-to-day experience; the reactive mind takes over in moments of "unconsciousness" prompted by injury or extreme physical or emotional pain.

The analytical mind stores a complete timeline of "mental image pictures" that builds up through our life. The reactive mind stores a special sort of memory called an "engram", in which all the elements of the traumatic experience recorded equate to all the other elements.

If you re-encounter such elements later in life, the engram can be "restimulated", causing a return of negative effects. This association may then in turn produce a mental image picture associated with the previous engram, called a "secondary"; or one at a second remove, called a "lock". It all silts up. This is a Bad Thing.

The process is more easily understood with reference to *The Basic Dianetics Picture Book* (Bridge Publications and New Era Publications, 1999).

At the top of page 35, there is a picture of a girl being mauled by an Alsatian. It is captioned: A GIRL GETS BITTEN BY A DOG. Standing over the dog-chewed victim, there is a distressed-looking woman in an A-line skirt and a polo shirt holding out one arm and saying, rather eccentrically: GET AWAY FROM THAT MAD DOG!

Below, there is a picture of the woman repeating her advice from the other side of an arm with a dog clamped to it: the scene as the victim might have seen it. The caption says: SHE RETAINS A PICTURE OF THIS EXPERIENCE IN THE REACTIVE MIND – AN ENGRAM.

Overleaf, we see the engram being restimulated. The dog-bitten girl, YEARS LATER, is walking past a woman with a dog. The reactive mind – even though the girl may not be conscious of having seen this benign dog – takes over TO "PROTECT" THE GIRL FROM WHAT IT PERCEIVES TO BE A DANGEROUS SITUATION. The girl's arm begins to hurt, and she feels an urge to go away.

An instance of this chain of negative feeling might be as follows. Silky the hamster bites me (pain: reactive mind takes over; engram forms). Silky the hamster is later squashed to death (distress and association with hamster causes formation of secondary). I start writing book about dead hamsters. The tip of my finger starts to hurt.

Scientologists claim to be able to break this cycle of suffering. Who is to say they are wrong?

SIKHS

MY CORRESPONDENT, a Mr Singh, was brief and to the point. I quote his letter in full.

"Sikhism states that there are 8.4 million different life forms, and the human life form is the highest rank. Only in this mould can you actually preach the name of God and achieve the ultimate reward, of reaching God. Sikhs believe that people who have a love and affection for their pet animals, do this because those particular individuals were related to them in past lives."

THE REST

WELL, I GOT as far as S. It would be nice to have been able to provide an A to Z listing of the teachings of all the different religious traditions, but this has already been rather hard work, and I can't find the Zoroastrians in the Yellow Pages. My apologies to them, and anyone else who feels his or her god has been unfairly overlooked. Take heart: gods can be expected to get over these things.

"For a few days, black and white, democrats and communists, republicans and royalists in all countries, islands and continents have one feeling, one language, one direction … one feeling of compassion for this little living being twirling helpless over our heads."

STUTTGARTER ZEITUNG

"The dog will die and we can't save it!"

DAILY MIRROR

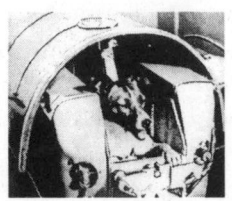

ORBITING FOREVER LOST:
LAIKA
AND THE DOGS' GRAVEYARD IN SPACE

FOR LAIKA, THERE WAS NEVER GOING TO BE A RETURN JOURNEY. SHE WAS MARKED FOR DEATH – BY HUMAN SELFISHNESS, BY THE TOTALITARIAN TIMETABLING OF THE SOVIET SPACE PROGRAM, AND, HEARTBREAKINGLY, BY HER OWN VERY SWEETNESS OF NATURE. SHE WAS TO BE – TO THE GREATER HONOUR OF THE UNITED SOVIET SOCIALIST REPUBLIC – THE FIRST LIVING CREATURE TO DIE IN SPACE.

SHE WAS NOT to know this when she was recruited for the Soviet space programme at the age of three. A sort of terrier-cum-husky-cum-samoyed mongrel of a sort known generically as a Laika, she was originally called Kudryavka, or "Li'l Curly".[53]

Sputnik 2's mission was conceived only three weeks before they shot Laika into space. It was October 1957, and Kruschev was riding high on the success of the first Sputnik. Whanged into orbit only days previously, on October 4th, it had been a giant poke in the eye for the prestige of the imperialist running-dogs in the US space programme. Schoolchildren in America could point their telescopes to the sky and see the satellite. Its radio transmission – blip, blip – will have sounded to listening stations across the Cold War West like: "Nyer nyer ner nyer nyerr".

It was, then, to the heavens that he looked when casting about for a spectacular to mark the fortieth anniversary of the Revolution. Regardless of the sort of planning that usually goes into a space launch (it is, after all, rocket science) Kruschev contacted the architect of Sputnik's success – the Soviet Union's most brilliant rocket engineer, Sergei Pavlovich Korolev. Something impressive had to happen in space, and it had to happen in the next three weeks.

The regime being what it was, Korolev knew well enough that "you must be joking" wouldn't cut it. So, as far as it appears, he thought, "Um. Um. A dog?"[54]

Pravda duly announced, on October 9th 1957: "The Soviet Union will launch a sputnik carrying animals as passengers. Detailed observations will be made of their behaviour."

Korolev and his team knocked up plans for something that was more or less identical to the original Sputnik – only with a box for the dog and a cosmic ray detector stuck on.[55] As Korolev's deputy Boris Chertok was (later) to admit: "The second satellite was created without preliminary design, or any kind of design."

Laika was to make her journey to space strapped into a harness, in a pressurised cabin. The cabin was lined with soft material to cushion her, and heat-proofed. It was just big enough for her to stand up in, though restraints prevented her turning around. Food was a sort of high-protein gel she had been trained to eat. She took no dog chews. There was no time to plan for how to bring Laika home again.

Reports now suggest she was placed in her capsule at lunchtime, on October 31st – four days before lift-off. She had been trained – as had her understudy, Albina – for the small space by confinement, over three weeks, in successively smaller and smaller cages. As she waited for the off at the freezing launch site, the air piped into her capsule was warmed through a heater, and two attendants were instructed to keep an eye on her.[56]

On November 3rd, 1957, Laika was chucked up into space from the same launch pad in Kazakhstan that Sputnik I had departed from a month earlier. Launched at 2.32 a.m. GMT, the little dog headed for her certain future at 17,895 mph. The world watched.

Many had been called to the canine space programme, but few chosen, and Laika was already a veteran. Over the preceding years, Korolev's team had conducted a series of sub-orbital high-altitude ballistic launches. Instruments were to record how the subjects reacted to noise, vibration, periods of weightlessness, changes in temperature, accelerations and decelerations ...

Originally strays kidnapped from the streets of Moscow, the dogs – mongrels were selected for their hardihood – were trained no less rigorously than, not many years later, the brave orange-suited possessors of the Right Stuff were to be. There were dozens of dog cosmonauts in the Soviet space programme. They were tested in capsules and in ordinary aircraft. They were whirled round in centrifuges and jiggled half to death in vibration chambers. First, they were locked into pressurised cabins and shot in the direction of the upper atmosphere. Not long after, dog space suits and dog space helmets were being used.

Laika had been up; but so also had less celebrated colleagues. Some were named to history; some unnamed. Their memorial is the stark table in a book about the early years of the Soviet space programme.

"26 May 1955", it reads. "Flight by two dogs. I Jun 1956 Flight by two dogs. 7 Jun 1956 Flight by two dogs. 14 June 1956 Flight by two dogs ..."

There was a breakthrough on Feb 21st, 1958, when Korolev's team managed to get the V-5A rocket up to an altitude of 480 km. Communist space-dogs were getting closer to orbit.

Not long after, they were coming back, too. On July 2nd, 1959, two named dogs – Otvazhnaya and Snezhinka – returned safely from "a great height". Snezhinka means "Icicle"; "Otvazhnaya" means "Courageous". With them, safe home, too, came a rabbit, called Marfusha: "li'l Marfa".[57] Li'l Marfa seems to have gone into retirement – but we know Otvazhnaya, living up to her name, was sent on a second mission less than a fortnight later, returning safely. Belanka and Pyostraya made it back alive from 448 km on August 29th of the same year.

†57
The names of the animals involved in the Soviet space programme are a source of some fascination, at least to me. Names like Albina ("White One"), Malyshka ("Little One") and Tsyganka ("Gypsy"). I asked my Russian friend Natasha to look over a list I had, and she burst out laughing. Kozyavka – a brave pooch who made more than one ballistic flight – translates, she swears blind, as "Little Bogey".

And so on.

It was her sweet temper that caused Laika to be chosen for the first mission into space. Her sweet temper sealed her fate.

The official version was this: Laika thoroughly enjoyed her outing into space. She suffered no ill-effects from weightlessness, panted happily through her first few orbits, and quietly lapsed into her final sleep when the oxygen ran out.

What actually happened was this: the crappy Jerry-rigged heatproofing fell off as Sputnik 2 entered orbit. Laika was baked alive.

Because it was bigger than the first Sputnik, Sputnik 2 was more easily visible from earth. As its orbit got more wobbly, it started to tumble end over end and so, towards the end, it flared ever more brightly in the sky. On April 4th, 1958, after 163 days and 2,570 revolutions, Sputnik 2 finally burned up. Laika's ashes were scattered across the sky.

The RSPCA was none too pleased. There were calls to protest at the Russian embassy, and the National Canine Defence League in the UK attempted to organise a minute's silence. Much as we all deplore the modern habit of reflex calls for a minute's silence, it's hard not to feel that the be-nice-to-dogs mob, in Laika's case, had a point. She was ill used.

Many years later, Laika's trainer Oleg Gazenko apologised: "Work with animals is a source of suffering to all of us. We treat them like babies who cannot speak.

The more time passes, the more I'm sorry about it. We shouldn't have done it. We did not learn enough from the mission to justify the death of the dog."

Laika appeared on stamps in Romania, Albania and Poland, has been posthumously honoured in chocolate bar form, and has given her name to several pop bands, none of whom have entered the top ten, let alone space.

Her sacrifice was not in vain. Well, not wholly in vain. Before she died, between five and seven hours and three orbits into the flight, the Soviet scientists were able to learn a little from their instruments about the effects of space flight on the body of a living organism. It established that spaceflight was survivable. And that only seems to have encouraged them.

Two years[58] after Laika burned to the abode where the eternal are, two huskies called Belka ("Squirrel") and Strelka ("Little Arrow") pelted into space in the fifth sputnik, known as Spaceship 2.

†58
August 19th
1960

Two things distinguished their flight from that of Laika:

1) They came back.

2) They were not alone. Their travelling companions on Spaceship 2 were two unnamed white rats, twenty-eight mice, several hundred insects, plants and seeds from onion, peat, wheat and maize. And – though this was kept hush-hush at the time – some flaps of skin from the thighs and shoulders of three doctors from the Moscow Institute of Experimental Biology.

TV cameras recorded the dogs' initial distress at the launch, but they seemed to relax a little once they were underway. When weightlessness kicked in they "jerked their heads up" and spent five minutes playing dead. But then they perked up. The cabin temperature stuck to an even 18 degrees. Belka was – it later emerged – space-sick on orbit four, but the story was suppressed in the interests of the greater glory of the Soviet space programme.

When their capsule bumped safely down on farmland the next day at 6 m/s, it was greeted by dumbfounded Russian yokels, who examined it and came upon a tag: "Please inform the Soviet Space Centre immediately on discovery."

Strelka, who had not been space-sick and was therefore deemed to have the Right Stuff, was also allowed to play a part in the give-and-take that kept the Cold War from becoming Hot. Her daughter Pushinka was presented as a gift to the

children of John F Kennedy, and her descendants are alive today – naturalised canine Americans.

It is of no real relevance to this section that Ham the Astrochimp – America's breakthrough experiment in flinging animals into outer space – returned safely to earth in January 1961. He died in 1983 and is buried at the Space Hall of Fame in New Mexico. When his colleague Minnie, the world's last surviving astrochimp, died in 1998, she was buried alongside him.

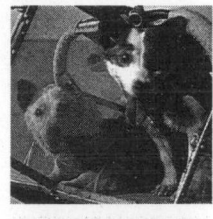

Ham co-starred in a film with Evel Knievel. Evel Knievel is, at the time of writing, still alive.

+ + + **FIVE INTERESTING THINGS TO DO WITH YOUR DEAD PET** + + +

3 : [OF 5] HOME BURIAL

PLANT IT IN the garden. This remains the preferred method of disposal for most modern animals, which may be buried flat. Micro-chimanks, it illegal were seen off a few years ago and – at present – the right to dispose of an animal corpse in one's own garden or compost heap remains the inalienable prerogative of any free-born Englishman. No such rights apply to human remains. There are, however, two obstacles to take into consideration: foxes, and the Deputy Prime Minister. The first is practical – if you don't bury your mutt deep enough, foxes will dig him up – the second, legal. Since the balkanisation of the old Ministry of the Environment, the burial of "working" or farm animals falls under the authority of DEFRA, and the disposal of pet animals under that of the Deputy Prime Minister's office. I don't make the rules, but you'd best follow them. If you have a pet cow, you may have an argument on your hands.

THE VILLAIN'S TROUSERS:
RIN TIN TIN

RIN TIN TIN STARTED HIS LIFE AS A TINY COG IN THE MIGHTY GERMAN WAR MACHINE, AND ENDED IT – WITH HIS DEATH IN THE ARMS OF A BEAUTIFUL HOLLYWOOD STARLET – AN ALL-AMERICAN HERO.

THE SCENE IS Fleury, France; a dismal, dark day with winds lashing heavy rain over man and dog alike. It is mid September, 1918; the dying days of the Great War, and Lee Duncan, a 29-year-old pilot in the US Air Corps, is dragging his way through a grim patrol towards – would he but know it – his destiny.

The exact details of what happened have been sufficiently mythologised that it's hard to arbitrate between competing versions. But, broadly, the unit came upon a decrepit old war-dog station that had been abandoned, along with its

canine inhabitants, by the retreating German soldiers. Cpl Duncan poked around, and discovered a starving German shepherd bitch – soon to be rechristened "Betty" – feebly nursing a litter of ten-day-old puppies.

Official Rin Tin Tin propaganda has it that these shivering wee rescue dogs represented the "oldest continuous bloodline in the history of the breed".[59] Hard to see how this can be proved one way or the other. I don't imagine the disarrayed Krauts left the pedigree certificate lying around, and the sire wasn't on the scene either. Daphne Hereford, of Crockett, Texas – custodian of the bloodline for 47 years and holder of "Rin Tin Tin" as a registered trademark – maintains anyway that Rin Tin Tin's sire was a dog called Fritz, and that "the lineage of Rin Tin Tin is traced to the first registered German Shepherd Dog, Horand, in 1899". Well. Whatever. It was a dog.

Duncan and his colleagues brought the dogs back to base and looked after them there. When the time came to return to the States, Duncan swiped two of the puppies for himself, and named them Rin Tin Tin and Nanette[60] apparently after the names given to the good-luck mascots carried by French soldiers. The hounds joined Cpl Duncan on his fifteen-day transatlantic passage by ship to New York.

Nanette's sea-legs were not, however, good. During the passage, she contracted pneumonia, and despite being left in the attentive care of a respected German shepherd breeder on arrival in New York, she died before Duncan made it home to California.

Given Rin Tin Tin's attested high intelligence, it seems odd and perverse that Duncan should have later replaced Nanette with another German shepherd bitch and encouraged Rinty to breed with her. Being presented with a girlfriend deliberately named after your dead sister is hardly going to get the juices flowing, but it seems not to have put Rinty off his stride. They in due course had four children, and that all-important bloodline was well under way.

The war was, meanwhile, over. Cpl Duncan went back to work in a hardware

†59
There exists an organisation fanatically dedicated to preserving the Rin Tin Tin bloodline, and calling itself The Legacy of Rin Tin Tin. Marginally less sinister than either the Knights Templar or, in Dan Brown's account of it, Opus Dei, it provides service dogs to disabled children under the cheery rubric of A Rinty For Kids. (A Rinty For Runty? Shame on me.)

†60
Some authorities spell her "Nannette", but I think that looks horrible. If I am wrong, may the spirit of the dead dog forgive me!

store, and Rinty – who Cpl Duncan touted round dog shows in his spare time – grew up to be an athletic and highly biddable creature, coloured an attractive shade of dark grey. In 1922, Rinty wowed crowds with a heroic thirteen and a half foot leap. It tickles me to imagine that this might have been vertical, but I have no evidence to support the assertion.

The leap caught the eye of the motion picture entrepreneur Darrell Zanuck, who offered the boy from the hardware store the princely sum of $350 to film Rinty's aerial hijinks. That quick hit planted a seed. Being in the movies, even by canine proxy, was bound to look like a step up from working in a hardware store.

Rinty landed a couple of parts as a stunt-dog, but it was in Duncan's own script that he finally got a starring role and the break that made him. The film was called *Where The North Begins* and it starred Rin Tin Tin as "Wolf-Dog". It attracted the notice of a film critic for the *New York Times*. The reviewer compared the newcomer unfavourably to established rival Strongheart, but spotted his potential: "in one sequence when he is shown a piece of the villain's trousers he is made to appear in a most vicious mood".

Rin Tin Tin was on his way.

That year, he was put under contract to Warner Brothers, and he became the most famous screen hound in the world. Many credit Rinty's success with having actually saved the studio; he was known as "the mortgage lifter", so bankable was his pulling power at the box office.

He enjoyed the spoils of success. Insured for $100,000 dollars, Rinty employed at the height of his powers a 100-strong retinue, and earned a basic salary of $1,000 per week. Rinty had his own valet, chef, production team, private limousine and chauffeur. He wore a diamond-studded collar. According to one book on the subject, he received a million fan letters a year, and never fewer than ten thousand in a given week.

Rinty did many of his own stunts. His specialisms? He was very good at sailing through sugar-glass windows, climbing up over doors (despite his aforementioned jumping skills, he cheated slightly here, typically using a sort of ladder of cleats attached to the door out of sight of the camera), and running through fire.

Rin Tin Tin made 24 movies with Warner Brothers before leaving the studio,

after making *Rough Waters*, his final film for them, in 1930. He went on to make a series of low-budget serials for Mascot Pictures before retiring from public life in 1931.

It was in August 1932 that the end came for the original Rin Tin Tin. In Raymond Lee's history of animal Hollywood, *Not So Dumb*, the scene painted is of Rinty and Lee Duncan enjoying "a playful twilight romp on their front lawn" in Clubview Drive, which came to an end when Rinty leaped into Lee's arms. When he left the ground, he was alive. When he landed, he was dead. Lee sunk disconsolate to his knees and howled. From across the street, their neighbour, the gorgeous Hollywood sexpot Jean Harlow, heard the cry and ran to comfort him. A man, a woman, and a dog – life expiring or expired – sitting dissolved in tears on the manicured front lawns of the Hollywood Hills. For some reason, the image in my head has, in the background, as its only sound the quiet hiss of the evening sprinklers all down the length of the street.

The United Press issued the following report:

> *Rin Tin Tin, greatest of animal motion picture actors pursued a ghostly villain in a canine Happy-Hunting Ground today. More than eighty years old as comparative human age is measured, his passing was announced this morning by his owner and friend, Lee Duncan.*

Barely in English it may have been – but the message got across. A dog-loving nation fell to silent prayer. Rinty was originally buried where he breathed his last – at Duncan's home in Clubview Drive. Subsequently (in a fit of sentimentality?) they dug him up and shipped the remains to be reinterred in France, the land from which he sprung.

His legacy was complicated. Lee Duncan had vowed: "There will always be a Rin Tin Tin." At first, Rin Tin Tin Junior, Rinty's son from his union with the second Nanette, took his place in the movies, most notably teaming up with the horse actor Rex for such features as *The Adventures of Rex and Rinty!* As one poster had it: "Rex – King of Wild Horses and Rin-Tin-Tin, Jr – The Dog Hero of Young America ... in *Law of the Wild* ... A Mascot Super-Serial in 12 Thrill-Inspiring Chapters."

It may have been thrill-inspiring on screen, but it was pretty iffy behind the cameras. Rex was by all accounts as vicious a chunk of horseflesh as Rinty was sweet-natured. "Rex was a mean horse to the end," one associate said. "Like some human actors are mean." "A vicious bay stallion." Their collaboration took its toll. In 1938 – four years after the cancellation of Rinty's radio show – Lee Duncan retired.

Were the best years behind them? It seems not. 1947 saw *The Return of Rin Tin Tin*, starring Rin Tin Tin III. Then, in 1954, he returned again. This time it was Rin Tin Tin IV's turn – and his prime-time TV series on ABC, *The Adventures of Rin Tin Tin*, returned him to the super league. Set in the Wild West of the 1880s, it told the story of Rinty and his feisty young master Rusty, a couple of misfits who had been adopted by a US cavalry troop and lived in a fort.

Every adventure would begin with young Rusty calling "Yo ho, Rinty!", and would close, after some mind-boggling adventure or other, with the just reward. "Okay Rinty," he'd say. "You've earned your milk bone."[61] It ran for five years. Nor was that even the end of it. In the 1970s another dog claiming to be yet another descendent of Rin Tin Tin popped up to film some colour intros and outros for a repackaged sepia-tinted relaunch of the old series. By this stage you would have to be a film historian or clinically insane to try to run down the Rintys. That's a lot of milk bones.

†61
What is a
milk bone?

And so, into the murk of apocrypha, the roots of the Rin Tin Tin legend plunge. More descendants than Noah; more comebacks than Jason Voorhees; more milk bones than one dog can reasonably be expected to eat.

CHAPTER 5

HENRY III

PETS OR PEOPLE? It is a question worth asking. Ezra Pound wrote the following on the subject:

> *When I carefully consider the curious habits of dogs*
> *I am compelled to conclude*
> *That man is the superior animal.*
>
> *When I consider the curious habits of man*
> *I confess, my friend, I am puzzled.*

Many distinguished figures in history – St Francis, Diane Fossey, Tippi Hedren, Brigitte Bardot and Carla Lane – have from time to time seemed more interested in their chimpanzees, gorillas, birds, or lions than in their fellow man. And quite right too. People are almost all ghastly.

Animals offer us unconditional love[62] – which if less rewarding than the conditional kind offered by our fellow humans – is at least a safe bet. Project onto them what you will – drown them, if you must, in the unhealthy

†62
Or, in the case of cats, unconditional indifference – which is nevertheless itself rather more comforting than it sounds on paper.

transference of your own stunted emotions. They will neither complain, nor charge by the hour, nor issue a cease and desist order, nor giggle with their friends afterwards about the pathetic client who "just wanted to talk".

As long as you feed them pretty regularly, and don't hit them or try to shag them, you're pretty much set. You can cry yourself to sleep with the sound of your sobs muffled in their warm fur every night of your life. Knock yourself out. They don't give a shit.

The problem, of course, is that far from being a device for escaping from humans, pet ownership all too often brings you right back into contact with them. There are, of course, exceptions. Sometimes too close an involvement with your pets can lead to informal shunning: consider the Mad Old Cat Lady, with her wee-scented cardigan, her sleeves lumpy with tissues, her peculiar hat and her shouted conversations with lamp posts. Consider the likelihood anyone will ever want to venture beyond the double glazing into the stifling heat of her home. Imagine the terrifying landscape of fur, doilies and cat poo that would greet you. Imagine the *smell*.

But mostly, pet ownership puts you into a community; sometimes whether you like it or not. So I noticed, at least, when I took Henry on his first outing to the V-E-T. I reckoned he'd need some vaccinations to prevent him catching something and dying, and he'd need his nuts off, to prevent him from catching something and making it his bitch.

The vet – a very nice one indeed in Herne Hill – is something like a drop-in centre for pet owners to socialise with complete strangers. It's weird. I parked the car outside the all-night pizza shop, hefted the cat, in his wire cage, where he was sitting on a towel growling, out of the passenger seat, and swung round the corner. I almost crashed into a girl carrying another cat in another basket.

So we had to do this sort of bashful grin/shrug. It conveys: "Huh! Cats! Both got 'em! You've just been to the vet, I don't mind hazarding a guess. Yup ... No, yeah, yeah. Nope. Yeah. Dead on: I'm just going. Got to get the li'l fella his shots. Seeya."

Then I arrived at the vet and the woman behind the counter was incredibly friendly. Everyone was incredibly friendly. The experience was oddly infantilising. The thing is, they sort of half talk to you and half talk to the cat. The vet's tiny outer office/waiting room was crammed with people and animals waiting to be seen, and I found myself standing by the door with my cat cage hoisted to upper-chest height.

"Hi," they said. "Oooh, you're a pretty little one, aren't you. Yeeeellow dere! Elloellodere." Kind of poking at the cat, which was uninterested. "What's your name?"

"Henry," I said, even though they seemed to think the cat was going to reply by himself. And so on. The cat was taking a close interest in the woman across the room who was holding in one hand the leads of a pair of boxer dogs, either one of which looked like it weighed more than its owner. The dogs were taking no interest whatever in the cat.

Their owner was reading the label on the side of one of the packets comprising the enormous mountain – the landslide – of Hills Science Plan products[63] that, now I come to think of it, was the reason this waiting room was so small.

Then, behind me, the door swung open and in came a grey-clad middle-aged woman with a transfixingly large, hairy wen on the side of her nose, and another cat in a cage. Her cage and my cage passed very close by each other. My cat did something I hadn't ever seen it do before. This is obviously a behaviour hard-wired into the cat. He arched – like a hairpin, like a cartoon cat – and raised every piece of fur along his back. He opened his mouth in a grimace, and said:

"…"

"Isn't he cute? You're a cute little kitten, aren't you?" said the lady with the wen.

"…" said Henry.

"Yes. You're a black Siamese, aren't you?"

"What's it to you, sister?" I thought. It was as if someone in the queue behind you at the checkout had peered over

†63
If you have a pet, the odds are you will have heard of Hills Science Plan. This is a special range of dry pet foods whose near medical-style packaging and marketing work to give the impression that Nobel-prizewinning scientists have toiled in laboratories to ensure that there is no form of food more nutritious for your cat or dog on the face of the earth. Certainly, there are few more expensive. They have different flavours (flavours in petfood – another hobby horse I may have to climb aboard shortly) and special types for every conceivable stage of animal life and characteristic (Kitten? Nursing mother? Fine or flyaway fur? On a diet? Sagittarian?) They are prominently on display in vets offices, and we're told that Science Plan is the number one choice for vets to feed their own pets on. Your cat will guilt-trip you into buying it Science Plan. Then it won't even want to eat it. Henry sulked for three days and begged for Sheba.

and made some remark about your choice of sliced bread.

"..." said Henry, arching a little further.

"I think it's a mog," I said, grinning soppily.

"Henry?" said the lady behind the counter.

Like I say: partly to me, mostly to the cat. Pets are registered under their own names, like children. It's bizarre. I sort of imagined taking my cat to the vet would be like taking my broken computer to the menders. I felt, childishly, a little peeved that I was marginalised in the transaction. It was clearly the cat's appointment. The doctor would see him now. I was just here as an interpreter, coping with the tedious consideration that cats don't talk.

It was in the consulting room that things got a little peculiar. The vet, like everyone, addressed most of her comments to the cat. She combed it for evidence of fleas, peered into its ears, and examined its mouth. The cat sniffed his way around the rubberised consulting room table in small circles, when left to himself for a moment.

What Henry needed, I explained on his behalf, was the first of his vaccinations, and his nuts cut off.

"Let's have a look at you then," said the vet. ("No. The cat," I thought.) She grabbed Henry by the back end, just as he was hunkering down in preparation for jumping off the rubber table and taking his chances with the boxers in the waiting room. She raised his back end, legs and all, off the table while Henry's front legs scrabbled for purchase and his face assumed a look of peevish dignity.

"Hmm. I think you have a little girl cat," said the vet, the first remark addressed directly to me.

"?" I said.

I explained that I was definitely told – by Ulrike, who had been definitely told by the guy whose advert in *Loot* she answered, who had in turn, presumably, sexed the cat with the expertise you'd expect from any reputable pedigree cat dealer who sells his cats through *Loot* ...

"Well, it is hard to tell sometimes when they are very young," she said, the tone of her voice indicating the kindly suppression of the exact opposite truth. "But, look, I can't see any testicles and ... " – she did something with her thumbs that I would not care to have done to me. Either I had a male cat with no testicles and two jacksies, I was forced to conclude, or Henry was Henrietta.

As I left the surgery, the lady on the front desk, having been apprised of my misfortune, kept her face straight as she asked me whether the cat, whose vaccination she was now registering, was going to be changing her name.

"No," I said crossly. "He's still called Henry."

DEADPETS
Case Study No. 8

"Bunnies *can* (and *will*) go to France."
JEREMY THORPE TO NORMAN SCOTT

"They'll harm what you love most."
"PETER KEENE" TO NORMAN SCOTT

"Rinka lives! Woof woof!"
AUBERON WAUGH
PARLIAMENTARY CANDIDATE FOR THE DOG-LOVERS' PARTY

THE DOG IT WAS THAT DIED:
RINKA

IT WAS ALL A TERRIBLE, TERRIBLE MISUNDERSTANDING.
RINKA THOUGHT SHE WAS GOING FOR WALKIES.

IT WAS NOT, however, a night as would favour man or dog. High up on the remote moorland on the Porlock side of Lynton, on the night of October 24th, 1975, a pale blue Ford Escort stopped by the side of the road in the driving rain.

A man got out of the passenger side, and walked round the bonnet to the driver's door. As he arrived, he saw the driver, too, had climbed out – and, behind him, there bounded out a very excited Great Dane, five years old and "the size of a donkey". The Great Dane started leaping up and down. The first man was called Norman Scott. The second man was called Andrew Newton. The dog was called Rinka.

This, as far as we understand it, is how events played out.

R: "Woof, woof."

NS: (Grabbing the lead): "I'm sorry. I meant just move over and then she wouldn't get out."

R: "Woof, woof."

AN: (Producing a gun) "Oh no. This is it."

GUN: (Shooting Rinka through head): BLAM!

R: "…"

NS: "You can't involve Rinka. You can't involve the dog."

AN: "It's your turn now." (Pauses. Waves jammed gun.) "Fuck it. Fuck it. Fuck it."

(**NS** runs off. Stops. Cannot bear to leave dog. Gives up. Comes back. **AN** re-aims.)

AN "I'll fuck it."

(Jumps in car)

AN: "I'll get you."

(Zooms off into the night.)

(**NS** tries to give Rinka the kiss of life.)

A little later, a passing car draws up, and finds a man, weeping in the rain, with the body of a dead dog cradled in his arms.

Andrew Newton later complained to a friend that the people he was working for were "a bunch of amateurs". Indeed they were. But he was one to talk.

Rinka was a martyr to the benighted social and political climate of the 1970s. She was the victim of a sad, sad story: a mixture of greed, selfishness, pettiness, hypocrisy and titanic, engulfing incompetence from which only she, the dog, emerges with any credit. It was a tale of Russian hats and bitten pillows and naff love-letters and sinister provincial carpet magnates.

A couple of days after the events described above, a report appeared in the *West Somerset Free Press*. "The Great Dane Death Mystery", the headline announced. "Dog-in-a-Fog Case Baffles Police."

From then on, the story unravelled backwards.

To understand what brought Andrew Newton and Norman Scott together, and Rinka to her rainy Golgotha, you have to go right back.

At one corner of the web was Jeremy Thorpe, a young man born with dazzling gifts. A photograph of him survives, from 1951, in a formal pose as President of the Oxford Union: a brilliant member of a brilliant generation. Among those with him in the photograph are William Rees-Mogg, later to become the editor of *The Times*; Asa Briggs, later to become one of the most distinguished historians of modern times; Robin Day, later to become the John the Baptist to Jeremy Paxman's Jesus; and a man called Dingle Foot, whose very name is distinction enough.

After leaving Oxford, Jeremy Thorpe's progress through the British political establishment was as rapid. Handsome, dashing, and a prodigiously gifted orator, he became Liberal MP for North Devon, and, by 1967 and at the age of only 37, the leader of his party. On the campaign trail, he wore a peculiar Russian hat and leapt athletically over garden fences to canvass housewives. In the 1973 election, he roved from Barnstaple over the surrounding countryside by helicopter. Powered by the white heat of technology, he toured the West Country beaches by hovercraft.

He was spoken of as a future Prime Minister. The First Lady of Fleet Street, Jean Rook, described him as a "a super-brilliant monkey with astonishing sex-appeal". His policies – who remembers them now? – need not concern us here.

But he had a secret side. Why should it have been secret? This was post-Wolfenden. It was a period when the electorate of Britain should have been entering a happy new era of liberalism and tolerance. But Thorpe seems to have taken the view – alas rightly – that the electorate were the same bunch of bigoted bastards they always had been, and that it would take many more years before you could reasonably be expected to have hopes of becoming even a Liberal prime minister if you were known to have had a passionate affair with a male model.

The other strand of the story is that same male model: Norman Scott. Norman was an animal lover from a very young age. Born Norman Josiffe, he grew up in Sidcup the fifth of Ena Josiffe's six children. He had no memory of his father, and his dearest solace in youth was Listowel, the pony he got when he was fourteen. He doted on the creature to the extent that, in April 1956, he was found guilty of larceny at Bromley juvenile court for stealing a saddle and some feed for Listowel.

His rather troubled early life intersected with that of Jeremy Thorpe in 1960. Norman was helping out at Kingham Stables in Chipping Norton when the new Liberal MP for North Devon, a friend of the owners, came to visit. The two were introduced and chatted briefly, a conversation that ended with a standing invitation from Thorpe to look him up if Norman was ever in London.

The following year, he did just that. He was unemployed, and seeking help to get back on his feet after a suicide attempt, and a brief stay in a psychiatric clinic in Oxford. He and Mrs Tish pitched up at the House of Commons in November. Mrs Tish was his Jack Russell terrier.

(Counterfactually enough, had Mrs Tish lasted the course and been on Dartmoor that terrible night, it's possible to speculate that the whole scandal might never have happened. During Thorpe's trial, Newton told the court: "If it had been a Yorkshire terrier or something not very big, that would have been all right." Being profoundly phobic about dogs, it is highly unlikely Newton could have told a Yorkie from a Jack Russell.)

Mrs Tish did not gain entry to the House. Norman had to park her at the nearby offices of the anti-vivisection league while he went in to visit Jeremy. Jeremy extended this unfortunate lad the hand of friendship, as any humane person would.

What happened afterwards was the subject of bitter dispute. Jeremy that night drove Norman and Mrs Tish down to Stonewalls, Jeremy's mother's house in Surrey. In the Thorpe version of events, Norman slept happily in the spare room with Mrs Tish, Jeremy in his, and Mrs Thorpe in hers. According to Norman, Thorpe came to him that night and made plain that his intentions were dishonourable.

In this version, seeing Norman cowering like a "frightened rabbit", Jeremy comforted him: "poor bunny". A little sinister, if you ask me, but there we are. "I just bit the pillow," Norman told the court. "I tried not to scream because I was frightened of waking Mrs Thorpe." Afterwards, he said, Thorpe patted his thigh and left. "I just lay there with my dog ... She was by the bed. I picked her up, brought her into my bed with me, and just lay crying."

Whatever happened that night, the two fell into a close relationship: Jeremy the benefactor, Norman the beneficiary. Jeremy helped Norman find a job with a farming family, and promised to fix it for him to go to France to study dressage.

"The really important thing," he wrote to his young protégé in February 1962, "is that you are now a member of a family doing a useful job of work – with Tish – wch you enjoy. Hooray!!" He signed the letter off: "Bunnies *can* (and *will*) go to France. In haste. Yours affectionately, Jeremy. I miss you."

By that summer, Jeremy started to cool off. Norman did not. Over the years that followed, the two were in intermittent contact: Norman, usually in trouble, seeking help or money; Jeremy, anxious, trying to sever ties.

Norman went to Ireland to work with horses, having started to style himself "The Hon. Lianche-Josiffe". That didn't work out, and he was back in touch for help after the 1964 election. Jeremy arranged to ship him to Switzerland at the end of the year. That didn't work out either. He returned almost immediately, without his luggage, and left for Ireland again. Peter Bessell, a friendly fellow MP who had started to serve as Jeremy's cat's-paw, managed to negotiate the return from Switzerland of the luggage. Norman noticed when reunited with his luggage, however, that his collection of letters from Jeremy seemed to have gone astray.

By 1967 Jeremy had become the leader of the Liberal Party, and his relationship with Norman was causing him no small anxiety. Norman, now calling himself Norman Scott, had decided he wanted to launch himself on Swinging London as a male model. Bessell arranged to put him on a retainer to help cover his start-up costs and remove the temptation for him to conduct shouty conversations in pubs and police stations about his friendship with Jeremy.

Then Norman got married. Hooray! thought Peter and Jeremy. Then, in rather

short order, Norman announced his plans to get divorced. Aargh! thought Jeremy and Peter; still more so when Norman made known that he planned to have Jeremy's name included in the filings to court about the divorce.

Utter panic reigned, and a plan was hatched to send Norman somewhere nice, like the Bahamas. Instead, unpredictable as ever, he went to Wales, settling in a cottage in Talybont with an Afghan hound named Apple, two whippets called Emma and Kate, and an unnamed cat.

There was a brief flurry of activity. Norman, and a kindly former sub-postmistress called Mrs Parry-Jones, who had taken pity on him and believed he deserved justice from the man who had "ruined his life", came to London to see David Steel, then the Liberal chief whip. An internal inquiry found nothing to worry about, and Norman returned to obscurity in Wales. He felt, as ever, hard done by.

1973 found him in a small cottage on the edge of Exmoor, near Simonsbath. He was low; borderline suicidal. He quarrelled with his landlady and, according to historians of the period, lived on a diet of "vegetables, mainly swedes". He continued to talk to anyone who would listen about his relationship with Jeremy. Then, while Norman was "woozy" with drugs, one Dr Ronald Gleadle persuaded him to hand over the dossier on the relationship, and sold it to David Holmes, who destroyed it. Norman was given £2,500, which can buy you a lot of swedes. But he would rather have had the dossier back, and he agitated – not knowing it had been destroyed – for its return.

Fishy things started to occur. He was done by the police for a DSS scam, when he claimed to have lost his social security book. Then the police arrested him over an unpaid hotel bill, and kept him in the ladies' cells of Barnstaple nick. There were menacing noises made. Was the establishment mobilising dark forces against Norman?

You bet it was. But the way in which it was mobilising them is perhaps the supreme 20th-century vindication of the unshakeable primacy in politics of the cock-up over the conspiracy.

In August 1975, Norman took lodgings with the felicitously named Edna Friendship, over the Market Inn in Barnstaple. He did odd jobs in lieu of rent.

And he took on a five-year-old Great Dane bitch called Rinka, a gift from a friend, as a companion.

Andrew Newton, Rinka's murderer, liked to be called by the nickname "Gino". His friends gave him another name. They called him: "Chicken Brain". If this was insufficient clue as to his suitability as an assassin, it's not as if there weren't other pointers available. "Chicken Brain" Newton was the muppet's muppet; a total fucking idiot.

How did he come to be the triggerman?

It seems to have happened like this.

David Holmes, a university friend of Jeremy, had by now taken over operational responsibility from Peter Bessell for what might be called Operation Shut Norman Up. Holmes was a friend of one John Le Mesurier, no relation to the *Dad's Army* actor. This Le Mesurier ran a carpet shop in Port Talbot, and happened to be friends with George Deakin.

Mr Deakin was a somewhat dodgier character than the respectable Mr Le Mesurier. A fruit machine entrepreneur known throughout the Port Talbot area as "King of the One-Armed Bandits", he was such a guy, as Mr Justice Cantley rather snobbishly told the eventual trial, as would pride himself on having "a cocktail bar in his living room".[64]

Anyway, this Deakin was introduced to Holmes by Le Mesurier, who apparently prided himself on his skills as a fixer in the shadowy underworld of Port Talbot. It was made plain to Deakin that Mr Holmes was in the market for a thug. Deakin made enquiries through David Miller, a trusted contact in a Cardiff printing shop.[65] His contact put him onto Chicken Brain.

[64]
Mr Justice Cantley presumably meant: "drawing room".

[65]
I am not making this stuff up

Were there other indications that Chicken Brain may not have been the safest pair of hands? Yes. Chicken Brain and Deakin were first introduced to discuss the little business proposition in question at the Showmen's Dinner in Blackpool, on February 26th, 1975. At that same dinner, Chicken Brain got into a fight with the boyfriend of a topless showgirl. The boyfriend had objected to Chicken Brain's attempts to dress the girl's private parts with meringues.[66] Nevertheless, Deakin gave him the benefit of the doubt. He gave him the benefit of the doubt, too,

when Chicken Brain tried to chat up Mrs Deakin on the phone when he called, later, to discuss the proposed arrangements for the "frightening job" on Norman.

Mr Deakin's contacts had assured him that Chicken Brain was "up for a laugh and a giggle". Mr Justice Cantley, at the trial, described him as a "chump". It is easy, I suppose, to be wise after the event. Deakin put Chicken Brain in touch with Holmes.

Chicken Brain set about his project, his first strategy being to subject poor old Norman to a series of odd phone calls. The original plan – as he told the court – had been to lure Norman to the Royal Garden Hotel in London and biff him with a chisel concealed in a bunch of flowers.[67]

Norman received a call from an "Ian Wright", who represented the "Pensiero Group" in Italy, and wanted him to come to London to talk about a modelling contract. Norman smelt a rat. He did not go.

Norman received a call from a "Mr Masterson", claiming to be a friend of Gordon Winter, a journalist and South African spy to whom Norman had talked about his relationship with Jeremy. Mr Masterson tried to lure Norman to the Bristol Holiday Inn, but when Gordon Winter told Norman that he knew no Mr Masterson, Norman again smelt a rat. He did not go.

By now, Norman would have been fully justified in feeling the clammy fingertips of paranoia brushing his neck. So we can only imagine how he felt when another man intercepted him en route to the laundrette one Sunday afternoon soon after.

History does not relate whether "Peter Keene", as he called himself, was wearing a stick-on moustache and sunglasses, but he might as well have been. Speaking in an accent that lurched unstably from one part of the world to another, Chicken Brain (for it was he, the Clouseau of assassination), claimed to represent a mysterious benefactor intent on protecting Norman. An assassin was even then en route from Canada, he said, drawing a terrified Norman into the lounge of the Imperial Hotel, Barnstaple for a beverage. "They'll harm what you love most," he hissed at Norman. Only through the good offices of Peter Keene and the mysterious benefactor would Norman's neck be saved.

Ten days later, Norman was in the "Pack of Cards" pub across the road, when the phone in the bar rang for him.

"It's Andy," hissed Chicken Brain in another fit of competence.

"Who?" said an ever more bewildered Norman, who didn't know anyone called Andy.

"Er, oops, it's Peter," Chicken Brain corrected himself, thinking on his feet. He went on to explain that the dreaded Canadian assassin was already in the country, and if he wanted to escape they were going to have to move fast. He made arrangements to meet Norman at 6 p.m. the following day outside the Delves Hotel in Combe Martin.

When they kept that assignation, Chicken Brain brought with him an ancient self-loading Mauser .25 pistol. And Norman Scott brought with him a Great Dane the size of a donkey.

The other thing about ole Chicken Brain, you see, is that he was morbidly terrified of dogs.

Rinka was by all accounts a sweet-natured creature. But she looked pretty menacing and, with a Canadian assassin supposedly on his trail, Norman needed all the back-up he could get. He refused to go anywhere without her. So, into the back of this blue Ford Escort, belonging to Chicken Brain's girlfriend, they somehow contrived to pile Rinka. I, for one, fondly imagine her great muzzle protruding forward between the two front seats at head height, the happy open-mouthed panting that dogs do in cars causing the dogophobic assassin inches away no small anxiety and discomfort. They drove to Porlock, where Chicken Brain dropped Norman off in the saloon bar of the Castle Hotel and told him to wait there, promising he'd be back at eight. Did he need a break from the dog?

Even this detail was botched. By 8:20 Chicken Brain still hadn't reappeared, and Norman went outside to look for a cab. Across the road, there was Chicken Brain waiting in the car. He flashed his lights. "I can't be seen with you," he explained, as Norman and Rinka piled back in. And off they went, up over the moor, to the safety of the mysterious benefactor.

By now, exhausted, nervous, and terrified of his four-legged passenger, Chicken Brain was not driving any too well. He was succumbing to exhaustion. All over the road. "Knackered," he admitted. So kind-hearted Norman volunteered to take over at the wheel. Indeed, when they stopped, he jumped out and ran round

the car so that Chicken Brain could just slide across, and Rinka wouldn't follow him out and track mud and wet fur back into the car. But it was one more cock-up for Chicken Brain. He, too, got out of the car, and Rinka, thinking she was game on for a yomp across the moor, followed.

And at that point, the scene described at the beginning of this chapter took place. Norman was later to tell the court: "I did not hear anything. The dog just fell against me and sank down. Newton had shot the dog. I couldn't really understand what he had done at that moment."

After the crisis had passed, Chicken Brain later said, "Scott still stood there. He made no move to go, so I got back in the car and said: 'I will see you another time' ... it's as stupid and simple as that."

Just as stupid and simple as that. That night, David Miller, the Cardiff printing shop owner, came home to find Chicken Brain in his house, stripping down the Mauser – he had borrowed it from a friend; it was nearly 70 years old – and claiming to have performed "a service to the community". The police were onto Chicken Brain within 48 hours.

When he was asked about the incident by the local newspaper, Jeremy Thorpe laughed. "Are they hunting dogs on the moors these days?" he said.

This was the other mistake he made. A dog-loving near neighbour, Auberon Waugh, who had never in any case liked the cut of the member for North Devon's Russian hat, took grave offence and determined to keep an eye on the matter. He wrote shortly afterwards, in *Private Eye*: "My only hope is that sorrow over his friend's dog will not cause Mr Thorpe's premature retirement from public life."

Meanwhile a terrier-like two-man team of investigative journalists, Barrie Penrose and Roger Courtiour, started digging away at the story. They were known collectively as "Pencourt", in homage to "Woodstein" (Bob Woodward and Carl Bernstein – the reporters who broke Watergate).

Their investigations led them to very high places – and give us an extremely eccentric cameo from Harold Wilson, who encouraged them in the belief that it was all some sort of South African plot. He seems to have fancied himself as the Deep Throat of Rinkagate. "I see myself as the big fat spider in the corner of

the room," he told them, incomprehensibly. "Sometimes I speak when I'm asleep. You should both listen. Occasionally when we meet I might tell you to go to the Charing Cross Road and kick a blind man standing on the corner. That blind man may tell you something, lead you somewhere."[68]

Pencourt took the sleeping spider's advice and kicked a few blind men. The blind men yelped. The web unravelled. The spider woke up.

†68
He was barmy, obviously, but he was right. Everyone *was* spying on him.

By 1978, Jeremy – who had by then bowed to the inevitable and stepped down as Liberal leader – and his alleged co-conspirators were committed for trial. The General Election of 1979 was called for 3rd May, and by happy chance, the trial was to start on the 8th. Auberon Waugh stood against Jeremy Thorpe in the election, as the candidate for the Dog-Lovers' Party; slogan: "Rinka lives! Woof, Woof."

Chicken Brain served two years for Rinka's murder. The trial of Jeremy Thorpe (he was acquitted) need not long detain those of us interested in Rinka – except to note a sour irony. At the trial, the prosecution alleged that Thorpe had told Peter Bessell that to murder Norman Scott would have been "no worse than shooting a sick dog".

There was widespread criticism of Mr Justice Cantley's directions to the jury. Considering Norman Scott, for example, he reminded them of "his hysterically warped personality", describing him as "an accomplished liar; very skilful at exciting and exploiting sympathy ... He is a crook ... He is a fraud. He is a sponger. He is a whiner. He is a parasite."[69] He added, in the interests of even-handedness: "But, of course, he could still be telling the truth." The jury got the message.

†69
And, as Peter Cook put it in his celebrated spoof of the judge's summing-up, a "self-confessed player of the pink oboe".

On the day he learned of Jeremy's acquittal, Norman was on the tiny farm he then lived on in Chagford, along with three horses, some chickens, ducks & guinea-fowl. And four dogs.

In 1999, Jeremy Thorpe published his memoirs, which he called *My Own Time*. He didn't have anything to say about Rinka. Nor was he keen, he wrote, to "rake over the embers" of his disgrace. He reported curtly: "With three co-defendants I was charged with conspiracy to murder one Norman Scott ... " (Even there, you see, the character of the man. Nobody is suggesting he tried to murder more than one Norman Scott. Even the prosecution conceded that one would have done the trick.)

Raking over the embers, Thorpe found time to describe Peter Bessell, his one-time right-hand man, as a character living in a "Walter Mitty" world, a "schizophrenic" "consumed by bitterness towards me, resentful of the fact that I had seen behind his façade". Bessell had given evidence for the prosecution.

Of the other issue, he wrote: "Scott claimed that there had been a homosexual relationship with myself – a claim that I have always totally denied. According to Scott this 'affair' had started with a chance meeting at the stables of a friend, when I had spoken to him at the most for five minutes." (Even there. "Denied": yes. "Refuted": not quite.)

Thorpe did not have the generosity of heart to condemn Andrew "Chicken Brain" Newton – nor to apologise for his insensitive remark about hunting dogs on the moor. But there was, as he looked back over his life, what seems to me like some plea, however sideways, for forgiveness. Jeremy, too, he revealed at the last, was a dog lover.

A whole chapter of his book is devoted to his own childhood pet: "I cannot make reference to the closer members of my family without mentioning George. George was a brown and white fox terrier of immense character. I was given him by my godfather after I had a long illness. He was chosen by my godfather's wife, from Harrods."

Thorpe arraigns George for theft, however: he stole a leg of lamb from a furnished holiday home and a "large cream bun" from a bakery in Limpsfield. He was very partial to brandy (a characteristic he shared with Chicken Brain Newton). George, untroubled by his sexuality, had "a long-standing relationship with a certain Georgina".

Also: "George had one distressing complaint from early age, namely that he had terrible wind. On one occasion in mid-winter, we were driving in the car with all the windows up when George gave us a really fruity one. My family turned on him and said: 'You filthy dog.' I, aged six at the time, unswervingly loyal to my dog, was alleged to have said: 'As a matter of fact, I rather like it!'"

Thorpe lives at Higher Chuggaton in North Devon now. At night, when the wind howls, is the wracked frame of the once and future leader of the Liberals tormented by bad dreams? Does he hear, away in the dark, the voice of little George commingling with the howl of a Great Dane? We will likely never know. One of his biographers told me a year or two back that "he opens all conversations these days with the words: 'I will sue you for criminal libel'."

By the mid 1990s, Norman Scott was still living in Dartmoor, and was reported to own seventeen cats, a sheepdog, a whippet, and two champagne pugs called Polly and Dora.

In the year 2000, according to a disreputable gossip column, edited by me, Norman took delivery of two pug puppies "orphaned" after their owners, a homosexual couple, separated. The pugs were called Apricot and Gucci. Norman was said to be "thrilled with them".

CHAPTER 6

HENRY IV

"I TOLD YOUR father that we were going to be grandparents," said my mother happily, "and he practically had a heart attack on the spot."

My mother – who is soppy about pets – has taken to putting Henry's welfare, activities re balls of string, sleeping arrangements etc. very near the top of the list of priorities in every phone conversation we have. And we seem to be having more and more. She at once despairs of her two older sons ever persuading a girl to stay still for long enough to produce a grandchild; and perhaps, in the back of her mind, worries that her feckless third son might end up doing so by accident.

She refers to Henry as "the grand-kitten".

That said, this is a woman who, while pregnant with her third child, dreamed that she had given birth to a litter of red setter puppies, and woke up infinitely happy and refreshed. Was she disappointed, finally, when humans came out?

The cat's contact with the outside world had so far been strictly limited, and its behaviour in cars didn't seem to promise a feline Dean Moriarty. But it was, sooner or later, going to have to make the journey to meet the folks, in a Wiltshire farmhouse two and a quarter hours from London.

At this stage, the cat was furthermore in the grip of acute gender dysphoria. Is that why it was ignoring the scratching post and shredding instead the ancestral bogey-green velveteen armchair? Pronouns, in conversation, skittered around like a fast cat on highly polished parquet.

†70

A brief note on what cats say. Convention has it that they say: "Miaow." I wish I could claim that it was my own scholarship that discovered the brilliant alternative here footnoted, but I stole it from Craig Raine. "Mkgnao," he reported, is what James Joyce's cats say. Also, in more conciliatory moods, Joyce's cats will say "mrkgnao" or "mrkrgnao". There's a bit of purr in there.

"Have you given her its food?" Alex might ask. "He still had some when I got home," I might reply. "Mkgnao,"[70] the cat, fed up with all this fannying about and reckoning even Hill's Science Plan was better than nothing, might interject.

We stuck the cat, one Friday evening, in its cage, and buckled it into the back of the car. All the way down the M4, it said: "Mkgnao mkgnao mkgnao mkgnao. Mkgnao. Mkgnao mkgnaaaaaaaaao." Half the way down the M4, we said: "Shhhhhh. There, there. It's all right," and other calming things that cats don't understand. The other half of the way down the M4 we said: "Shut *up*, cat."

Cat arms protruded right up to the shoulder through the bars of the cage, claws out, waving frantically in space. Cat face got pushed up against the bars until the eyes were at serious risk of escaping from the cage without their owner. Occasionally, one of us would reach back and push

†71

This is the noise, X-Men scholars will note, that Wolverine makes when he "pops" his adamantium claws.

our fingers through to stroke her head in the hopes of calming her. Alex did this from the driver's seat, reaching back blind with one long arm. For a time Henry scrabbled at his fingers with the velvety pads of her front paws. Then – SNIKT![71] – she dug all ten claws simultaneously into the pad of his thumb. The car swerved across two crowded lanes of traffic.

When we finally arrived, we were all a bit tense. Naturally, the tension evaporated when we pulled up outside the house, opened the car doors, and into each door shot the head of an overexcited German shepherd, each one leading with a slobbery, football-scarf-sized tongue. Henry thought that was just hilarious. "Fssscccchhhhhh!" She looked like she'd been drawn by Charles Addams.

She was carried at head height, still in her cage, Lupus and Raksha the dogs surging and bounding up underneath, through the hall and up to a room at the very top of the house, where, with the door safely closed, we opened the door to the cage. Litter tray, food and water … all check. The mother and little sister took it in turns to coo. Henry came out of her cage very slowly. I diagnosed this as meaning: I do not know what those noisy hairy things were, and I do not care above half to find out.

As well as the long line of cats I described earlier – Damn, Blast, and Jennifer; Ferdie, Friday, Faraday,[72] Saturday, Sunday, Ferdie II – my folks have also had dogs. My dad hates dogs, or pretends to. The story goes that on the day he proposed to my mother, he laid down one strict rule for the marriage. "The day you get a dog," he told her, "is the day you get a divorce."

Many years later, on one of their wedding anniversaries, he staggered in from the car carrying a big smelly cardboard box. He plonked it on the kitchen floor. Inside were two red setter puppies, one male, one female, covered from head to hairy toe in vomit and dogshit. My mother fell instantly in love.

"One of them is called Dog," said my father. "The other one is called Divorce." My dad is sentimental like that.

Red setters, as anyone with even a glancing acquaintance with one will know, have the looks of a canine Apollo, the energy of a small nuclear power plant, and the brains of a stick of celery. Dog and Divorce were hopeless. The moment they were big enough to knock us down, that was all they did, all day long. They meant well. These were such creatures as would go down to the bottom of the garden, and get lost. Not lost in woods, or lost in a back paddock. Lost within sight of their home.

You would look out of the sitting room window, and see a confused-looking russet blob ambling in circles. "The dog's lost again," you would say. You would walk down the bottom of the garden. When the dog noticed you, it would drool a bit. Then it would knock you over. Then it would lie down in the wet grass and wait to be rescued. You would have to pick the dog up and carry it, staggering – an adolescent red setter weighs, if memory serves, about as much as an eight-year-old child – all the way to the house. Once it arrived safely back at the house, it

†72 Faraday left this world in grand style. Sometime during the middle of the night, she made to leap up onto my parents' bed. At the instant her front claws made contact with the covers, she expired. My parents woke to find her hanging, stiff as a board, down the side of the bed, claws still embedded in the eiderdown.

would perk up, and bound off down the garden again.

We finally had to give Dog – who being male was even bigger and more boisterous than his sister – away. All my parents were left with was Divorce. Divorce eventually disappeared. Her disappearance was blamed on her having been kidnapped by gipsies,[73] though it seems perfectly likely to me that she simply went to the bottom of the garden and managed to get a tree between herself and the sightline from the sitting room window.

There followed a succession of Great Danes. There was loping, sandy-haired Gustav, who narrowly avoided being called Hamlet. He was chasing a deer across a road near our house, and he was hit by a car. The car, in an irony nobody found funny at the time, was a Triumph Stag. Deer deer.

There was Ballou. He was a very pleasant mottled grey (i.e. blue, i.e. Dog Ballou) hound. Then he developed some sort of brain disease, whose outward manifestations were unpredictable episodes of homicidal mania. We had him put down, on the first strike principle of pre-emption; get the dog before the dog gets you.

Their memories were kept alive by the mild but persistent form of nominal aphasia that seems to afflict my mother. If she wants to summon one of her children, she forgets, at that precise instant, what it is called, so shouts a string of names at random, in which will be included some combination of the names of children and the names of dogs living or dead: "Jack! Peta! Lupus! Sam! Gustav!"[74]

By the time Henry came to visit, we had moved onto Alsatians: Lupus, a big, shaggy, gentle, black-and-tan monster, with weak hips at the back; Raksha, a younger, smaller, more excitable bitch.

The cat count stood at two. There was Nonnie, a white Birman of the very very fluffy variety – surviving replacement for Saffy, an ickle-bitty fwuffy pedigree Birman given to my sister a few years back, and eaten by the mad Great Dane in short order, and Saffy's successor, a pedigree Maine coon, also eaten by the Dane within 24 hours – and Mouse, a smaller Siamesey-type off-white shorthair. In my mind's eye, Henry by now having approximately doubled in size, these two cats were approximately the

[73] This is not intended as a slur on the Romany community, nor any other travelling folk. I report only the received wisdom of the time. It always struck me as odd, since I never saw any evidence that gipsies were involved. But the prevalent myth had it that the common land that backed onto our then garden was periodically the haunt of gipsy dognappers. A received suburban prejudice.

[74] Boy, girl, dog, boy, dead dog

same size as my cat. When I first saw Mouse, I practically collapsed with shock. She was cruising along the kitchen worksurface in search of, presumably, a dog to eat or something. Not only was Mouse twice as long as Henry, she was *really* fat. I didn't realise cats got that big. This was more like a hairy zeppelin than a cat. Nonnie, who was if anything even bigger, didn't actually bother walking around that much. She mostly just lay on my sister's bed all day, growling.

Also, there were some chickens. My money was on Henry meeting the chickens and thinking: what devilry is this? (In the event, the bookies were paying out.)

The interaction between cat and cat, and between cat and dogs, was pretty much predictable. Mouse smelled Henry and made her way to the other side of the door to Henry's room. She lay there, nose at the chink under the door, and made a low persistent rumble of hostility. Henry, inside, said: "Mkgnao?" Or she lay at the foot of the stairs, while Henry peered down at her from the balcony. The sound effects were the same. Nonnie, when she came out, hung back. The scene was triangular. Come down those stairs, cutie-pie, was the message, an' we gon fwuck you up. Negotiations continued.

With the dogs it was more straightforward. Carry Henry downstairs past her tormentors, let her get a sight of Lupus, and watch how nimbly she leaps from ꝗꝰ ꝓ ꝣꝺ ꝑ ꝓ ꝣꝺ ꝑ ꝓ ꝣꝺ, ꝑ ꝓ ꝣꝺ ꝑ ꝓ ꝣꝺ, ꝑꝺ ꝑꝺꝑꝺꝑꝺ, to the top of your head. Enjoy the feeling of blood trickling down your forehead. Install her safely in a warm sitting room with the door closed, and watch her calm down. Then wait for your mother, who, completely ignoring the lessons of Darwin and Hobbes alike, believes that all creatures just want to get on with each other and live in harmony, opens the door and brings Lupus in so they can get to know each other. Lupus, sure enough, ambles in, sniffing, in a mood of benign curiosity. Henry – who happens to be curled up on the other side of the door – crosses the room briskly, at head height, and installs herself in the two and a half inch gap between bookcase and wall. It takes the best part of an hour to coax her out.

It was while all this is going on, that one night Alex raised the alarm.

"I think our cat," he said, "is falling to bits."

POOR BUT INTERESTING:
GREYFRIARS
BOBBY

SOMEONE HAD BEEN TELLING LIES ABOUT GREYFRIARS B.

YES. WE ALL know about the tombstone; where it stands, in red granite, on unhallowed ground in old Edinburgh. "Died 14th January 1872 Aged 16 Years," it reports underneath his name. That much is true. "Let his loyalty & devotion be a lesson to us all," it exhorts. That much is unexceptionable.

But there's a lot more to it all than that, and I am indebted for the contents of this chapter to the scholarship of Forbes MacGregor. The story of Greyfriars

Bobby – the faithful dog who lingered on his master's grave, and was never suspected of simply trying to remember where he had buried a bone – is part of Edinburgh's cherished history, and yet more cherished tourist industry. His posterity – the red granite fountain, surmounted by a bronze pooch, that stands at the head of the Cowgate; Bobby's grave and that of his master – remain a part of the city's daily life.

Mr MacGregor, however, is made of less soppy stuff. He seems to have made it a point of principle not to rest until the myths about this long-dead pooch have been torn into a million pieces, and the armature of drab truth over which they were arranged restored to public view. There is, as you can see from the introduction to his *Authenticated Facts Relating To Greyfriars Bobby* (Miniprint, Edinburgh), something steelily Presbyterian about Mr MacGregor's project.

"The fictitious embellishments," he writes, "not only lingered on, but were fed, and prospered into the monstrous myth believed universally all this century ... Justice to John Gray, whose affection for Bobby was so uniquely rewarded, has been delayed for one hundred and twenty-two years.[75] By persevering search, helped by good fortune, I have been able to find out many authentic details   I have, on the negative side, completely disproved the existence of 'Auld Jock', the shepherd who was associated with an equally fabulous[76] 'Cauldbraes' farm."

One focus of Mr MacGregor's disapproval is Eleanor Atkinson, author of the 1912 book *Greyfriars Bobby* and de facto high priestess of the Bobby cult. "It sold by the million and is still selling well, published as a paperback by Puffin Books," reports Mr MacGregor without bitterness. "Although she states categorically that the story is absolutely true, it is largely a pure fiction. Apart from this," he adds, "the style is not easily intelligible to children, although the book states it is for 8-year-olds."

In order, then, to undo all this badness, Mr MacGregor arranges the facts he has discovered in alphabetical order for ease of scholarly reference. For the general reader, however, he offers his own novelistic re-telling of the story, which

[75] Whether long-dead Mr Gray still thirsts for justice after all this time is moot.

[76] He means this as in *in and by* means Fictitious 19th-century Scottish farms – especially those named Cauldbraes – are not such places as you will find transvestites in gorgeous sequinned dresses, glitterballs, feather boas and uplifting bursts of four-to-the-floor happy house music.

he calls, to drive the point home: *Greyfriars Bobby: The Real Story At Last* (Steve Savage, London and Edinburgh, 2002).

†77
This may confuse readers. John Gray is a different "Auld Jock" from the one who doesn't exist, and he is in a different line of work.

His story starts among the benighted poor of Edinburgh in the chilly January of 1853. His hero is 40-year-old John Gray. Gray is a labourer who has come to Edinburgh with his wife and his 13-year-old son, in vain hope of finding work as a gardener. Gray is a sandy-haired man, standing 5' 7" in his stockinged feet. He is known as "Auld Jock".[77] His father,

†78
The existent "Auld Jocks" so far outnumber the non-existent Auld Jocks two to one.

before him, was known as "Auld Jock",[78] but Gray has broken with family tradition; his son is known as "Young Jock". And yet the family's fortunes remain low. With the winter ground

untillable, work is scarce. They are living in a stinking Cow Market slum, down to their last portion of "tatties and herring", and the poorhouse is starting to look like the next stop on their journey.

So Auld Jock Gray takes a decision. He joins the police. He will patrol for eight hours, six days a week; for which he will be rewarded with thirteen shillings a week, and a house to live in off the Cowgate (a low-lying street in the Old Town, slightly rough then, as now), in the middle of his beat. When he patrols he will be equipped with a leather belt, a lantern, a baton, a whistle, a rattle, a notebook, a pencil, and a sandwich.

†79
A watch-dog that will bite bad men.

He will also, he promised his wife, be equipped with "a watch-dug that kens whaur tae meet his teeth".[79] After the

loss, in circumstances unknown, of his first watch-dog (did its teeth meet in the wrong place?), John Gray takes on another. The year is now 1876, at best guess, and Bobby, the Skye Terrier he acquires, is a bit over six months old.

When you look now at R W Macbeth's 1868 etching of Bobby, done from life, he does not look like the sort of watch-dog who would strike terror into the heart of a man with a stripy shirt and a sack marked "swag" – still less one of the steaming drunk brawlers Constable Gray was expected to round up on a Saturday night.

He looks droopy; placid. His thick eyebrows and thick moustache and thickly furred ears droop and taper down to either side in near-identical curves. Buried

in all that pale fur, his eyes are wide apart, and don't both seem to focus on the same point. He looks a little bit like an elderly, and more hairy, version of Harold Macmillan.

He is also very small.

Bobby's name was not an accident. MacGregor suggests it was chosen – after a children's chant, "Here comes Bobby, keekin' in the lobby" – because this improbable wee creature was a police dog. History tells us that Bobby's legs were six inches long.

He liked picking fights with larger dogs, was notably patient, and was more or less omnivorous. MacGregor directs us to an authority, too, who describes Skye terriers as having a distinctively tripodic gallop: proceeding on three legs with a hind leg raised aloft as if kept in reserve.

Bobby proved well suited to his duties. His vocabulary included the words "walkies", "bone", "good doggy" and "Bobby", apparently – and if told "on trust, Bobby!", he would lie doggo for as long as required in a fixed spot, and would prepare to kick up Skye terrier hell if approached by any suspicious characters.

Auld Jock and Young Bobby were not to be partners for long, however. In November 1857, Auld Jock was invalided out of the force with a case of TB brought on by any combination of long cold nights on patrol, foully stinking slums, or the coal smog known as "Auld Reekie". On the evening of February 8th, 1878, a day on which there were no walkies for Bobby, Auld Jock reinvented himself as Dead Jock.

Two days later, Bobby – who had the night before seen out the candlelit vigil with the body, sustained by a smidgeon of bread and butter – joined the funeral procession down Cowgate to Greyfriars Kirkyard. Bobby's thanatotic seriousness, MacGregor conjectures, was not yet in place. The route of the funeral procession, during which Auld Constable Jock's coffin was carried by his fellow officers, passed by the market and then veered in the direction of the tasty pie and bone shop – each time, causing a burst of soon-to-be-thwarted anticipatory wagging in Bobby's stumpy tail.

Alongside Young Jock, watching Auld Jock going underground, the penny perhaps dropped for the pooch. When Bobby was brought back home, along with the other menfolk, he found he had no stomach for the funeral tea. Bread and jam delighted him not; no, nor boiled ham neither.

Rather, while the mourners got stuck in, Bobby lay growling fractiously under the table. Periodically, he would howl; a sound considered to be bad luck in Scottish tenements at the time. He scratched to be let out and, when he was, he pelted off down to the kirkyard. Both the gates were barred to prevent dogs getting in, but Bobby slipped in unnoticed as a pair of policemen went through the main Kirk Gate on patrol.

He spent there the first of many nights on Auld Jock's unmarked grave, taking occasional shelter under one or other of two large table-shaped stones nearby.

†80
The hardest-working man in Greyfriars Kirkyard.

In the morning, he encountered the Greyfriars gardener, James Brown.[80] Brown tried to chase Bobby off with a spade, but Bobby attacked his assailant's ankles with such peculiar ferocity that, when Brown's feckless gravedigging assistant Jamie turned up for work a few minutes later, he found Brown trembling at bay, out of biting reach, on the higher of the two table-stones.

The snappy beast was pacified with some porridge. Resisting all further attempts to move him that day, Bobbie held his ground, and stayed another night. And another. And another. He became a fixture. James Brown, anxious now to stay on the right side of him, took to feeding him, and put down a bit of sacking under one of the table-stones for him to lie on. Policemen on their nightly patrols shared a nibble of a sandwich as circumstances warranted. Bobby's unique privilege – as the only dog allowed to stay in a churchyard full of cats – was de facto rather than de jure, but it became entrenched.[81] Bobby in due course acted territorially. He saw off the indigent cat population of the kirkyard, and attacked unfamiliar humans.

He started to attract a wider circle of patrons, too. James Anderson, a kind-hearted upholsterer in Candlemaker Row, whose back windows overlooked the kirkyard, started taking Bobby in when the evenings were chilly. He accepted these invitations – and nor was he averse to the odd free pie from Mr and Mr Ramsay's Eating House. Bobby, being a dog, was a pragmatist. But he homed to the grave; refusing attempts to return him to his slum home. This was not, as far as scholarship can tell, a bereavement-for-pies scam worked on sentimental humans.[82]

Things got even better when Sergeant Scott, a dog-loving soldier of the Royal Engineers then stationed in Edinburgh Castle, started to take an interest in Bobby. Sgt Scott took to buying the mutt a once-a-week steak treat from the ever-useful Eating House (now Currie's Eating House). Sergeant Scott even took Bobby on a tour of his garrison at the castle, and he was allowed to attend – as a special guest – the firing of the one o'clock gun. The event was commemorated with a drawing in an 1862 edition of Good Words magazine.

Bobby ever after associated the one o'clock gun with food. So powerful did this association become that, in due course, crowds of spectators would gather daily by the cemetery gate and watch Bobby streak out towards the door of Currie's Eating House to fill his greedy, hairy little face. He kent well whaur tae meet his teeth.

† 81
What, incidentally, happened to Bobby's poo? History does not relate. But if you live in a churchyard, it is the sort of issue that can make or break your popularity. We assume Bobby's instincts told him to steer clear of the graves.

† 82
Had it been, mind you, it could scarcely have worked better. By the middle of 1862, his fifth year of vigil, Bobby had made arrangements to be regularly fed by four successive proprietors of what had been Mr and Mrs Ramsay's Eating House.

A weekly feed of steak; a daily *plat du jour* from a professional kitchen; a limitless supply of cats and bones; VIP walkies with a dashing soldier; the chance of shelter from the cold in the warm and, presumably, well-upholstered parlour of kind Mr Anderson; crowds of adoring acolytes … Did any of this help to blunt the edge of Bobby's grief? We must, however faintly, hope so.

In spring of 1862, Bobby's myth was given a fillip by a distinctly hucksterish character called John Traill, who took over the eating house and rebranded it Traill's Temperance Coffee House. Mr Traill saw that Bobby was what might be called a selling proposition.

So, like most successful entrepreneurs, he made a whole bunch of stuff up, rebranding himself as Bobby's patron and selling his customers a romantic yarn about it. He claimed "Auld Jock" (who actually died four years before Traill showed up on the scene) had been a regular customer of his, along with Bobby. He claimed that this "Auld Jock" had been a farmer, and that chowing down at the one o'clock gun, too, had been one of Auld Jock's quirks.[83]

†83
And yet, as the steely Mr MacGregor demonstrates, John Gray died three years before the one o'clock gun was first fired.

But – the rotter – when in 1867 Bobby's very life came under threat over his not having a dog licence, did he volunteer to pay the seven shillings? No he did not. Rather, he denied any duty to Bobby, sat back, and was prepared to let the dog-catcher have his way.

Our scholar, Mr MacGregor, reserves special anger for Mr Traill: "a humbug" who "monopolised Greyfriars Bobby" and "served himself" with deliberate falsehoods. "Rarely," he writes, "has the world seen such a contrasting tale of canine fidelity and human perfidy."

John Brown and other of Bobby's patrons endeavoured to scrape together what meagre contributions they could. But in the end, it was the intervention of the wealthy Lord Provost of Edinburgh, a very bearded man called Sir William Chambers, that saved Bobby. Hearing the story, Sir William – President of the Scottish Society for the Prevention of Cruelty to Animals – took Bobby's licence on, in perpetuity, himself. Bobby thenceforth wore a collar stating: "Greyfriars Bobby from the Lord Provost, 1867, licensed."

Thereafter, Bobby was, as Americans would say, all set. He moved from grave,

to pub, to parlour until he died, at the very ripe old age of sixteen, on the evening of January 14th, 1872. In the last few years of his life, he had made his peace with his perfidious Svengali, and he was toasting his old bones by the Traill fireside when life departed.

His passing was marked in the *Scotsman*, on January 17th. "Many will be sorry to hear," their staff reporter wrote, "that the poor but interesting dog, 'Greyfriars Bobby', died on Sunday evening."

John Traill buried Bobby in a flowerbed outside Greyfriars Kirk. Like suicides, murderers, and unbaptised children, Bobby was barred from consecrated ground. Auld Jock was going to have to get through eternity without him. The gravestone that Traill and co. erected, bearing just Greyfriars Bobby's name, was removed soon after. R T Skinner reported in the *Scotsman* in 1934, that, thirty years before, a session clerk had indicated to him the best guess at where "the dog's dust" lay: "the centre of the triangular piece of ground between the gate-way and the older Church as the spot at which Bobby was buried."

Today, you can visit the Museum of Edinburgh and gaze with your own eyes on Bobby's untenanted collar. His empty dinner dish, donated to the City of Edinburgh by John Traill's grand-daughter, stands beside it.

It says on it: "Bobby's Dinner Dish."

from the the grave to the table

PART ONE

Cooking with Bunny

There are as many different ways of preparing rabbit as there are of killing them. Though, like mutton, rabbit is seldom now eaten in the average family home, there's no reason this delicious, economical, plentiful source of food should not enjoy a revival. As I understand it, rabbits afflicted with myxomatosis are not actually poisonous to humans, and are undoubtedly easier to catch. However, they have very unappealing buggy-out eyes and I would counsel against trying to eat one.

You have to be a bit more careful with wild rabbits – the flavour will be better but you don't know where they've been – but with farmed rabbits (which will tend to be bigger and less lean and milder tasting than their wild counterparts)[84] and with pet rabbits, you should be fine. Rabbit can be cooked in most of the ways chicken can. It goes very well with mustardy sauces and has a delicious, delicately flavoured sort of flesh. The great Hugh Fearnley-Whittingstall reports that they make very good burgers when mixed with around 20 per cent good fatty minced pork.

Rabbits are generally eaten fresh. You hang them, with the skin on to keep them moist, for only 24 hours, and make sure you 'paunch' them – that is, pull the giblets out – beforehand. To paunch a rabbit, just open up its front and let the innards fall out. Make sure, as they flop onto the floor, that the liver isn't horrible and diseased and spotty.

Then wipe the cavity clean. Once you chop off its head and hands, the skin should comes off pretty easily like a little jacket. Young ones are good to roast. Older ones want a bit of stewing or boiling.

>> 84

This does raise welfare issues. Intensively reared flopsies, like intensively reared chickens, won't taste of much and will hurt your conscience.

Mrs Beeton's Simple Boiled Rabbit

From Mrs Beeton's *All-About Cookery*
Preparation time: 20 mins / Cooking time: 1 hr / Serves: 4

Ingredients

1 good-sized rabbit

1 onion

1 carrot

Half a turnip

**A bouquet garni
(parsley, thyme, bay leaf)**

6 peppercorns

A pinch of salt

Place a large open pan of water on the hob, and bring it to a brisk boil.

Place rabbit – skinned, gutted and trussed – in pan, and return it to the boil.

When the water re-boils, add the vegetables, cut into good-sized chunks, the bouquet garni, peppercorns and salt. Mrs Beeton recommends a whole teaspoonful, but in this sodium-conscious age, I'd err on the side of caution.

Turn the heat down to a gentle simmer, and let the rabbit cook for up to around an hour, depending on the size and age and toughness of the meat. Mrs Beeton recommends garnishing it with onion sauce, and serving fried bacon as an accompaniment. The cooking liquor can be served separately as a broth, or used as the basis for a sauce. Personally, I'd sieve it through muslin or a very fine sieve, then boil it down fiercely till it colours pleasantly and concentrates in flavour. I'd let it cool, and pour it into an ice-cube tray. I'd leave this in the freezer for several months and then, when I came across it again, I'd throw it away.

Alex Forrest's Simple Boiled Rabbit

From *Fatal Attraction*
Preparation time: 15 secs / Cooking time: variable / Serves: him right

Ingredients

1 good-sized rabbit

A pinch of salt

Place a large open pan of salted water on the hob, and bring it to a brisk boil.

Place rabbit, unskinned, in pan, and return it to the boil.

Replace lid, being sure to leave rabbit's ears sticking out so as to allow steam to escape.

Leave.

PART TWO /

Cooking with Dog

Human beings, at least in Western Europe, pretty seldom eat land-dwelling carnivores. Dogs – inasmuch as they are involved with the human food chain – are generally there to tidy up. A specialised few tidy up sheep, while still alive; and the rest skulk under tables hoping to tidy up leftovers. But dog is edible.

The cuisine best known for its dog recipes – and most commonly excoriated by animal-lovers in the West on the grounds that pigs may be intelligent, but dogs are cute – is that of Korea. But dogs have also been eaten in Africa, and, though less frequently, in Western Europe when, as during the sieges of Paris and Stalingrad, the citizens have grown extremely peckish. The explorer Richard Francis Burton did not eat puppy himself during his visit to Zanzibar – but he did report as follows:

A stunted Pariah dog is found upon the Island and the Continent: here, as in Western Africa, it is held, when fattened, to be a dish suitable for a (Negro) king. Some missionaries have tasted puppy stew – perhaps puppy pie – and have pronounced the flesh to be sweet, glutinous and palatable. The horse is now a recognized article of consumption in Europe; the cat has long served its turn as civet de lapin, without the honours of publicity; and the day may come when "dog-meat" will appear regularly in the market. I have often marvelled at the prejudices and squeamishness of those races who will eat the uncleanest things, such as pigs, ducks, and fowls, to which they are accustomed and yet who feel disgust at the idea of touching the purest feeders, simply because the food is new.

ZANZIBAR: City, Island and Coast (Tinsley Brothers, 1872)

The classic Korean dog dish is a soup, credited with health-giving properties, which goes by many names. Since the 1940s, it has been widely known as Bosintang. Its appearance on menus was discouraged by the authorites during the 1988 Seoul Olympics, however, and a number of alternative names, among them Youngyangtang, Sacheoltang, and Mungmungtang, came into use.

One of its names, gaejang, is pretty literal: gae ("dog") and jang ("stew"). Youngyangtang is kind of its full name. It means "health stew". Bosintang has similar connotations of healthiness. Then there's Mungmungtang, which is onomatopoeic. Mung mung is how a dog's bark sounds to a Korean. "Woof woof hotpot."

An extremely sagacious older friend who knows Korea very well is able to testify to the deliciousness of dog, properly prepared. He once ate Bosintang with a pal of his – a Korean gourmet – in the Korean countryside. I swear, his eyes almost mist as he recalls how lovely it is, on a very hot day, to sit down with an ice-cold cup of rice wine and sip this warming canine broth.

I went, initially, the official route, leaving a long and detailed message for

the press office of the Korean Embassy in London. "I don't think they ever comment on that," said the press officer I reached. I explained that I was after a recipe, really, rather than a comment, and some guidance on what sort of dog is the most suitable to use. She promised to pass the message along to the relevant authorities, and took my number and my email address. I didn't hear back.

Then I asked my ex-girlfriend, K, who was born in South Korea and whose parents still live there. I was faintly nervous of approaching K about it, just in case she suspected some sort of implied slight to her homeland. But she couldn't have cared less, and was on the case like a shot. Eventually, K came up with the goods, and offered helpful annotations, to boot.

Bosintang

Preparation time: 20 mins / Cooking time: 1¹/₂ hrs / Serves: 4

Ingredients

500 g of lean dog meat

2 large onions, chopped

3 leeks, trimmed and sliced into rounds

2 handfuls of perilla leaves

400 g of taro stalk soaked in water

Cut the meat into largish chunks, and boil in a thin broth with soy paste and taro stalk until tender. Remove the dog meat with a slotted spoon, and reserve. Bring the broth to a boil again. Add the other vegetables. Return the meat to the mix. Boil until the flavours have combined (about 40 mins).

Dress with a paste made from ginger, garlic, perilla, and chilli peppers mashed together with plenty of salt. Serve in an earthenware bowl, with side-orders of kimchi (delicious spicy fermented cabbage), sliced fresh red peppers and batons of cucumber. Wash down with Soju.

The original translation K found was peculiar in its idiom – it had the unmistakable marks of having been processed through cheap translation software – but one of the things that came through pretty clearly was the effort that goes into making the ingredients taste less like what they are.

"In Kyungsang province, to get rid of the smell," it notes, "perilla purple are put in the soup. Perilla are also used for ridding the smell. Taste of perilla is similar to that of dog, and it becomes a good match to dog meat. Side dishes of dog meat are Kimchi, fresh peppers, and cucumbers. Adding a glass of Soju (liquor) enhances the taste."

Soju, K's marginal scribble explained, is the Korean version of sake. Perilla is wild sesame. K marked taro with a question mark.[85]

Taro stalk is evidently not very nice, either. My recipe advises that, before you start to cook, "the stalk of taro is to be kept in cold water one or two days to get rid of its smell and taste". K added that, though it's not in the recipe, she'd recommend using some gochujang, too, which is a sort of chilli paste and "delicious".

There is a recipe for kangaroo soup in Australia that goes as follows. Put your kangaroo meat in a large pan of water, along with a selection of diced vegetables, and a rock about the size of your fist. Bring the water to the boil, and leave it at a tremulous simmer for not less than 24 hours, topping up as necessary. Remove from heat. Discard kangaroo meat. Eat rock.

But I digress.

Most to the point, I have no confidence that I have disentangled the instructions properly, and I have no wish to be responsible for enthusiastic citizens suffering not only prosecution by the RSPCA, but succumbing to dog-soup poisoning also. Make this at your own risk.

For balance, a Western European recipe. This one is reproduced by kind permission of Hugh Fearnley-Whittingstall, one of the UK's foremost omnivores

---

>> 85
Turns out it's some sort of perennial succulent.

and author of the *River Cottage Meat Book*. It should be set in context. Writing in the *Observer* a couple of years ago, Hugh described how he just selected one of his four piglets for early slaughter (she was going to be his annual spit-roast), and remembered how puppyishly playful they had been as youngsters. At the time, he happened to have, too, a litter of puppies, a circumstance that prompted the following reflections:

It seems to me somewhat arbitrary though, more or less an accident of culture, that the pig went to slaughter today, while the puppies are earmarked for a decade of pampering and play as family pets. There's no doubt whatever that pigs can make affectionate pets — there are dozens if not hundreds of Vietnamese pot-bellied pigs curling up on suburban sofas all over Britain. They can also be trained in a similar way to dogs. Everyone knows they can hunt for truffles. Less celebrated is their performance as "gun-pigs" — but apparently in parts of Eastern Europe they were once as popular as dogs for retrieving shot game in dense woodland.

And the edibility of dogs, of course, is as culturally relative as the petability of pigs. It is not the eating of dogs, in eastern cultures, that is barbaric. It is only surely the husbandry — or woeful lack of it — of the canine fatstock, that may rightfully incite moral outrage. Reports suggest that in Korea, dogs destined for the pot are treated with extreme cruelty. But for the sake of fairness, we should perhaps imagine our family pets living the life of an intensively farmed pig in a British pig unit. It's no picnic in there either.

So perhaps the time is right for a bit of a cultural experiment. We have already found homes for eight of the nine puppies. With one for us, that leaves one whose fate is still undecided. I say we should keep her for a while longer, and lavish just as much love and affection on her as we do on her sister and mother. We might vary her diet a bit though — plenty of milk, cheese and cereals to help her pile on the pounds. All in all, we shall do everything to ensure she is happy, healthy and gets to do what dogs like to do.

My free-range, outdoor-reared, organic puppy should be oven ready just in time for Christmas.

He included a proposed recipe — "A nice spicy dish for a summer barbecue. Naturally I would prefer you to choose puppy that is outdoor-reared – preferably organic" — and added that it would be equally suitable for pork. It was as follows.

Hugh Fearnley-Whittingstall's Puppy Satay

Preparation time: 2 hrs / Cooking time: 6–8 mins

I n g r e d i e n t s

500 g lean puppy shoulder

2 garlic cloves, crushed

**Juice of 1 lime
(or $^1/_2$ a lemon)**

2 tablespoons soy sauce

**A thumb-sized nugget
of ginger**

**A good pinch dried chilli
flakes**

**2 teaspoons soft
brown sugar**

Trim the puppy of any tough sinews and cut into smallish (2 cm) cubes. Combine all the other ingredients as a marinade, and toss with the puppy. Leave for at least an hour, preferably two, tossing again halfway through, if you remember.

Mount the marinaded puppy on wooden skewers, and grill on a hot but not too fierce barbecue, turning occasionally, for 6–8 minutes, until nicely browned and sizzling.

Serve with a simple peanut sauce, made by gently heating crunchy peanut butter, and thinning to dipping consistency with equal quantities of lime or lemon juice, soy sauce and water. Pep it up with a bit of chilli if you like.

PART THREE

Cooking with Guinea Pork

Cuy bono? Muy bono, we have every reason to believe.

Since before even the times of the ancient Incas, unsentimental South American folk have been chowing down on the little furry beggars. The bone record is scanty, but some reckon that they may have started to be domesticated as long ago as 5000 BC in Bolivia and Southern Peru. They call them "cuy", because of the high wheeeep sound they make as they snuffle around the place: "Cuy! Cuy! Cuy!"

Your unpretentious Andean family will tend to let the cuy live in the kitchen for ease, convenience and warmth, and let them run round like chickens. A breeding pair makes a nice wedding present.

There are thought to be around 100,000 guinea pigs kept as domestic pets in the United Kingdom. In Peru, 65 million a year are cooked and eaten. You can't argue with those numbers. They have obviously caught onto something we haven't. Grub's up.

The good news is that, soon, you won't even have to butcher your guinea pigs yourself.[86] A company in Peru, which already exports guinea pig meat to the US and Japan, in 2004 announced its intention to start shipping cavy to Britain.

In fact, they aren't just going to ship any cavies – they are going to be shipping scientifically modified super-cavy. Fruit of a three-decade long experimental breeding programme at La Molina University in Lima, the "Raza Peru" variety of edible guinea pig is a breakthrough in super-sized rodent grub. Most guinea pigs weigh about a pound and a half; these babies weigh 2.5lb.

Those who have tasted cuy – among whose ranks I regret to say I am not yet numbered – report that it is delicious, and tastes a bit like rabbit. It's good for you, too, being lower in fat and higher in protein than chicken, lamb, beef or pork.

>> 86

Not so hard. Skin in hot water. Leave the head on. Pull its guts out. Wash in salty water and leave to drip dry.

The experience of the Rev. Phil White, who contributed to a BBC survey on exotic food, is roughly representative. "It looked a bit like crispy duck with its leg in the air and its head intact, but still with its front teeth and whiskers. It was surprisingly tasty. Once you got going you forgot it was guinea pig!"

It gets better than that. A 17th-century painting of the Last Supper still hanging in a church in Cusco, Peru, shows Our Lord about to tuck into a nice spot of roasted guinea pig.

Q: What Would Jesus Do?
A: He Would Munch Cavy.

And here's how he might do it.

Roasted Cuy

Preparation time: 1 day (inc. marinating) / Serves 4
Cooking time: 15 mins or so, depending on the heat of the grill

Ingredients

2 large guinea-pigs

2 red onions, chopped

4 cloves of garlic, chopped

2 tsp cumin

1 tsp white pepper

2 tsp of salt

2 tbsp water

2 tbsp oil

Annatto (for colouring)

Mix ingredients well and spread over the inside and outside of the animal. Allow to marinate for up to one day to allow flavors to meld. Before roasting, remove excess marinade to avoid scalding. The spit should be inserted into the back part of the animal and exit from the jaw. Once on the stick, tie the front and back feet, stretching out the legs. Put on grill, turning manually. Continue to apply lard to the skin to avoid drying out the meat. The cuy is ready when the skin is close to bursting. Serve with boiled potatoes sprinkled with coriander, chillies, and the following peanut sauce[87] (overleaf). If your community is especially progressive, rice may be substituted for the potatoes.

>> 87
Those allergic to peanuts or who, like me, simply think they are disgusting, could, I'm sure, make do with a smear of delicious perilla. If it works for dog ...

Peanut sauce

Ingredients

1 large cup of roasted and ground coffee with peanuts

2 tbsp lard

2 white onions, chopped

2 cloves garlic

Pinch of salt

Pinch of cumin

Annatto

Fry onions until golden brown, then add other ingredients. Simmer for at least half an hour. Serve.

PART FOUR /

Not Cooking with Horse

Horse will do for anything you'd otherwise use cow for, milking aside. But the best thing to do with a dead dobbin, now your local hunt will no longer be able to feed his mortal remains to their hounds, is to turn him into delicious steak tartare.

This has obvious advantages for the gourmet. In the first place, using horse meat helps foster the European dream by forging closer links with our continental neighbours. In the second, particularly if it has died of old age, it will allow you to have a good old go at tenderising the meat. Bash bash bash. In the third, it offers a belt-and-braces food safety approach, since the raw egg/raw meat combination so frowned on by the busybodies of the international environmental health community is less scary when the raw meat is horse. Raw horse is more wholesome, apparently, than raw cow.[88]

>> 88

In Japan, raw horse meat, sliced very thinly, is eaten either as sushi or sashimi. It is called Basashi.

 138

My auntie, who is herself a bit of a cook, was able to help me out with the following advice from her cherished copy of *Larousse Gastronomique*: "Horse meat lends itself to all beef dishes, but is especially suitable for raw dishes (such as the authentic steak tartare) as the animal is unaffected by tuberculosis or tapeworm."

The origins of "authentic" steak tartare are not simple, but the Ravening Mongolian Hordes are understood to have had something to do with it. The most popular legend, pace Larousse, runs that the RMH – aka the Tartars – used to strike down the local cattle on whatever steppe they were ravaging at the time, and then tenderise the cuts of meat by putting them underneath the saddles while they galloped off to the next pillage. By the time they'd worked up a good appetite sacking, raping, ravaging etc, the meat would be all soft and mushy. This is, at least, the theory propounded in Panati's *Extraordinary Origins of Everyday Things* (HarperPerennial, 1989).

Problems with this theory:

1) Historical records from China and the Middle East make no mention of this practice.

2) Have you ever taken a horse's saddle off after a long ride on a hot steppe? Are you familiar with the indescribably pungent smell of sweaty horsehair? Do you really think you'd fancy eating anything that had been sitting underneath, however tender it might be. If these guys did, they really were barbarians.

3) It means they weren't eating horse, which undermines my original theory.

4) It doesn't account for the raw eggs. The Ravening Mongol Hordes did not, surely, take chickens on their adventures. Even at a gallop, a chicken can't keep up with a horse.

It has been suggested, too, that even if they did put meat under the saddles of their horses, it was to help ease raw saddle-sores on the horse, rather than to make it more digestible. This seems to me more plausible.

Another theory has it that the Tartars regarded their horses as packed lunches.

They'd stop, chop a lump of meat off the well-muscled hindquarters of their mount, sew it up again, eat the morsel raw, and ride on.

Problems with this theory:

1) Come on. There is only so much raw lunch you can chop off a living horse before you start seriously to diminish the animal's performance as a form of transport, let alone as an engine of war.

Another theory has it that low quality meat was simply shredded to make it more palatable. This is plausible but boring.

The truth is: no-one has a scooby. So here, by way of thanking her for her scholarly contribution, is this adaptation of my auntie's groovy late 70s recipe for the dish.[89]

Steak Tartare

Preparation time: 15 mins / Cooking time: None / Serves 4

Ingredients

450g lean fillet or rump of horse

Salt and freshly ground black pepper

4 tbs olive oil

3 egg yolks

Worcestershire sauce

3 tbs chopped onion

1 tbs chopped green pepper

1 tbs chopped capers

1 tbs fresh parsley, chopped

Crisp lettuce leaves for garnish

Chop the horsemeat very finely. Mix with the other ingredients to taste. Shape into pretty round patties. Adorn with lettuce leaves. Chow down.

The classic restaurant version of the dish has a pleasingly do-it-yourself aspect. Your chopped steak, nicely seasoned with salt and pepper, will tend to arrive with a little well on the top in which your raw egg yolk sits, frequently cradled in half an eggshell. You can go mad with the capers and onions and Worcestershire yourself, to taste.

>> 89
From Leith's *School Of Food And Wine: Intermediate.*

PART FIVE

Mice are nice

The edible dormouse, it has to be conceded, is no longer so widely popular as an entrée as it was in ancient Roman times. Nevertheless word is that it made good eating. There is, at least, a bit more meat on it than the ordinary white mouse that nowadays serves as a domestic pet, laboratory fodder, or the staple diet of your pet snake. But we must make do. I see no reason that the determined omnivore need not substitute Mus mus for Glis glis in the recipe below.

It may not be impossible, mind, to find your actual Glis glis. Commuters from north-west London will be encouraged to learn that the dormouse has a toe-hold around Amersham. It thrives in the Chilterns, and in particular the leafy Chesham Bois area.

They had been hens'-teeth rare since Roman times, but in 1902, Walter Rothschild imported six of the little furry bastards, and turned them loose around Tring. They bred with enthusiasm, and a pretty robust population continues to roam as if it owned the place through the couple of hundred square miles between Beaconsfield, Aylesbury and Luton.

They look a bit like squirrels, only with cute fat little faces and no tails, and the noise they make is described by one authority as being: "Woofle, woofle, woofle." They may be hunted with airguns, catapults, bows and arrows, and on horseback if need be. If you chase them with dogs, however, I refuse to be responsible for the legal consequences.

The classic recipe for mouse comes from the Roman cookbook prepared by Apicius. The principal aromatic here is silphium, or laser. This is, apparently, like extra-pungent garlic. So use garlic if you can't find laser in the organic section of your supermarket.

Apicius writes, in his *De Re Coquinaria*:

> **Glires: isicio porcino, item pulpis ex omni membro glirium trito, cum pipere, nucleis, lasere, liquamine farcies glires, et sutos in tegula positos mittes in furnum aut farsos in clibano coques.**

Translated – in Ilaria Gozzini Giacosa's *A Taste of Ancient Rome* – that is:

> **Dormice: Stuff dormice with pork filling, and with the meat of whole dormice ground with pepper, pine nuts, silphium, and garum. Sew up and place on a baking tile, and put them in the oven; or cook the stuffed (dormice) in a pan.**

You can improvise. I have a sneaking hunch this may do nicely for guinea pigs, too.

DEADPETS

Case Study No. 10

Other dogs may be thy peers
Haply in these drooping ears
And this glossy fairness.

But of thee it shall be said,
This dog watched beside a bed
Day and night unweary
Watched within a curtained room
Where no sunbeam brake the gloom
Round the sick and dreary.

FROM "TO FLUSH, MY DOG"

FLUSH

FLUSH, ELIZABETH BARRETT-BROWNING'S GOLDEN COCKER SPANIEL, IS PROBABLY THE MOST CELEBRATED GOLDEN COCKER SPANIEL IN THE HISTORY OF ENGLISH LETTERS: THE DEDICATEE OF TWO POEMS BY EBB, THE SUBJECT OF A BOOK BY VIRGINIA WOOLF, AND THE GOLDEN THREAD RUNNING THROUGH ONE OF THE GREAT EPISTOLARY LOVE AFFAIRS OF ALL TIME. HE EVEN STOLE THE SHOW IN THE FILM OF THAT LOVE AFFAIR, *THE BARRETTS OF WIMPOLE STREET*. HE IS ALSO, ARGUABLY, THE MOST SPOILED PET IN HISTORY.

FLUSH WAS BORN Flush, son of Flush, in the summer of 1840, near Reading. Little is known of his early life, though his biographer Virginia Woolf conjectures that it involved "gambols" among leaves and brambles and bean fields and such. Further, she asserts, "Love blazed her torch in his eyes; he heard the hunting-horn of Venus. Before he was well out of his puppyhood, Flush was a father." Flush's bloodline may survive in the Reading area, though I can't find evidence to support Woolf's claim.

His wild oats aren't our concern here. Flush's public life began, effectively, in January 1841, when at the age of six months he joined Elizabeth Barrett on her sickbed in Torquay. Flush made the journey by hamper via Basingstoke. Elizabeth had been sent to Torquay from the family home in Wimpole Street in 1938, in the hopes the fresh air would do her frail constitution good. It didn't.

Elizabeth was at the time in deep mourning: nearly demented with grief at the death the previous year of her favourite brother, "Bro", by drowning. Tormentingly, brother and sister had last parted on "a pettish word". She thought that she would die. Flush had been pressed on her as a solace and companion by her friend Mary Russell Mitford, the owner of Flush's sire and namesake.

In his youth, Flush had a glossy coat and distinguished, floppy ears. He had "eyes like agates" ("hazel bland" in colour), "legs like a Bantam's", and wore a fancy dog collar made from a mosaic-beaded necklace. One imagines him resembling a small, hairy occasional table. Because he spent so much time on Elizabeth's bed, he bathed daily, whether he needed to or not.

Woolf, who the reader may intuit I trust neither in accuracy of reportage nor plausibility of conjecture, fits Flush into her world-view by claiming marks of spaniel aristocracy about him: viz, no topknot, a dark nose, and eyes that are "full but not gozzled". As well as being a poor swimmer, Virginia Woolf was a howling snob.

Did Flush help cheer Elizabeth up? It seems he did. Elizabeth was receptive to pet animals. According to her biographer Margaret Forster, she had previously owned a squirrel she tamed herself, a number of rabbits, a hen, a goldfinch, and a Shetland pony called Moses. Flush – at a time when another Shetland pony would have been an impractical and unhygienic bedside companion – gave her especial comfort. He was, as her many letters on the subject, and her poems "To Flush, My Dog" and "Flush, or Faunus", attest, exceptionally patient and docile in her sickroom.

He was spoilt, but it is possible that Elizabeth put more pressure to succeed on Flush than the average spaniel could be reasonably expected to bear. She had a very high opinion of Flush's intelligence, and believed that, once he had mastered arithmetic, he would play dominoes with her. To this end, she tried to teach him to count by dangling bits of cake in front of him and enjoining him to gobble them up neither before, nor after, the count of three. When her brothers came upon her teaching Flush to read – "Kiss 'A', Flush … Now Kiss 'B' … " – they "laughed the tears into their eyes".

What do we know of Flush's character?

He disliked travel. He was a martyr to seasickness, and EBB wrote to her younger sister Arabella in 1846 that Flush "moans & wails on the railroad, when the barbarians insist on putting him in a box".

He disliked beards. In Pisa, he barked so violently at them that EBB banned him from restaurants, causing him to lose weight.

He disliked open fires.

He disliked watermelon, having once taken it in error for beef.

He disliked mountain-climbing.

He disliked living geese, and feared them. He had to be carried past any gathering of geese that approached rabble size.

He disliked Italy, where he lived for the later years of his life. Italy made his hair fall out; a malady he sought to counteract by eating grapes.

He disliked strangers. These, he bit.

Italian fleas liked Flush. Him, they bit. EBB combed him every morning into a bowl of water until it turned black with hungry Italian fleas, but considered this nasty task the only way she had of preventing him being "eaten up bodily, all but his teeth".

Flush was particular about his food. He liked cakes, especially macaroons, but flatly refused to eat bread unless it was thickly buttered. He preferred muffins. He drank sugared milk, instead of water. He took a dim view of mutton.

His favourite foods were toasted cheese, roast partridge, and chicken with cayenne pepper. He was a bastard for ice cream.

He was particular, too, about who he took food from. His détente with Alfred Barrett, Elizabeth's father, was brokered with cakes. Before he was quite reconciled

to Mr Browning he treated with contempt an attempt by the poet to buy him off in a similar manner. Instead, he bit Mr Browning, and left the cakes to go stale. In Woolf's somewhat rosy account of their conciliation, he finally scarfed them down, once they were "bereft of any carnal seduction … mouldy … fly-blown … sour", as "symbols of hate turned to love". I wonder. A dog as spoilt as Flush would have found stale cake very unpalatable.

Flush was a loyal and affectionate dog, but certain facts must also be faced. He was undoubtedly both a coward and a hypochondriac.

"Duke" Flush, as he was known below stairs in Wimpole Street, was generally held to be extremely good at starting fights and extremely bad at ending them. When he arrived at Wimpole Street – with Elizabeth's return from Torquay in September 1842 – he joined a menagerie that included a bloodhound called Catiline, a mastiff named Resolute, and a terrier called Myrtle, whom Elizabeth believed "the ugliest dog of all Christendom".

Flush's characteristic trick would be to goad the other dogs beyond endurance and then hightail it into Elizabeth's petticoats before revenge could be properly exacted. On one occasion, Catiline managed to catch him in time, and bit one leg hard enough that the yowling return to the petticoats was made tripodically. Flush was agreed to have Brought It Upon Himself. Flush was all bark and no bite. He frequently feigned illness. As EBB wrote: "Flush always makes the most of his misfortunes – he is of the Byronic school – *il se pose en victime.*"

Flush arrived in Elizabeth's life to help supply a lack. Where went Bro, there came Flush. In some ways, the story of Flush's subsequent career – and the key, perhaps, to the attention-seeking and truculent behaviour he sometimes exhibited in later life – is a painful story of perpetual replacement. First, Flush had to deal with the irruption into his cosy sphere of Robert Browning. Then, later, with the arrival of another Robert Browning: Elizabeth's son Robert Wiedemann, known as "Pen".

He did not go quietly. A cornerstone of the romantic myth of the Browning courtship is their secret marriage and flight to Italy. Flush nearly wrecked the whole shebang. In September 1846, just as their plans for elopement were reaching completion, Flush contrived to get himself kidnapped by a gang of "organised dog-banditti" called The Fancy.

Not only did it threaten to scotch the elopement plans, the kidnapping caused tensions between the couple. Who did Elizabeth love more: Flush, or Robert? The poet – a man of immense spiritual generosity but high principles, and a certain pragmatism when it came to Flush – did all he could to prevent his wife paying the ransom. He subtly started speaking of Flush in the past tense, which Elizabeth did not much care for.

Elizabeth – who knew The Fancy were in the habit of posting paws and heads back to recalcitrant owners in bloody parcels – was adamant. She would pay. What would Robert do if she were kidnapped? she asked. He said that he would pay the ransom and then devote as many as 50 years of his life to tracking down and shooting the kidnappers. (The author of *Sordello* makes a comically unlikely nemesis, but we must take his word for it.) Anyway, one Mr Taylor, the Shoreditch-based archvillain in charge of The Fancy, was paid 20 guineas for Flush's return.

That was not the first time this had happened. Flush had been pinched in September 1843, spent 48 hours in captivity and was ransomed for 5 guineas. In October the following year he was lured from the Wimpole Street doorstep with a canine honeytrap. Cost of return: 7 guineas. The Fancy made £4,000 a year from the dog pinching business.

Flush was exceptionally good at getting kidnapped, and it isn't impossible to suppose that he may have had a touch of Stockholm Syndrome. "Did all that barking … spend itself on such enemies as … myself, leaving only blandness and waggings of the tail for the man with the bag?" asked Mr Browning on the occasion of the 1846 kidnapping – dropping the heaviest hint possible that Flush might have colluded somewhat with Taylor's mob.

We can't know. The marriage went ahead on September 12th, 1846, and a week later the Brownings, with Flush in tow, skedaddled for Italy. The long summer of their married life was to be spent in their Florentine palazzo, "Casa Guidi". Italy did not agree with Flush. Flush preferred Wimpole Street. His hypochondria increased.

A further blow – and a further occasion for Flush to *se poser en victime* – came when, on March 9th, 1849, the Brownings' son Pen was born. Where went Flush, there came Pen. EBB reported to Miss Mitford: "For a whole fortnight he fell into a deep melancholy and was proof against all attentions lavished on him."

Pen adored Flush, especially his ears. Flush was less keen on Pen. EBB and RB both fell into the common difficulty of calling the dog by the baby's name and vice versa. (Easily done: my little sister, in infancy, answered to Gustav.) But Flush and Pen came to an accommodation. Flush appears to have realised that what can not be changed must be borne.

By the time of his death, he had borne enough. The young Flush that EBB remembered as "Full of prank and curveting, / Leaping like a charger" was long gone. He was, like many old persons, bald and very smelly. He snuffed it either just before, or just after, his fourteenth birthday.

"Dear Flush," EBB wrote to her sister in June 1874. "He is gone, Arabel. He died quite quietly – I am sorry to say Penini found him, & screamed in anguish. There was no pain, nothing to regret in that way – and our grief for him is the less that his infirmities had become so great that he lost no joy in losing life. He was old you know – though dogs of his kind have lived much longer – and the climate acted unfavourably upon him. He had scarcely a hair on his back – everyone thought it was the mange, and the smell made his presence in the drawing room a difficult thing. In spite of all however, it has been quite a shock to me & a sadness – A dear dog he was …"

A manuscript letter from Robert Browning to an unidentified correspondent identifies Flush's final resting place as "in the vaults under Casa Guidi". Margaret Forster places him "in the courtyard", however. She speculates that the sadness of his passing was alloyed, for young Pen, by the ceremony with which he was interred.

Death separated him geographically, as well as spiritually, from his masters. EBB lies not too far off, at the English cemetery in Florence; Robert Browning is in Poets' Corner in Westminster Abbey.

EBB had high hopes of meeting Flush in the hereafter. She noted in one letter that, when introduced to a church, Flush made straight for the high altar to perform his peculiar canine devotions. This embarrassed Robert, but was indulged by Elizabeth. She wrote, in a letter to a friend ten years before his death: "Flush has a soul to love. Do you not believe that dogs have souls? I am thinking of writing a treatise on the subject."

Her treatise was never written.

CHAPTER 7

HENRY V

ALEX THOUGHT THE cat was falling to bits. Henry was gnawing on his hand just now he said, when he noticed he was all smeared with blood. Now, the wee claws had been known to inflict flesh wounds from time to time, but there was more blood than you'd expect from that, and it wasn't coming from Alex. It was coming from the cat's mouth, and ... he opened his fist and held it out to me.

A tiny, hooked, perfectly white feline tooth, no longer attached to its owner.

"Is that supposed to happen, do you think?" My other brother Jack chipped in the further intelligence that he was pretty sure he'd seen her lose a claw on a wooden beam that afternoon.

We looked at the cat, who happened to be sitting, at the time, on the mat. Perfectly placid. It appeared that her teeth falling out wasn't the source of bother to her that it would be to me.

Long story short, it turns out that cats – notoriously lactose-intolerant though they may be – have milk teeth. Henry was not being dismantled. Henry was not dying. Henry ever after this instant took to fishing under duvets and pillows with her claws out – she was probably wondering where the hell her 50p was.

It turned out, in fact, that it wasn't Henry we needed to be worried about. It was Lupus. A fortnight or so later, Mum called to say that there was something wrong with the older dog. He had stopped eating, and was barely moving from his mat. The incident of the abrupt introduction and the flight behind the bookcase was to be the first and only time Henry and Lupus would ever meet.

Mum took the big gentle creature to the vet, who discovered a huge lump of something very nasty in his abdomen. An X-ray revealed that it was a sarcoma on his spleen. They took a blood test to see whether he had leukaemia – if he did, there'd be no point in even trying an operation to remove the sarcoma. It came up negative. But when they took him in for the operation, a pre-op X-ray showed something else up: a shadow on his heart. The sarcoma had spread. An operation would only delay the inevitable.

When Mum emailed to tell me that Lupus was gone, I didn't know what to do. This was supposed to be my specialist subject. I sent her Kipling's "Dinah in Heaven".[90] She said she was crying too hard to be able to read it.

Grief, a man who lost his son in 9/11 once told me, ambushes the heart. I thought that sounded like a quotation, but I haven't been able to find it anywhere since. And he was right: it hits you unexpectedly, at odd times, in odd places. And grief, for those who lose their pets, isn't any different in form – isn't, in some cases, any different in scale – than it is for those who lose their friends, or their relatives, or their children.

There are problems, too, with pet loss. Some people are weirdly angry to see a human being in deep mourning for a hamster. But some human beings go into deep mourning for their hamsters. And if you are in deep mourning for a hamster, you may find it more difficult to share your feelings than if you are in deep mourning for a child.

But you feel what you feel.

There are books, now, to help you through. I have beside my keyboard a selection of them. They are generally called something yucky. *The Heart That Is Loved Never Forgets*[91] has a

†90
See Appendix I

†91
This is quite an interesting one, in fact. It deals not only with human grief, but with animal grief, and the author, Kaetheryn (sic) Walker, is a veterinary homeopath. Several pages of tables at the back describe which homeopathic remedies are appropriate to the relief of grief-related symptoms in companion animals. Fear of thunderstorms, for example, should be treated with carbonate of sodium, chloride of sodium, phosphorus, yellow snow rose, inky juice of cuttlefish, and nitric acid. That'll larn him!

picture of a very fat, dozy-looking cat on the cover. *Absent Friend* shows what looks like a King Charles spaniel gazing wet-eyed and mournful up towards the camera from a blue and red rug. Beside him on the rug is a brush, an empty dog collar, and a condolence card from which a German shepherd's face looks out, framed by a black-fretted heart. The card says: "You're truly ... in my heart." †92 There's *The Loss of A Pet*, *Goodbye Dear Friend*,[92] *Goodbye, Friend* and so on and so forth.

†92
This is by the famous agony aunt Virginia Ironside. Word.

The gist of most, except the weird homeopathic one – see note 91 – is more or less the same. There are a number of stages of grief. These can come in any order, can repeat on you, can take more or less time for different people, and so on. You need to allow yourself to grieve and accept your feelings. Yadda yadda yadda. It's all very good, very sensible stuff, and you could pretty easily use these grief manuals for a human as well.

Pet bereavement proceeds like human bereavement, and its severity isn't to be underestimated. Cat owners grieve more severely than dog owners. Women grieve more severely than men. *Absent Friend*, whose naff cover and twee title I so freely mock, nevertheless does contain some very interesting statistics. The authors conducted a survey of more than 1,000 adults in the UK on the deaths of their dogs and cats, and found that one person in ten had mourned so severely that they had been driven to seek help from their family doctor.

You're not alone. In the past, some who have lost pets have felt awkward seeking help from the sort of bereavement counselling services traditionally dedicated to those who have lost human beings. No longer. In 1994, the Society for Companion Animal Studies established for the first time a network of "telephone befrienders", in response to the growing number of letters they were receiving from grieving pet owners with no outlet to express their loss. The system – initiated and run by volunteers – was simple. Callers to a central helpline number would be put in touch directly with the "befriender" nearest to where they lived. Befrienders were given proper training, and the service is accredited with the British Association for Counselling and Psychotherapy.

†93
The PBSS number is 0800 096 6606 (8.30 a.m.-8.30 p.m.). Email: bssmail@ bluecross.org.uk. For further details see www.bluecross.org.uk

It took off. By 1998, the Pet Bereavement Support Service[93] became too big to be co-ordinated by a single person, and the pet welfare charity Blue Cross became involved.

Most callers are women, though some call on behalf of men. Most call within a week of the animal's death. "It's mostly dogs and cats," says Jo-Ann Dono, who now heads the service, "but we do get calls about horses, and some small furries."

By 2004, the service was taking 2,000 calls a year, had 90 befrienders on its books, and had also started corresponding with the bereaved by email.

"It's the loss of a relationship or attachment," says Jo-Ann. "Lots of non-pet-owners don't understand that. There was not much recognition, and so this was an avenue to explore those emotions: a listening ear that you could talk to confidentially. Someone to reassure you that what you are feeling is normal."

If you think about it, we shouldn't be surprised pet loss hurts so much. It is a truism that has almost attained the status of cliché, by now, that we are really mourning more for ourselves than we do for the departed: our loss, not their death. Hopkins, in "Spring and Fall", describes young Margaret "grieving" over the autumn unleaving of Goldengrove, and finishes:

> *It is the blight man was born for,*
> *It is Margaret you mourn for.*

†94
Some specialist pet publications have been doing this for years, mind. *Dogs Today* accepted pet obits from issue one. The bi-monthly official journal of the National Fancy Rat Society, *Pro-Rat-a*, has its own sort of Births, Marriages and Deaths page, known as "Hatches, Matches and Dispatches".

That emotion can surely sometimes be all the purer when you're talking about an animal onto whom you have been able to project so much of yourself.

In 2004 the *Daily Telegraph* started accepting "Pet Obituaries" on its Court and Social pages, alongside the human death notices and the announcements of births, engagements and marriages. The *Telegraph* was the first newspaper, as far as I know, to do so.[94] Really, they were death notices rather than obituaries proper, as they were composed and paid for by the pet owners, but you could not fail to be moved by them. Each told a tiny story of affection and loss.

BECK AND BELLA — *Two guinea pigs, suddenly and cruelly taken by a fox on May 31. Sweet, gentle and playful, the first real pets of Cornelia Furneaux, who loved them, fed them*

and looked after them every day for two and a half years, and now misses them very much. "Their spirits are in heaven but they had a lovely life as well."

FLYN OTWAY *aged 11 years 10 months, euthanasia at Cliffe Vets, Lewes, Wednesday 18th August 04. Loyal dog and expert rabbit exerciser. Leaves favourite chair (and fleas) to Clovis.*

TYSON *You liked to box but you were a gentle, handsome cat who loved us all. You were purring as you died and it broke our hearts. We'll never forget you.*

The feature petered out, to my disappointment, after a few months – but I believe that was more down to people not remembering it was available than to a lack of will. The longest one published, a tribute to an Old English mastiff called Grumble ("'Grumby', we miss you terribly.") ran to 28 lines.

Gertie and Hector and Zippy Haworth and Misty Pendragon and Becky Boo and Charlie Dog and Twinkle and Heather and Tabitha and Muttley and Pimms will not be forgotten.

Nor will Lupus.

Not long afterwards, Mum received a letter from her pet insurance company, Dog Breeders Insurance, opening: "We have considered your claim."

It set out the details of the claim in itemised sequence.

Euthanasia – 26 November 04. Claim amount: £48.53. Excess: £0. Payment: £0. [The policy didn't cover euthanasia. Fair enough.]
Treatment for sarcoma – 17 November 04. Claim amount: £387.39. Excess: £60. Payment: £327.39.

It further advised, presumably against the eventuality that we were planning to hit them up for postmortem treatment: "Please note: the time limit for treatment received ends on 17th November 2005 unless the maximum cost of treatment covered by your insurance is reached first."

Nice.

CHAMPION
V.
TRIGGER
HORSE OPERAS AND THE TWILIGHT
OF THE SINGING COWBOY

MARENGO AND COPENHAGEN — RESPECTIVELY THE STEEDS OF NAPOLEON AND WELLINGTON — WERE ALL VERY WELL. BUT OF FAR MORE IMPORTANCE TO THE CULTURAL HISTORY OF THE WESTERN WORLD WAS THE LONG RIVALRY BETWEEN TWO OTHER RIDERS, AND TWO OTHER HORSES.

ANYONE WHO, LIKE me, grew up in the 1970s, will remember the comforting tea-time cry of "CHAMPiyaaaarn, the WONder ho-o-o-o-orse!", signalling the imminent arrival on the small screen of another instalment of the adventures of the horse equivalent of Lassie. I had no idea, as I watched Champ, that magnificent chestnut stallion, rearing on his hind legs and boxing the air with his front hooves, what a distinguished history he had. I had never heard of Gene Autry, whose "Flying A" production company made the show. Still less was I even aware that I was watching a sort of twilight of the gods. The *Champion* television series was the sunset of Champ's career. Or, if I am accurate – something else I didn't know either – it was the sunset of Champs' career. But more of that migrating apostrophe later.

The Lassie/Rin Tin Tin formula – boy befriends animal; boy suffers weekly disaster; animal rescues boy and friends from collapsed mine shaft; cattle rustlers detained – was one that captivated the American small screen for decades, with a number of different animals taking the Lassie role. Its bizarre zenith was Flipper: the dolphin Lassie.[95]

†95
There was never a cat Lassie, however, or a sea-monkey Lassie. Cats are hard to train, and show little or no interest in rescuing humans from collapsed mine-shafts. Sea-monkeys, while quite easy to train, are very small indeed and not very telegenic.

Champ was successful in this mould, but his glory days were behind him in the "horse operas". This was a sort of movie, now entirely disappeared, that once captivated the world. But to set it in context, we have to go back even further.

It did not take long, once first man learned to exploit the power of the moving image for fun and profit, for his mind to turn to cowboys and Indians. And this meant that the very early days of Hollywood were no place for a horse.

There is a joke told about the making, back then, of a huge movie showing Custer's Last Stand – it runs like this. A journalist has been allowed on set, and is watching the last climactic set-piece battle. The embattled troops of poor ole General Custer are circled in the centre of a low bit of land, and down upon them from all sides, every mounted injun in the Western world rides a-whoopin' and a-shootin' and a-wavin' his tomahawk. It is bloody carnage. Bodies and horses and such like are biting the dust everywhere you look.

Awed by the scale of the production, the journalist asks the director: "How on earth can you afford to make a film on this scale? The extras alone must be costing you a fortune." And the director, from around the smouldering stogie he is obliged to have in order to appear in this sort of joke, says: "It's simple, son. On the last take, we use real bullets."[96]

†96
I did not say it was a good joke.

But if extras got a hard time, none got a harder time than horses. They were expected to race trains, tumble spectacularly in battle, rear on demand, leap improbable gaps and from great heights, and gallop off happily, rather than collapsing with an injured spine, when some musclebound stuntman in a cowboy suit jumped from a second floor balcony directly into the saddle. They died in droves. Nobody seemed to mind much.

Among the tricks used to help horses fall over in an impressive manner, for example, was something called the "Running W". The special effects man would attach cuffs low on the horse's front legs, and run long fine wires back from each one to where they would be attached, at the other end, to a log buried in the sand. When the effect was needed, the horse would be given a mighty slap on the rump and sent at a full gallop in the desired direction. In due course, the wires would pull taut and dobbin would go spectacularly arse-over-ears for the camera, almost certainly breaking his neck.

If the "Running W" was impractical, they would use a camouflaged pitfall to trip the creature. And if they wanted a horse to leap over the edge of a cliff, they wouldn't take a chance on persuading the horse to do it himself. The shot you'd see of the horse flying through the air would be genuine enough. What you wouldn't see was the preceding moment, when he had been tipped out of a greased chute positioned on the edge of the cliff. It was carnage.[97]

†97
There was only one horse in the history of the movies who actually enjoyed pretending to be shot. A horse called Ghost was able to die, at a gallop, on cue. Its owner earned $300 a "death".

The equine death toll on certain early films, *Jesse James* and *The Charge of the Light Brigade* in particular, was one of the most effective galvanisers of public opinion when it came to getting the American Humane Association involved in movie-making. This charitable organisation now supervises animal welfare on all mainstream motion pictures, and refusing to allow AHA access would mean pariah status with the Academy and distributors for any film going on release.

Indeed, the AHA became so closely involved in the movie industry that they distributed their own equivalent of the Oscars for animal actors. The Patsies – Patsy being an acronym for Picture Animal Top Star of the Year Award – were first issued in a ceremony in Los Angeles in 1951.[98] One old photograph shows a delegation of the AHA earnestly presenting an award to a horse called Fury (who seems more or less indifferent to the presentation). But there is evidence that, whatever the good work of the AHA, their predilection for giving dumb animals awards encouraged showboating and queeniness among animal actors. By the time Marilyn Monroe's career was underway, levels of animal upstaging were such that she expressed reservations about appearing in a Western. Was she worried, a friend asked, that her leading man would eclipse her? "It's not him that worries me," she said. "It's those hammy horses."

The arrival of the AHA and a general feeling that horses in movies should be well treated coincided with a shift in the tenor of the standard Hollywood Western – and, indeed, with a gorgeous sunniness in the American popular psyche. The Depression was a memory; the Second World War a nightmare barely yet imagined.

The darker and more violent cowboy flicks of the past were giving way to a new style of film – something like a harbinger of Busby Berkeley on four hooves. It was the era of the singing cowboy. And the greatest singing cowboy of them all was Gene Autry. Gene Autry was a good man who owned at least 300 pairs of cowboy boots, and did more than his fair share of yodelling.

Born on September 29th, 1907 in Tioga, Texas, Gene Autry[99] grew up baling prairie hay on his uncle's farm, and learned to sing in his Baptist-preacher grandfather's choir. Gene saved up, and got his first guitar – for $8 cash – from a Sears & Roebuck catalogue when he was just twelve years old.

In 1927, as he relates in his genial and absorbing autobiography, *Back In The Saddle Again*, he was working as a telegraph operator in Chelsea, Oklahoma, when a customer came in, heard him picking idly at his guitar, and suggested he go to New York and seek his fortune on the radio. That customer was the Oklahoma

†98
Francis the talking mule – a forerunner of the legendary Mr Ed the talking horse – was the first winner.

†99
Real first name: Orvon. 'Gene' was his middle name.

cowboy legend Will Rogers, and he spoke in a voice, Autry remembers, "which had the sound of a man chewing on cactus".

Autry dismissed the idea at the time, but in due course, as it was foreseen, so it came to pass. Autry's filmography is awesome, and spans decades. He is the first to thank his stars for the distance his good luck and genial persona propelled his modest talents. When he looked back over his films, he found it hard to remember even the sketchiest details of some of them. "Trying to single out one of my movies," he wrote, "is like trying to recall a particular noodle you enjoyed during a spaghetti dinner."

What distinguished the movies was a particular style and outlook on life. There were songs. Violence, death and the dark side of life played no more role in a Gene Autry movie than they did in *The A-Team*.[100] And there were songs – often featuring Autry's distinctive sexy yodelling.

"I came along," he recalled, "owing more to Bing Crosby than Bill Hart.[101] My movies offered crimes of cunning instead of crimes of violence." There was a formula. As Autry saw it, there were two principles that were established from the earliest of his films.

†100
Although, paradoxically, Gene's own-brand guns held hegemonic dominion over the enormous American cap pistol market for several years.

†101
William S Hart was an early, non-singing cowboy star. His horse was called Fritz.

1) There wasn't a Reo truck or a wood-panelled station wagon on the road that my horse, Champion, couldn't outrun.
2) Big Business and Special Interests and High-Handed Villains always lost out to the Pure of Heart.

Imagine that now. It was a formula with which Autry was very happy (he should have been; it made him his fortune), and one that he declined to deviate from, even when tempted with offers to branch out into playing romantic leads. A cowboy, he pointed out, if he keeps his nose clean and doesn't disappoint his public, can still be lassooing steers into his fifties. A matinee idol can be burned out in five years flat.

Autry had more than just his sunny disposition and his yodelling to recommend him to the public. He had Champion.

The familiar image we have of Champion – rearing, of course – is of a brown horse with four white "knee-socks" and a handsome white blaze on his nose. The original Champion, in fact, only had three "socks". A dark sorrel horse out of Oklahoma, Champ became a sort of trademark. What the public didn't know is that there were, in fact, at least three screen Champions over the years – film historians still struggle to disentangle which was which, and Autry's "spaghetti dinner" memory doesn't help them much – and that's not counting the stunt horses and the understudies.

To Autry, though, they all shared in the essence of Champion-ness. And Autry's closeness to the horse, who for ease of use I shall call Champion rather than Champion(s), may shed interesting light on his less enthusiastic relationship with his leading ladies.

In his autobiography, Autry feels the need to issue a denial early on.

"Let me dispose right now of a malicious rumour that has haunted me all my life. I did not kiss my horse!" he wrote, before conceding: "We may have *nuzzled* a little, but we never kissed. Never. I can take a joke, but it bothered ol' Champ. That was one way of pointing out, I guess, that Autry was about the most reluctant Romeo the screen had produced up to that time. I never kissed my leading ladies either ..."

Autry chooses not to explain his reluctance to kiss his leading ladies. It may relate to his previous, shrewd assessment of the professional shelf-lives of romantic leads. It may be something to do with his wholesome, old-fashioned morality. And it may not. We can but return our cherished, scratched old yodelling cowboy record to the gramophone, and speculate.

In only one of Autry's films, *Loaded Pistols*, when the *Hopalong Cassidy* starlet Barbara Britton shared billing with Autry above the title, did any leading lady ever get billed ahead of the horse. Quite right, too. Autry *owed* Champ. And this is where Roy Rogers entered the scene – and with him, not long after, Champ's hated rival Trigger. It was 1937. Gene, then as famous as famous can be – a box office draw who had completely reversed the fortunes of the studio for which he worked, Republic – discovered that the studio was diddling him.

Basically, they had hit on a 'bundling' system whereby movie houses would

have to buy a package of films from the studio, so if they wanted the new Gene Autry movie, they also had to take (and pay for) a whole raft of rubbish films the studio was trying to offload. When he learned about this, Gene took grave exception to what he saw as a breach of fair dealing, and one with which the yodelling cowboy did not care to be associated.

So Gene and Champion went on strike. And not only did they go on strike, they went on the run. If he wasn't going to make the film they wanted him to make, the studio was damned if he was going to make money touring on stage. They took out an injunction to prevent Autry from doing any work at all; an injunction that would take effect as soon as Autry had been officially notified. So Autry and Champ, like small-time hoods fleeing a subpoena, hightailed it off across the Midwest, with process servers chasing them from stage show to stage show.

They finally caught up with Autry in Nashville, just before he was due to go on for the first of a sold-out three-night run at the Paramount Theatre. He would now have been in serious legal trouble if he appeared on stage. Solution? He bought a ticket for his own show, and sat down in the front row to watch while Champ – along with Autry's then sidekick Lester 'Smiley' Burnette – did the show for him. The audience loved it: "people enjoyed being a part of events that are out of the ordinary, so they reacted warmly to everything we did". Perhaps it was in Nashville that there first appeared in Champion's eye the seed of a glimmer; the idea that one day, he might be able to strike out on his own without a yodelling buffoon on his back.

Meanwhile, however, back at the studio, opportunity knocked for a young man from Ohio who went under the stage name of Roy Rogers. Autry and Champ had been just about to start shooting a film – a sort of *Mr Smith Goes To Washington* on horseback – to be called *Washington Cowboy*. Autry's absconsion had left the film without a star. So they retitled the film *Under Western Skies*, and put Rogers in as the lead.

Did Gene – who in due course fell back in with the studio and resumed churning out his films – consider Roy a "scab"? He claims not. "There was never any animosity or jealousy between Roy and me ... A break came, and he took it, just as anyone would have, myself included. Of course the studio tried desperately

to create the impression of a rivalry, a feud, between us ..."

Well, possibly.

It is hard now to get a sense of quite how big a star Champion was. Champion's skills were as follows. He could kneel, bow, waltz, hula, rhumba, untie knots, smile, kiss, and – his signature display – leap heroically through large paper posters. At one time or another, he would jump up on top of a grand piano. He was tidy with flaming-hoop work, too. Plus, he was a comedian. During a live show in Chicago, when Champ had completed his routine and Autry had strolled downstage of him to deliver a song or two. Champ quietly, but very visibly, took a dump onstage. Autry, unaware: "Well, now that Champ has done his act, it's time for me to do mine ..."

At the peak of his fame, Champion, like Trigger, travelled around in an enormous luxury horse-box with running water, servants' quarters, and an attached trophy room to display his gongs.[102] I am not able to establish for sure whether Champ is the first horse to have flown coast-to-coast on a DC-3 aeroplane, but we can be confident that flying horses were, at the time, rare. The plane was specially adapted, with five rows of seats taken out and a personalised stall put in. Champ was slipped apples to keep him quiet during periods of turbulence, and ever after, according to Autry, he was an "apple junkie" and shunned oats.

†102
He received thousands of fan letters, none of which he read. In 1945, Champion was invited to place his hoofprint in the walk-of-fame sidewalk outside Grauman's Chinese Theater.

His arrival in London in July 1939 was the cherry on the bakewell tart. In the very shadow of war itself, Champion was "treated with a courtesy and respect given few other American entertainers", even attending a lunch in Autry's honour at the Savoy, becoming the only horse, to my knowledge, to have eaten in that hotel.

"I led him through the lobby of that elegant hostelry, where the princes of Europe have met," wrote Autry, "and later he walked among the tables at my reception, while the startled guests protected their plates."

The Nazi threat hung over the proceedings, and at a lunch on August 21st, Autry was cheered to the echo when he pulled out his six-shooters in the middle of lunch and declared: "Look, I ain't a'saying yes, and I ain't a'saying no, but if those Nazis cross the border in the morning I'm a'coming in, shooting."

Hitler wasn't, apparently, scared of singing cowboys. As Germany invaded Poland, Champion invaded Liverpool. Two headlines, almost equivalent in size, on the same newspaper front page:

HITLER SAYS HE IS LOSING PATIENCE

COWBOY TAKES LIVERPOOL

In Dublin, 300,000 people lined the streets to see Champion – "what was then thought to be a world record for anyone less than the Pope". That record stood, Autry claims, until the Beatles toured New York.

War, however, was to separate the singing cowboy from his steed. In 1944, while Autry was doing his wartime service, the original Champion keeled over and died of a heart attack. He was 23. Autry was out of the country and didn't learn about his death for a month. Champ was succeeded by a four-socked Tennessee walking horse also called, obviously, Champion; and he in turn by a third Champion, who starred in the *Adventures of Champion* TV series I describe above, and died in 1976.

How did Champion stack up against Trigger?

For a start, he had ole Trig outnumbered. Remarkably, Trigger was a single horse: a golden palomino.[103] Born Golden Cloud, his sire was a thoroughbred Caliente race-horse and his mother a palomino. Trigger had a white mane and tail and boots. He was billed as "The Smartest Horse in the Movies", and supposed to be able to perform 60 tricks.

He never attended a luncheon at the Savoy, but he did check into a hotel for a press conference, signing his name X[104] with a pencil held in his teeth, and trotting upstairs to meet the journalists afterwards. He was commended for being able to display "self-restraint" when indoors – which I take to mean he was house-trained. Unlike Champ.

Trig first appeared in public at the age of three, underneath Olivia de Havilland in Errol Flynn's *Robin Hood*. He was working, at the time, for Hudkins Rental Stable in Hollywood.

†103
Like Mr Ed, The Talking Horse. I have not space here to go into Mr Ed's long televisual history, but his death is worth mentioning. Mr Ed, like Trigger, was 33 when he died , on Feb 28th, 1979. All that talking – they moved his lips with a strand of see-through nylon – had done him no good. By the time of his death he had lost all his teeth and was addicted, for some reason, to beef-flavoured baby food. His last owner, animal trainer Clarence Tharp, buried him without ceremony in the backyard of his trailer home in Cherokee County, Tahlequah, Oklahoma.

†104
Trigger was illiterate.

Roy Rogers bought him outright from Hudkins in 1938 for $2,500.[105] It was, apparently, love at first sight. Trigger walked out, and Rogers told the stable's owners: "This is it. This is the color I want. He feels like the horse I want, and he's got a good rein on him."

It was actually the fickle Smiley Burnett – who served at one time or another as sidekick to both Autry and Rogers, who named Trig. He told Rogers: "As fast and quick as the horse is, you ought to call him Trigger. You know, quick-on-the-trigger."

And Trigger he became. One Glenn Randall, who had been training show horses, was introduced to Rogers and became Trigger's trainer: "a lucky day for all three of us". Rogers commended Trigger as being "tough as a boot", and boasted: "I'm the only cowboy, I think, that started and made all my pictures with one horse."

Trig retired in 1957, at the age of 25.

On the death of the original Champion, a colleague consulted a taxidermist and told Autry that for $1,500 he could have Champ stuffed and put on display. "Johnny," said Autry, "the horse had a good life. Let's not make him work for us now. Go ahead and bury him." Autry was none too pleased when, this story making its way around the circuit, his response was boiled down in popular wisdom, to: "*Fifteen hundred dollars? Drag him out and plant him.*" Champion rests at Autry's Melody Ranch.

Years later[106] when Champ's arch-rival Trigger pegged out, Autry's arch-rival Roy Rogers took a different decision.

"When Trigger died I had mixed thoughts about what to do," he told an interviewer. "I'd seen what a beautiful job they did mounting animals. If I put him in the ground, I knew what would happen to him. If I put him here in the museum, people could see him from now on. So I had him mounted. He looks beautiful. I'm so happy I did it. He appeared in all my pictures and countless personal appearances. It would have been a crime to bury him."[107]

†105
Gene Autry claimed never to have spent more than $1,500 on a horse. H F Hintz's book *Horses In The Movies* claims, however, that Champ Jr was bought in 1956 from Charles Auten of Oklahoma for $2,500. It is possible that – for reasons that will become clear below – Autry was retrospectively fixated on the figure of $1,500.

†106
June 1965, to be precise. Trigger died at 33 – more than 100 in human terms.

†107
Trigger, stuffed, is further immortalised in the song "P F Sloan", by Jimmy Webb.

In fact, he went taxidermy crazy. Not only Trigger, but Trig Jr,[108] Buttermilk – the horse belonging to Rogers's wife and screen sidekick Dale Evans – and Bullet the dog all ended up on proud display at the Roy Rogers Museum in Victorville, Texas.

Dale Evans said that when Roy died, she would have him stuffed and place him atop Trigger in perpetuity. Though her husband predeceased her,[109] Dale never lived to see her dream come true.

Trigger, to this day, remains riderless.

✦✦✦ FIVE INTERESTING THINGS TO DO WITH YOUR DEAD PET ✦✦✦

4 : [OF 5] CRYONIC FREEZING

YOU CAN, IN theory, put your terminally ill gerbil into suspended animation, on the understanding that it will be defrosted and restored to life when gerbil vetinerary science is sufficiently advanced to guarantee her a new lease of life in some unimaginable future. This is really a very select option. The two firms that will subject pets to cryonic freezing are the Cryonics Institute and Alcor. Both specialise in humans. They only accept medium-size animals (horses are out), it will cost you an arm and a leg – several thousand pounds, in fact – and, more to the point, it is a service at present open only to clients of those companies. You have to let them freeze you, too.

CHAPTER 8

HOW TO
STUFF A
SONGBIRD
(NOT VERY WELL
AT ALL)

PART ONE
BOOK LEARNIN'

I AM IN ONE OF THE BIGGEST BOOKSHOPS IN ONE OF THE BIGGEST AND MOST LITERATE CITIES IN THE WORLD. WATERSTONE'S, PICCADILLY, LONDON. THIS IS A GREAT VERTICAL WAREHOUSE OF BOOKS: EIGHT FLOORS OF WALL-TO-WALL PRINTED MATTER. BILLIONS OF WORDS. MILLIONS OF PICTURES. DOZENS OF BORED-LOOKING BOOKSELLERS. AND I AM HAVING NO LUCK — REALLY, NONE AT ALL — WHEN IT COMES TO FINDING A DOG-STUFFING INSTRUCTION MANUAL.

I HAD NO luck in Hatchards, down the road, either. There wasn't a sausage. I looked under Arts and Crafts. Nada. Sports. Zip. I even tried Cookery. Not a thing.

"Taxidermy?" the assistant had said. "We used to store them in Crafts, but we don't keep them anymore." There had been plenty of books on the care of cats, the psychology of dogs, the training of budgies. But there had been nothing post mortem.

And now, here I am, in the enormous, fastidiously alphabetised fifth-floor craft section of Waterstone's, and I am panning — fruitlessly — through the Ts.

It goes like this, from left to right. *Creative Tabletop Fountains. Tea Bag Folding. More Tea Bag Folding. How To Make Award-Winning Teddies.* Spot the lacuna.

I pan back, from right to left. Do they give *awards* for home-made teddies? *Who* gives awards for home-made teddies? How do you apply?

And — somewhere, somewhere in this country — there are people just gripped by tea bag folding. One book wasn't enough. The sheer weight of popular demand forced a second into print. That's not including the people, countrywide, sitting in with the curtains drawn and the radio droning softly in the background, turning their living-room fucking tables into scaled-down Diana Memorial Fountains.

Tea-, Tab-. Tab-, Tea-. No Tax-.

The problem, I guess, is this. Stuffing animals was once pretty rock and roll,

when you had things to stuff like tigers and bears. Many of these animals did not die of natural causes, and many of those around when they died were not too fussy about their places in the ecosystem. But fewer people are killing things, especially tigers. Shooting things is going out of fashion; and displaying them, glassy-eyed and permanently roaring in your front room, is going even more out of fashion.

Taxidermy – in its various forms – has been around since before almost everything we associate with modern civilisation. Tunnel to the centre of a pyramid, and there you will find, alongside a mummified person, a mummified cat.

Stuffing pets – or, in the old days, taking the stuffing out of them – is as old as civilisation itself. Many take the view that the mark of civilisation in a society is bound up with the respect it shows to its dead. But taxidermy's on the back foot. We don't even do humans any more.

Taxidermy is losing ground to tea bag folders and tabletop water features.

This is a grave state of affairs, and no mistake. I retreat, hurt.

PART TWO
IN WHICH I LOOK
TO THE LAND OF THE FREE

WE MAY BE letting taxidermy die out here. But in the States, where shooting things is popular with disaffected teenagers and practically compulsory for presidential candidates, where no backwoods cabin is complete without a trophy, and where if you have a rack of guns and you choose to exercise your constitutional right to dismantle a moose in your outhouse folk probably won't bother you none less'n you bother them first, there's a little more play.

In the States, authors like Russell Tinsley can flourish. Russell is the author of *Taxidermy Guide – The Complete Illustrated Guide to Home Taxidermy* (Third Edition, Accokeek 2002). I took delivery of this pretty, coffee-table-sized paperback a week or so after my failed

expedition to Waterstone's. The fact that his excellent book is in its third decade suggests exactly what I'd hoped; and what Russell affirms in his introduction.

"If old ten-thumbs could do a reasonable mount job," he wrote, self-deprecatingly, "anyone could . . . Yes, taxidermy can be learned from a book, and it can be very rewarding."

I'm already finding it rewarding. My purchase has been worth it, in fact, for the author photograph alone.

Russell Tinsley wears a shirt in a cheesecloth check, whose long 70s-style collar, open at the neck, spreads out over his dark V-neck tank top. Russell wears big glasses, and big ears, and has big grey sideburns that go down from his hairline to the line of his jaw, and spread halfway down to his chin. He is smiling toughly, showing his teeth. He has a pipe clamped between his teeth, in no way jovially. On his head, he has a trucker-style baseball cap which says "Ducks Unlimited" on it.

Russell Tinsley looks like the sort of guy you could trust to peel a polecat.

Russell himself learned from a master. Lem Rathbone is the Yoda to Russell Tinsley's Skywalker. Sensei. Master stuffer. In some of the many black-and-white photographs that follow, documenting a collaboration that goes back to 1967, you can glimpse Lem Rathbone. He is a balding man, maybe 60 years old. He looks serious; lugubrious even. He wears a shirt of an almost identical check to Russell.

†110
I should explain. Taxidermists don't mostly, talk about "stuffing" animals. They talk about "mounting" them. "Get Stuffed", the celebrated taxidermist on the Essex Road in London, should, properly, be called "Get Mounted". But that would attract police attention. Actually, it did anyway – but that's another story. See below.

Here he is, deeply concentrating; shaving the flesh off a stretched hide with a currier's knife, his trousers mysteriously stained. Here he is, holding a six-foot sailfish he has just mounted,[110] eyes reproaching the camera.

Chapter One is called Beginning Taxidermy, and, again, it's a photograph that catches the eye. Fig 1-1: Basic Tools Required To Get Started In Taxidermy. They look very much as you would imagine Basic Tools Required To Get Started In Serial Killing would look. They look industrial. Knife, hammer, screwdriver. Heavy duty wire brush. Electric drill. Electric saw. Check.

I don't even own a shed. This is never going to work.

1-1. Basic tools required to get started in taxidermy: saw, brush, hammer, knife, drill and screwdriver.

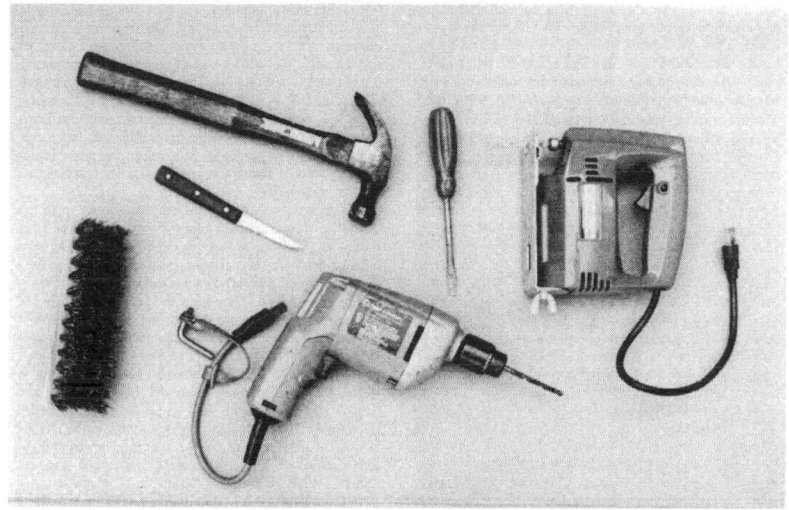

4-24. On an open-wing mount, cardboard strips should be placed top and bottom along each wing and also across tail feathers to hold them straight while the mount is drying.

PART THREE
IN CONFERENCE

SO IT IS that I come to get in contact with the UK Guild of Taxidermists – an organisation that gives me hope, at least, that the melancholy long withdrawing roar of the sea of Victorian and Edwardian taxidermy has not yet, at least, given way altogether to silence.

Many of my friends suggest I get in touch with the guy who runs "Get Stuffed", a North London taxidermy emporium that has become a sort of landmark in the area. I think twice.

"Get Stuffed" is a landmark for two reasons. One is that it mounts extravagant and amusing window displays – in the festive season, for example, residents of the area would barely bat an eyelid to pass its frontage and be saluted by a stoat, poised on its hind legs with a little floppy Santa hat on its head.

The other is that such was the owner's enthusiasm for stuffing furries of every shape and size, and the more exotic the better, that back in 2000 he ended up being raided and sentenced to six months inside, when it was discovered that he was harbouring a quite staggering collection of exotically posed, glassy-eyed endangered species.

This man, it became clear, was a renegade. He has of course done his time, paid his debt to society, and deserves no further punishment – and, indeed, his business seems to be thriving once again – but I am a character at once cowardly and ridiculously impressionable. Even were I to have won this understandably cautious character's trust I feared I might tempt him into recidivism. I had nightmare visions of being cajoled into stuffing a polar bear. So I bottled it.

My point of first contact with the Guild was Dave Astley, the organiser of their annual conference – a sort of all-purpose social and jamboree, which offers amateurs and professionals alike the opportunity to mix, learn from the masters, and display their proudest efforts for peer review.

I was originally hoping Dave would be able to help direct me to a reputable sensei – a Lem Rathbone, if you like, to my Russell Tinsley – so that I could learn taxidermy myself, my ambition still being, to learn at least in theory How To Stuff A Schnauzer. But he mentioned, in our initial conversation, that one of these very conferences was upcoming – and that anyone was welcome. Would I like to come as a delegate?

You bet your bippy I would.

I sent a cheque. And, in due course, on notepaper headed with a handsome rust-red logo which read: Taxis Derma,[111] I received a letter, accompanied by a leaflet giving details of the venue – the biology department of York University – and opening: "Dear Delegate."

It advised me, during my time on campus, to please wear my name badge at all times,[112] and enjoined me to "as usual, please bring any spare taxidermy related items or other contributions you may wish to donate for the raffle to help boost Guild funds".

> †111
> It's Greek for taxidermy.
>
> †112
> This, as it turned out, was good advice. Taxidermists are not so easy to spot, first off, as you would think – and particularly not because we were to be sharing the campus (out of term) with an enormous delegation of chemistry students from the Open University.

It ended, without comment: "Pets are not allowed on the campus. I look forward to meeting you and wish you a very pleasant stay in York."

Ten days later I am in a taxi, on a sunny afternoon in September, rolling past the historic castle walls of York towards the campus of the university, just a little way out of town.

The campus is set around a lake, from which a fountain gushes prettily. There sit on the lake a number of ducks. It may be the present mood, but I notice, breezily, that they seem to be entirely motionless. The biology department, where we're due to register, is eerily empty. I collar a security guard.

"Seen any taxidermists?" I ask. He gestures. He thinks there are some taxidermists down there somewhere. And, not long after, I stumble by accident into the back of a quarter-full lecture theatre where a Wisconsin man is spray-painting a fish before a raptly attentive crowd. I seem to have arrived.

Many people, when you mention the idea to them, seem to think taxidermists are a bit weird. Mention an ambition to stuff a badger, and they think you're some

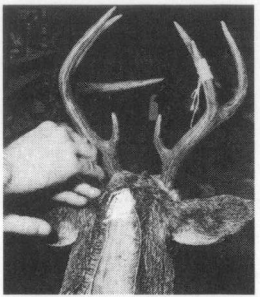

10-4. This ashtray was made from a buffalo's foot, but a cow's foot could be substituted, or that of an elk or moose

4-23. Cover the long feathers with cardboard and wrap the bird lightly with thread.

odd alloy of Burke, Hare and Ed Gein. Actually, nothing seems to make more sense as an activity for a person interested in art, and in the natural world. Good taxidermy is a sensational demonstration of knowledge, manual dexterity, and aesthetic touch: of sleight of hand and sleight of eye.

So, what are taxidermists actually like? Answer: like most people, they are a nice bunch once you get to know them. A kindly, whitish-haired man called Brian, over from Doncaster, takes me up first. Nine years retired from his job as an ICI

executive, he's a hobbyist. He pays tribute to how absorbing the art of taxidermy can be, and how difficult.

"I don't know how anyone can do this as a hobby who's working," he says. "I can be in there from the time my partner leaves in the morning, and the kids go to school, and I'm still there when they come back and ask: what have you done? Messed it up, usually. I must have skinned hundreds of magpies ..."

It's from him that I first hear, too, of the late Don Sharp, whom Brian seems to have regarded as something of a mentor: "He'd never keep any of his secrets to himself. If he could help you with something, he would. Anyone in this Guild, in my experience, if you get them on the phone they'll help you. There's none that" – and he curls his hand into the centre of his cobalt-coloured gilet, as if covetous – "keeps a secret to themselves."

On the first evening I fall in with Dave, for example, who used to work as a bricklayer but broke his arm in a motorcycle accident and decided to retrain as a taxidermist. He runs his own taxidermy business now, and has recently started to pass the knowledge on. He's here with a sidekick, a huge and taciturn Scot called Robert, who runs a mobile phone company and was Dave's first ever pupil. Dave shows him around with what seems like pride. Robert lodges in my head as "Silent Bob". He wears slightly tinted glasses and chews his food, in the canteen, thoughtfully.

Afterwards, we all play pool. I'm very happy to report that despite knowing nothing about taxidermy, I enjoy that sudden access of undeserved skill that all pub pool players will recognise: the Four Pint Plateau. I whup them.

I hear Emily Mayer talked about before I meet her properly. "Emily, there," says Brian with some awe. "She's a professional. She's lovely with it ..." Another: "She always gets best in show." Another: "She's a weird one ..." Another: "She slept in her van rather than digs last year ..." Another: "She's often seen carrying a small dog under her arm ..." Another: "She talks on the phone just like a man ..." Boys, boys.

Emily is, within the world of taxidermy, a bit of a legend. She was the only ever female chairman of the Guild; and is one of very few female members. Plus, she's shit-hot. She has mounted kills for game-crazy Marco Pierre White. She is the taxidermist Damien Hirst turns to when he needs artisan help with his art. The cultural critic Jonathan Meades, a friend and admirer, occasionally announces in print that he would like her to stuff and mount his body after his death.

Emily also makes fine art sculpture. She left taxidermy for some years "for personal reasons", but returned to the fray and is now going as strong as ever.

She's as striking in person as in reputation. Leggings, leather, very garish colours – as if Janet Street-Porter had got dressed in an S & M shop in the dark. A tall, wiry middle-aged woman, she has short spiky hair, a wide dry mouth, a gravelly voice and, um, an array of knives dangling from her ears. From one ear, there's a lime-green miniature clothespeg; from the other, in order, a conventional lockknife a shade under an inch long, and two tiny meat cleavers.

"Tools of the trade," she explains, when I mention them, but she adds a bit later: "What I do now is very specialised. I haven't skinned anything in ages." But it's what she does now, rather than her sex or her deep voice or her star quality, that makes her of real interest.

Emily is, though not exactly its inventor, far out in front of any others at the cutting edge of a technique that – though some think it's kind of cheating, kind of *not* taxidermy, in the old sense – is to others "the future of taxidermy". It is, if you like, photography to traditional taxidermy's realist painting.

It is called "erosion casting", and it is very difficult, very expensive, and very yucky. When it works, it produces really amazing results. Basically, what she does is this. She takes her dead furry animal, and she covers its body all over with rubbery liquid silicone. She rubs it right into the fur, all the way down the skin, all over the corpse. You can't afford any air-bubbles whatever.

When that sets, she rots the animal out. Boiling water can speed the process, but, basically, you have to wait. The bugs do their work, and the body turns to a mixture of liquid and mush. Then, through an aperture in the silicone case, and helped by the bendiness of the set silicone, you haul all this stinking goo out, guts and bones and rotted skin and all. (One of the reasons Emily seems to be in such a minority in embracing this technique, she concedes, is that "most people won't work with decaying flesh".)

But once you've got all the horrible stuff out, and the inside of the silicone is perfectly clean and scrubbed and flesh-free, what you are left with is an effect a

little like suede: the soft roots of the fur, protruding into the emptied body cavity just as far as they did into the skin.

And then, the clever bit: you can pour and smear a coat of tinted resins around the inside of the cavity, and it will grip the roots of this fur. You could think of it as an artificial skin. And, when it has dried, you use solvents to dissolve away the silicon from the outside – and, a lot of brushing and brushing and cleaning later, you are left with a perfect, not approximate, but absolutely perfect, recreation of the animal's coat, follicle by follicle. You just use the fur. Isn't that cool?

The results are spectacular. People still talk about the foxhound with which she won best in show the previous year. It isn't cheap, though. A rat, Emily reckons, would cost you a couple of thousand quid. She has been working on this stuff for ages. An early experiment involved a pig's head, covered in plaster, rotting at the end of her garden.

She appears to be something of a workaholic. The presentation she gives at this year's conference is a taxidermist's What I Did During My Summer Holidays, complete with slides. She calls it "Adventures With Latex In Mexico", and it describes, as she puts it, a "three-week holiday in search of roadkill" in Central America. She itemises her luggage: "Six litres of latex, a kilo of silicone, a couple of pairs of knickers and a pair of shoes."

Initially, her discoveries were disappointing: a very smelly three-months-dead donkey, and a dead iguana. But when she headed for the beach she hit paydirt: dead turtles. She describes in some detail how, spooning latex over the shells and layer by layer, reinforcing it with scrim and muslin, she was able to produce a very handy set of latex moulds suitable for casting likenesses of dead giant turtles to her heart's content.

She cast the dead iguana, meanwhile, in silicone, on a mould base cobbled together out of paper and gaffer tape. While the silicone was drying in the sun, the iguana inside cooked. The kindly taxidermist fed the chunks of it, as she removed them from her mould, to the slavering beach dogs attracted by the smell.

She returned to England with a set of latex turtle moulds nesting in her luggage, the full skeleton of a dead pelican, and a snake.

PART FOUR
THE COMPETITION,
A LOTTERY

IN ONE ROOM, just above and behind the lecture theatre, delegates to the conference have put their specimens on display, and it's here that I first see the results of erosion moulding: a handful of detail-perfect little rats scurrying around an anglepoise; and a rescue-dog called Rosie, a collie with a broken foot, resting curled as if sleeping.

But in this same room there are many other beauties. There's Dave's hare – posed dramatically mid-leap in the setting of a field of corn-stubble. There's a whole cheetah. There are antelope heads, and a leaping – is it a springbok? – and a vole, and a tawny owl, and a handful of squirrels, and a magnificent looking gyrfalcon ... There are countless birds and fish.

They all look extremely professional to me; but by the end of the weekend, I will have been disabused of some of those notions. These are in competition with each other for prizes with names like Best Small Mammal and Best Amateur Fish; and their makers – amateur and professional alike – are subject, too, to judging for credits by a panel of the professionals.

The publicly posted judging notes are exacting, to say the least. It's constructive criticism – but it would be easy not to take it that way. Owl's head all wrong. Squirrel's feet overstuffed, too chubby. Thrush's legs on backwards, and such like. I won't even go into what was wrong with the cheetah.

It isn't unknown for recriminations to take place in the bar afterwards.

The awarding of prizes on the final evening, however, is a very jolly event. I glow with happiness for my new friends. Brian's mink wins Best Amateur Mammal, and his tawny owl gets Best Amateur Bird. Dave's "Running Hare" comes third in the mammal section overall – which is something, considering Emily's erosion-moulded dog and rat easily take first and second respectively. Best Fish is a sea

bass; Best Head is a kudu. A song thrush by Jack Fishwick, a drily witty Lancastrian bird taxidermist who competes internationally, shares the Best In Show trophy with Rosie the rescue dog.

Afterwards, there comes the fundraising raffle. Tickets are selling like hotcakes at a quid a pop. Arrayed on the table at the front of the lecture hall is the panoply of prizes that have been donated for this year's conference.

Among them are:

- A bottle of wine
- A plastic reindeer souvenir
- A set of eight potter's sculpting tools
- Two electric glue guns
- A big book about game and hunting with an eagle on the cover
- Many, many packets of reindeer moss
- A bottle of Famous Grouse whisky
- A yellow polyurethane mount for a deer's head
- A case of half-litre bottles of meths
- A box of rubber surgeon's gloves
- Some silicone cartridges
- An enormous ball of string

"Any more for any more?" calls Dave over the crowd. "Any more raffle tickets? Some good prizes! Some good prizes! Look at that," he says, hoisting *Game and Hunting* aloft, "Brand new! Never been out of its wrapper!"

As each winning ticket is announced, the winner comes down and chooses his or her prize. The wine and the whisky go early on. There are rumbles of approval and, occasionally, heckling, as the good prizes go. But we have underestimated how much meths there is. Two more cases appear, as if from nowhere.

Forty-five minutes on, they are still drawing tickets. On the table is nothing but bottle after bottle of meths. Three-time winners trot wearily down to collect yet another bottle of meths. The fun is starting to go out of this. We want to go to the pub. Some of the bottles seem to be leaking. It smells of meths.

A common consensus emerges that winners will start to be allowed to take two bottles of meths rather than just the one. Then they stop bothering to come down, and a couple of helpers at the front just start chucking the meths up the raked seating of the lecture hall.

Then, just when it starts to look as if we've got through it, someone discovers, lurking under the desk, an enormous green binliner... full of more bottles of meths.

The dam bursts. The methylated and methless alike pour from their seats and down to the exit doors. It's time for a drink.

PART FIVE

ONWARD

"THAT'S WHAT YOU want to look out for," says Emily, later, rubbing her right thumb over the heel of her left hand. "Slippage. You just do that to the stomach. If the hair starts coming out, forget it. You can't do anything with it."

It is just gone midnight, and we're in one of York's student bars. The bar is furnished like an airline departure lounge. The drinks are not as cheap as I remember student drinks being. The rival delegation of Open University chemistry students seems to have made itself, at last, scarce – and the UK Guild of Taxidermists is letting its hair down.

Slippage is a key early indicator of decay. It starts, apparently, on the belly and around the orbits of the eyes. It means the epidermis has started to detach itself, the hair roots have come adrift, and there's no use trying to mount the specimen. You'll end up with something bald, messy and, probably, pretty smelly to boot. Ripeness is all.

Taxidermists have learned this from experience. Being able to tell how far gone what you might call a "found specimen" is is very helpful. The high days of Victorian and Edwardian taxidermy – when it was permissible to go overseas and pot away at more or less anything with a hide – are long gone.

DEFRA is at one shoulder. The RSPB and its bunny-hugging fellow travellers at the other. If you get raided by the police with a freezer full of goshawks or, for that matter, unprovenanced otters, you are in dead trouble.

There are, of course, a few things you can be sure will be fresh, and you can be sure will be legal. Things you kill yourself. DEFRA still lets you take, *inter alia*: rabbits, squirrels, foxes (provided you don't have your dogs with you), hares, wild and feral pigeons, game birds in season, otters less than one year old,[113] the odd corvid, and badgers.[114]

†113
Joke: you mustn't shoot baby otters.

†114
Or badgers.

But there are few of those, and many determined taxidermists – particularly city-dwelling ones – do not own guns. It is impractical to chase urban foxes and dispatch them by strangulation.

Many unskilled taxidermists, particularly hobbyists like myself, have little or no chance of striking up the sort of relationship we would like with a zoo, or a farm. Nobody's going to cart round a dead giraffe for us to practise on. We must make do. The obvious candidates are roadkill and catkill. You're driving down a country lane, and pass a dead badger. Screech of brakes. Four legs intact? Still warm? No slippage? Disco. Sling it in the boot of the car, wrap it in newspaper, and chuck it in the chest freezer at home. Defrost, skin and mount at leisure.

That's one source. The other, which concerns us here, is domestic pets. If you own an animal, you are welcome – within the limits of health, safety and common decency – to do what you like to it postmortem. You do not have to apply to DEFRA for an Article 10 certificate to skin, tan, and mount your dead schnauzer.

I should make clear here that I do not encourage you, however tempted, to run your domestic menagerie as the supply side of a taxidermy hobby. Not only is this unethical and, depending on how the specimens are dispatched, cruel, it will almost certainly attract the attention of the RSPCA. If you return tearfully to Battersea Dogs' Home, only a fortnight after you and your new doggie set off home to start your new life together, you will excite sympathy. If you do so twice, you might elicit a hard stare. At my guess, three times will be enough to bring the bizzies round.

But if Flopsy the bunny has hopped his last, and you have decided you would like to see him, for all time, casting a benign ceramic eye over you from the top of the telly, go ahead. There are three[115] good reasons to mount your own pets:

1) You like making things.
2) You can.
3) A professional taxidermist will be very reluctant indeed to do it for you.
4) It will cost a fortune to get it mounted professionally.

†115
Number 2 is not
a good reason.

There is, of course, one very good reason not to, which is that you will almost certainly make an incredible hash of it and, in doing so, magnify your grief and upset unbearably. But even using a professional doesn't guarantee that's not going to happen.

The Guild is a highly respectable body, which accredits taxidermists and encourages high professional standards, but it is voluntary. As far as I can tell, pretty much anyone can put a sign outside his or her door, or on the Internet, advertising himself as a taxidermist. So *caveat emptor*.

This is a sore point. Members of the Guild still talk about an episode of *That's Life*, from years and years and years ago. This episode involved a most distressed old lady, and a beloved cat which she had entrusted to a taxidermist. The man in question was not of the best. The climax of the item was when someone lifted the mounted specimen from a cardboard box for the camera's inspection. It was, like, a Frankencat. A horrorcat. It barely had the right number of limbs, and was, to hear them tell it, held together with a visible cross-hatching of running stitch. It would have passed for a frisbee from a distance. A furry frisbee. With three eyes. It was really, really funny. But less so for taxidermists.

This is held to have been bad publicity for the honourable trade of taxidermy altogether. It also illustrates, albeit in a particularly horrible form, exactly why, as I mention in 3, above, you will probably find it hard to talk a professional into doing a pet; and why, consequently, as in 4, they will gouge your wallet for the privilege. In fact, if you are determined to go to a professional, you should think twice about any taxidermist who seems too keen to do your pet.

When you mount a specimen of a wild animal, be it a sparrowhawk or a rabbit, your aim is a sort of generic verisimilitude. You are trying to recreate, as accurately as possible, and in a pose of your choice, what a good specimen of sparrowhawk or rabbit would look like alive: essence of sparrowhawk; essence of rabbit.

This is a sort of sculptural/necrotic subcategory of natural history – and good taxidermists are experts on animal anatomy, habitats, markings and so forth. Many professionals work in, or have trained at, museums. At the conference in York, the lecture on tanning techniques was delivered by Phil Howard, who works full-time for the National Museums of Scotland (he has huge great walk-in freezers, and talks cheerily about how long it takes to dismantle a dead gorilla).

Attention to detail is all. In the hall outside the lecture theatre, Jack Fishwick was selling acrylic eyes in the coffee breaks. He had hundreds and hundreds of sets of tiny eyes arranged by species, in little zip-loc baggies. The man ahead of me in the queue asked for a wood-pigeon, and Jack retrieved the specific eyes in moments. Not cheap. He pointed out a dark circle that comes just off the pupil (they have them: grab a wood pigeon and look), and explained at what angle it should be positioned in the mount. The pair of vole eyes, I picked up, incidentally, set me back only 30p: beady black ones are the easiest to make. Now seeking vole.

Generic verisimilitude poses one sort of problem. Specific verisimilitude poses a whole other sort. The best taxidermist in the world will make your Rover look like a border collie (provided that's what he started as), but the best taxidermist in the world can't necessarily make your Rover look like your Rover.

Home videos and/or pre-mortem photographs are close to essential. Only you know how that offside rabbit ear flopped, or exactly how your Alsatian's hips sagged; or how he held his tail.

"Nobody – unless they're very unusual – knows what colour their pet's eyes are," one taxidermist said to me. "But they know if it's wrong. They won't be able to say, but they know something's wrong, and they won't be happy."

"Every week, I get someone in tears, calling me up, asking me to mount their pet," says another, shaking his head. "They're at their wits' end and they say no other taxidermist will do it."

Some refuse outright. The odd one, though, relents out of kindness. More than one I spoke to did have a pet on the go – but was determined it would be their last; like the man who had succumbed to a tearful entreaty from a desperate old lady.

It was a chihuahua called Kim. Many of them view people who want their pets mounted as "a bit weird" in any case.

Standard practice seems to be to insist on half the money up front, and to talk the customer into a cooling-off period, letting the animal cool its heels in the freezer while, grief subsiding, the owner can rethink whether cremation or burial might not be the better way. Some customers do change their minds. Many, by the time the mount is complete, are too worried about raking up the bad feeling to return and pick it up.

So. You are determined. Be warned. Taxidermy, regardless of what author Russell Tinsley may have you think, is very difficult.

4-22. Stumps cut from limbs also make likely perches.

BRUIN

GEORGE GORDON NOEL: LORD BYRON. ONE OF THE HIGHER ACCOLADES A WRITER CAN EARN IS TO HAVE HIS OR HER NAME PASS INTO COMMON CURRENCY AS AN ADJECTIVE. USUALLY, THESE ADJECTIVES – JOYCEAN, SHAKESPEAREAN, BECKETTIAN AND SO ON – APPLY TO QUALITIES OF STYLE OR MOOD IN WRITING. WITH A SELECT HANDFUL, HOWEVER, THE ADJECTIVES ARE APPLIED TO A STYLE OR MOOD IN LIFE: ORWELLIAN, KAFKAESQUE, BYRONIC...

EVEN PEOPLE WHO haven't the first interest in Geordie Byron's uniquely foxy way with a feminine rhyme know what "Byronic" connotes. Curly-haired, dashingly aristocratic, Hellespont-swimming, club-footed, impulsive, very interested in having sex ... *Jane Eyre* wasn't by Byron, but Mr Rochester was, ironically, Byronic. *Lord* Rochester, was probably also Byronic. But neither of them owned a pet bear.

Bruin the bear may be considered the peak of Lord Byron's very distinguished pet-owning career. In this as in all else, Byron was precocious, taking possession

of Bruin before he was twenty, while still an undergraduate at Cambridge.

Why a bear? Because he wasn't allowed to keep a dog. The then authorities at Trinity – whose writ expressly proscribed undergraduates keeping dogs – may have had cause to reflect on the Law of Unintended Consequences. Byron, in truth, had pretty bad luck with dogs, anyway. Dogs, too, had bad luck with him. The trouble started not long after he had inherited his title.

Byron grew up in Aberdeen, a grey Scottish city that had not yet been cheered up by the arrival of the North Sea oil industry or the right to vote in the Scottish Parliament elections. As his biographer Fiona McCarthy points out, it was a place that offered excellent opportunities for the trainee depressive. Byron was not overjoyed, either, by his club-foot. One imagines the young, curly-haired child, who used to amuse himself by sticking pins in his mother during church services, with a deep frown fixed on his alabaster brow.

He brought a certain tetchiness with him, then, when he travelled south to Newstead Abbey in 1798 after his great-uncle pegged out and he inherited his title and property. Newstead was a splendid old pile, with abundant moss, vaulting and damp. While he was there, little Geordie, still frowning, had a dog called Woolly. Woolly's mother was a wolf, and Woolly was enormous and – smarting under the indignity of his name – we must assume spoiling for a fight. When Woolly finally gave young Byron a painful little nip, the response shows us the character of the man.

Still frowning, Byron stomped back into the Abbey, and returned with a loaded pistol he had borrowed from the gamekeeper. Pushing Woolly to the ground, Geordie levelled the gun at the monstrous half-wolf's head and shouted:"Woolly, you shall die!"

Geordie Byron was around ten at the time.

Though the threat was not carried out, that incident seems to have damaged Byron's relationship with Woolly.[116] He later complained that the vengeful creature "doted on me at ten years old and very nearly ate me at twenty! He bit away the backside of my breeches and never would consent to any recognition in despite of all kinds of bones which I offered him."

†116
Some authorities seem to record the half-wolf as being called "Lyon"; I prefer "Woolly".

He went on to own several dogs. Two for whom clear records of his affection survive were called Nelson and Boatswain. Nelson was a bull mastiff; Boatswain a black and white Newfoundland. Neither met happy fates, though Boatswain's greater longevity – he stuck around long enough to pose for portraits – assured him a place in canine history.

Byron took Nelson and Boatswain with him on a pleasure trip to Harrogate he made with his medical student friend John Pigot, in 1806. Nelson met a horse in the courtyard of the Crown Inn there, and tried to eat it. His attack was so vicious that he had to be shot, plum ruining the holiday, but bringing a certain sprightliness into Boatswain's step. Boatswain and Nelson had, themselves, fought viciously. Nelson's replacement, a bulldog puppy called Savage, died not long after his arrival.

Then, three years later – on November 10th, 1808, at the age of five – Boatswain himself went mad and died. According to his early biographer, Moore, Byron tenderly wiped the slobber from the mad dog's jowls with his own hands.

Boatswain's magnificent marble tomb, surmounted by a stone urn, stands among the ruins of the Abbey. It was the only building work Byron did at Newstead. Byron wrote gloomily at the time: "I have now lost everything except old Murray." Joe Murray was the wrinkled factotum Byron inherited along with the house.

Anyway, the bear. Legend – tacitly encouraged by modern Trinity undergraduates hoping to impress their friends – has it that the pet bear Byron kept as an undergraduate, and for whom he professed the dearest affection, was chained up in the tower at one corner of Trinity's enormous Great Court. According to Fiona McCarthy, however, the bear Byron described as "the finest in the world" was actually kept in stables in Ram Yard, along with Byron's horse, Oateater. (Like Woolly, Oateater had a silly name. The bear was known, as bears will be, as Bruin.)

Bruin ate bread and milk, but had fire in his belly. Byron put Bruin forward for a fellowship, keen to give his friend a leg-up in life, and, peripherally, by way of protesting against the dumbing down of the curriculum.

Byron complained that the bear "kept by me at Cambridge to sit for a

fellowship" had been thwarted in his quest for success by "the jealousy of his Trinity contemporaries". How sadly far that is from the hopeful start of Bruin's academic career, when Byron's friend Ned Long wrote to him to say: "I have no doubt Bruin would receive a fellow of Trinity with a friendly hug."

Bruin did became a minor academic *cause célèbre*. It was, in the opinion of Pigot's mother, a Mrs Pigot, the legacy that would survive him. "I hope the poor Bear is well," she wrote to Byron. "I wish you could make him understand that he is immortalised, for if four-leg'd Bears have any vanity it would certainly delight him."

Though no portrait survives, McCarthy guesses that Bruin was a smallish bear, probably a rescued former dancing bear. (Perhaps a four-leg'd Bear may have vanity; he was once in showbusiness.) Was Byron trying to make a point about political emancipation? That might explain how cross he was about the satirical poem another Cambridge scholar, Hewson Clarke, published about Bruin in a London magazine:

> *Sad Bruin, no longer in woods thou art dancing,*
> *With all the enjoyments that Love can afford;*
> *No longer thy consorts around thee are prancing,*
> *Far other thy fate – thou art slave to a lord!*

Was Clarke suggesting that Bruin was being unfairly deprived of sex; or suggesting something rather darker? His poem concludes:

> *... when with the ardour of Love I am burning,*
> *I feel for thy torments, I feel for thy care;*
> *And weep for thy bondage, so truly discerning,*
> *What's felt by a Lord may be felt by a Bear!*

Byron went on to dismiss Clarke as "a very sad dog, and for no reason that I can discover, except a personal quarrel with a bear".

When Byron left Cambridge, Bruin came back with him to Newstead, and a house guest in 1809 reported that the principal diversions to be enjoyed there were "playing with the bear or teasing the wolf". Occasionally, the dogs could be persuaded to have a fight with the bear, though the largest of them, Thunder, was

a noted coward in this respect. A former Newstead servant was to complain that Thunder "could seldom be induced to face the bear".

During his years on the continent, Byron kept his menagerie lively. In Ravenna he kept ten horses, eight enormous dogs, three monkeys, five cats, an eagle, a crow and a falcon. When Shelley went to visit, he recalled being greeted by "five peacocks, two guinea hens and an Egyptian crane", and in 1819 Byron reported cheerfully: "I have got two monkeys and a fox – and two new mastiffs ... The monkeys are charming."

The bear was interred in the family crypt at Hucknall Torkard, near Newstead, in 1810, cause of death unknown. Byron joined it in 1824 – his frowning corpse having been turned away as unsuitable by the deans of both Westminster and St Paul's – after a fever claimed his life while he was limbering up to lose it in heroic action during the Greek civil war. So it goes.

✦✦✦ **FIVE INTERESTING THINGS TO DO WITH YOUR DEAD PET** ✦✦✦

5 ∙ IDEAL FREEZE-DRYING

A NUMBER OF taxidermists in the US now do this as an alternative to traditional stuffing. It is cheaper than most of the above, and the results don't look half bad. Essentially, the dead pet is placed in a powerful vacuum chamber, and the moisture in its body slowly escapes as water vapour and is sucked away. The process does take anything from two to six months. When it's finished, however, Fido will sleep as contentedly beside the fire as ever he did – and, as a bonus with endless potential for playing pranks – he will weigh only one fifth or so of what he did in life. The freeze-dried pet, adds a leading American proponent of the technique, "requires little maintenance, other than an occasional fluff and spray of cedar residue to maintain gloss".

CHAPTER 9

STUFF IT YOURSELF

PART ONE

WHY NOT MAKE WAX FISH?

"WHY NOT MAKE WAX FISH?" ASKED THE GREAT DON SHARP.

WHY *NOT* MAKE wax fish? Goldfish are, in the normal run of things, among the least durable of companion animals. Overfeeding kills them. Underfeeding kills them. Dirty tanks kill them. The process of cleaning the tank, half the time, seems to kill them. Separation anxiety kills them. Cats kill them. Herons, given half a chance, kill them. A fright kills them. With their alleged three-second memories, it's a wonder they even remember to breathe, or gill, or whatever it is they do.

Wax fish, kept out of direct sunlight, are more durable than their real-life counterparts, and about as interesting. Moreover, they are at the easier end of the fish taxidermy scale. I am given to understand that doing a "full skin mount" is bastard hard. Casting in wax is an easy, fun and hygienic way of immortalising your goldfish and, what's more, once you've got your mould made, you can make a limitless number of them. Goldie may have passed away – but his little body can bequeath a whole shoal of creepily identical Goldies to posterity. I daresay that, as well as aiding the grieving process, casting fish in wax will be fun for kids. Make sure you get an adult to help, however.

MAKING WAX FISH THE DON SHARP[117] WAY
IN EIGHTEEN EASY-TO-FOLLOW STEPS

1) First, you immerse your fish in an alum solution, haul it out, and gently rub off the slime and mucus from the surface of the fish. Don't dry it off completely. You'll need that little thin coating of alum water to stop the fish sticking to the plaster.

2) Now take a pair of scissors or clippers, and clip off the fins on the side of the fish, nice and neatly, where they meet the body. The ones in the vertical plane (stare at the fish: they go up and down, in line with the tail) should be left intact. Set these fins aside.

3) On a bit of old newspaper or, better, a plastic sheet, set yourself up a four-sided frame. For a small, thin fish this need only be a few inches deep, but it's better to leave too much room than too little. It should comfortably be able to accommodate the fish. It should be pretty watertight. This is where you're going to make your mould. (The carpentry aspect of this is best done before you start farting about with the fish.)

4) Now, you want to mix some plaster. Ordinary plaster of Paris is fine – but if you use a harder form of dental plaster your mould will be stronger, and surface definition,

†117 Don Sharp was a founder member of the Guild, a taxidermist since he was fourteen years old. He had died only a few months before the conference, aged 62, of cancer. Everybody seems to have loved him – and from amateur hobbyists to professionals, described him as a fount of advice and encouragement and good humour. The Best In Show trophy, which was this year shared between Emily Mayer (dog) and Jack Fishwick (songthrush), has been renamed the Don Sharp Best In Show trophy. His posthumous appearance, projected onto the screen in the lecture hall, is greeted with real emotion.

potentially, better. Don strongly cautions against using tap water. Air bubbles are fatal to the project. Use still mineral water or rainwater if possible. Sprinkle handfuls of plaster gently onto the surface of your bowl of water. The plaster will sift pleasingly down and sit underneath. Keep sprinkling until the surface of the plaster is just level with the surface of the water, and it's poking out in tiny islands here and there. Add a pinch or two of salt. Then, very gently, agitate it to let bubbles rise, and give it a slow stir round with a spoon. Remember, air bubbles are the enemy.

5) Gently pour the plaster into your frame, filling it just about halfway. If you can, agitate the table gently to get them bubbles out. Smooth any bubbles to the side of the frame with the back of a spoon so the plaster is level and white and pristine in the middle.

6) Soon, the plaster will have reached the consistency of thick yoghurt, or delicious crème fraiche. Now take your fish. Very gently, lower the fish onto the surface of the plaster, on its side, until it's snugly floating, half in, half out. If you wiggle it very slightly as you put it in, you may help eliminate the dreaded air bubbles. Spread the tail or dorsal fins out a teeny bit if you like. It's your fish. (Advanced learners can inject a bit of formaldehyde into the base of the fin beforehand to help it stick out. Do not accidentally inject yourself with formaldehyde. This HURTS.)

7) As you are doing this, half submerge four small marbles – or, as Don does, you could use old glass eyes – as "keys" around the shape of the fish (but not, obviously, touching it). These knobbles, when they fit into their corresponding declivities on the eventual other half of the mould, will make it easier to align the two halves accurately for casting, and keep them in place.

8) Wait. The plaster will dry.

9) Now for the second half of the mould. Paint a very thin film of barrier cream over the surface of the dry plaster of the bottom half of the mould. Then make up a fresh batch of plaster, and dribble a thin skin of it all over the exposed surface of the fish. Agitating the table a little may help to get rid of air bubbles. Once Goldie is wearing his wet plaster pyjamas, pour in the remainder of the plaster to the depth of the mould.

10) Wait again. Once the plaster is thoroughly dry, separate both halves of the mould, and carefully remove Goldie. You may now, if you feel the need, give him a Viking funeral, or flush him down the loo. Best not to eat him, as plaster dust and alum are bad for the digestion.

11) Make sure there's none of the dead fish left clinging to it (ie – gently clean the inside of both halves of the mould). Now, using a small cylindrical file or suchlike, carve a narrow channel from the edge of the mould, to an unobtrusive point on the fish. The idea is to create a passage for hot air to escape during the casting process – a conduit from the hollow heart of the fish to the outside world once the two halves of the mould are pressed together. If your wax fish is filled with hot air when cast, it will collapse as the air cools and contracts.

12) To prevent the dry plaster of the mould sticking to the wax, soak both halves of it in water for at least half an hour, then pat them dry.

13) Now, the fun bit. On top of a bain-marie, melt and keep molten a 50/50 mix of beeswax and paraffin wax. To this, you should add a thimbleful of molten rosin. This will toughen the mixture. The rosin has a higher melting point, so needs to be melted separately over a direct flame – using an old bean can will do fine. Once it's mixed in with the molten wax, though, it'll all stay good and liquid over the bain marie. If you want to colour the wax, you can stir oil – not acrylic – paint into it.

14) Ready the lower half of the mould. Make sure it is more or less level. Lie a length of wire along the channel you cleared for the hot air in 12, above, so that a good few inches protrude out over the edge of the mould. This will act as a sort of valve closure for the channel. To reinforce the tail and fins, lay bits of very dry, light gauze or scrim over those bits of the mould. They don't need to be cut exactly to shape; you can trim them later.

15) Pour on the wax: first, carefully, onto the areas of fine detail around the fins; then into the central fish-shaped concavity of the lower half of the mould.

16) Slap the top half of the mould down, squeeze them tight together, and then shake, rattle and roll like mad. You're trying to get the molten wax to slop all round and coat the inside of the mould evenly and entirely. As you do this,

pause frequently to wiggle and poke the wire valve in and out to release any trapped air.

17) Plunge the whole cast into cold water. Take it out. Ease the two halves of the mould apart and, with any luck, you will find yourself with a just-cooling wax fish. While it's still warm, you can use the residual flexibility to put a slight bend into it, or position the fins and tail in the way you want them. Before it sets entirely, cut round the fins and trim off the excess gauze. The raised seam, too, where the two halves of the mould met, can be pared carefully down with a knife, and rubbed smooth with a little white spirit.

18) Paint your fish as you see fit. The professional taxidermist, particularly with a larger specimen, will probably put in a couple of glass eyes. The experimentalist may attach sequins and/or go-faster stripes.

PART TWO

MAKING FLEXIBLE
TAILS THE EASY WAY

ANOTHER INVALUABLE AND inventive shortcut that emerged in one of the masterclasses at the Guild's conference, was the following. It's easy as pie and fun to boot. As well as working on tails, it'll do for the legs of small mammals.

First, you need to "skin out" your tail. It is possible to buy specialist tail-skinners from the US – but a pair of nutcrackers will do. Essentially, you grip them round the tailbone, and haul them down to the end of the tail so the skin comes off like an old sock. Do this with care – the skin is supposed to go back on your model tail in due course, and you don't want to be darning.

The skin will want attacking with borax to preserve it – or, if you are feeling especially enterprising, and/or are dealing with a biggish animal whose skin will be too thick for borax to work its magic, proper tanning.

Take the tail bone, and lay it down flat on a bit of cardboard, wide enough to accommodate it with a few inches of clearance all round. Now, grab a tube of silicone, and a skeleton gun. Set the tailbone aside a moment. Lay down a generous layer of silicone on the cardboard, smoothing it out so it is pretty even. Plonk the tailbone down atop it, then simply squirt silicone up and down all over the tailbone, building it up so the whole bone is encased in a thick layer of silicone, and stuck to the cardboard by it.

Wait for it to dry fully.

Taking a very sharp Stanley knife, cut through the silicon down the length of the tail, down to the bone. Then pulling the rubbery slit apart, you can peel out the tailbone. Depending on how long you left it, this may be a bit smelly. If need be, wear a cycle-mask dabbed with aftershave, and/or surgical gloves.

Wash out the inside and let it dry ... Bingo. You have a mould.

Now you need a glue gun. A crappy glue gun can cost as little as a couple of quid – but a super-duper gas-powered glue gun, which will make you the envy of your rivals in the home taxidermy community, can set you back a good deal more.

Take a couple of bits of wire, and bung them in your tail bone mould, so they reach down more or less all the way to the thin end, and stick out a few inches from the fat end. You can always trim them. Then, with the nose of your glue gun stuck through the slit in the silicone, squirt hot glue into the mould, all the way down the length of the tail. Once it's all full up, you can just gently press the sides of the mould together to make sure they meet properly, and massage out any air bubbles.

Wait for it to dry fully. Then just pull apart the two sides of the mould, and strip out your new, bendy, fully poseable, made-of-glue-and-a-couple-of-bits-of-wire tail.

Re-glove with skin. Attach to stuffed cat. Make yourself well-deserved cup of tea.

Cat, s. a domestic animal; kind of ship
Dog, s. a domestic animal; a lump of iron

FROM DR JOHNSON'S *DICTIONARY*

DR JOHNSON'S CAT

YOU WOULD NOT KNOW FROM THE ABOVE THAT DR JOHNSON WAS A "CAT PERSON". HE WAS, IN FACT, DEVOTED TO HIS CATS, OF WHICH THE BEST KNOWN WAS HODGE.

IN HIS *Life of Johnson*, Boswell records Hodge "scrambling up Dr Johnson's breast, apparently with much satisfaction, while my friend, smiling and half whistling, rubbed down his back, and pulled him by the tail; and when I had observed he was a fine cat, saying 'Why, yes, Sir, but I have had cats whom I liked better than this'; and then as if perceiving Hodge to be out of countenance, adding, 'but he is a very fine cat, a very fine cat indeed'."

Hodge was never far from Dr Johnson's mind. He regularly bought the cat oysters to eat. Once, he and Boswell were chewing the fat about a young toff who had gone so much to the bad that he'd last been sighted running round London shooting cats. Johnson, in a "sort of kindly reverie", said: "But Hodge shan't be shot; no, no, Hodge shall not be shot."

Hodge is presumed to have escaped both shellfish poisoning and being shot, dying of natural causes.

Not all that tempts your wand'ring eyes
And heedless hearts, is lawful prize;
Nor all that glisters, gold.

GRAY'S CAT

ALMOST EVERYONE REMEMBERS THE "MORAL" TO THOMAS GRAY'S "ODE ON THE DEATH OF A FAVOURITE CAT, DROWNED IN A TUB OF GOLD FISHES".

FAT LOT OF good that does the cat. It is much easier to be wise after the event as a poet, than it is to breathe water as a cat. She probably expired in about the time it takes to write the title of Gray's poem out in that fancy copperplate they used in olden-day times.

One suspects – looking at it from the cat's point of view – that Gray's "Ode", pretty though it was, didn't come from the heart.

Gray's "Ode" is the feline "Lycidas". Like Milton, Thomas Gray did not know the subject of his poem particularly well. The subject of Milton's great elegy was Edward King, an old acquaintance of the poet's, and probably not a close one. He drowned in the Irish Sea. Selima, the cat in the "Ode", did not belong to Gray. She drowned in a blue and white china pot, at 17 Arlington Street, London.

We remember Milton and Gray. Do we remember in any particularity those their elegies were supposed to commemorate? That's what poets are like.

Edward King, in real life a theological scholar and Fellow of Christ's College, Cambridge, was transformed for the purposes of "Lycidas" into a warbling, sheep-herding swain who cavorted with nymphs. Selima was, for the purposes of the "Ode", transformed into a nymph – a process that, as Dr Johnson sensibly remarked, required Gray to do "some violence both to language and sense".

So, by the magic of metaphor, are scholars and cats transformed into swains and nymphs. Would Edward King have had congress with a cat? That's his business.

I digress.

Selima was a "handsome" tortoiseshell cat with black ears and green eyes, belonging to Gray's childhood friend Horace Walpole, son of the former prime minister. Walpole is remembered now for his gothic house, Strawberry Hill, and his gothic novel, *The Castle of Otranto*. He was a bit camp, in other words, and Selima's exotic, oriental-sounding name was to be expected.

Like *Lycidas* – Milton's contribution to an anthology for King – Gray's Ode was written to order. It was Walpole's request that he commemorate Selima in verse; and the emotional tug behind the poem is between Gray and Walpole, rather than Gray and the cat. The two men had only recently been reconciled after four years of not speaking.

Their intense and passionate friendship – generally thought to have had an implicit if not express homosexual character – had ended in a furious gap-year tiff. After leaving university, they travelled together through continental Europe on the Grand Tour. Gray was by character depressive; Walpole was up for a party. They grated on each other.

"I treated him insolently," Walpole told Gray's biographer after his death. "He loved me, and I did not think he did. I reproached him with the difference between us ... I often disregarded his wishes of seeing places, which I would not quit my amusements to visit, though I offered to send him to them without me. Forgive me," he added, with a twitch of the old bitterness, "if I say that his temper was not conciliating ..."

That's as much as either was ever prepared to say about why they quarrelled.

Gray wanted to hang around gloomy old churches; Walpole wanted to have Fun. There must have been more to it than that. They parted company at Reggio in 1741 and, but for the conciliatory offices of a mutual friend in 1745, would never have spoken to each other again.

So it mattered that Walpole asked Gray for the poem after Selima's death at the beginning of 1747. At first, Gray demurred, however; Walpole had two cats and Gray wasn't sure which was which.

"One ought to be particularly careful to avoid blunders in a compliment of condolence," he wrote on February 22nd. "It would be a sensible satisfaction to me (before I testify my sorrow, and the sincere part I take in your misfortune) to know for certain who it is I lament. I knew Zara and Selima (Selima, was it? or Fatima) or rather I knew them both together; for I cannot justly say which was which.

"Then as to your handsome cat, the name you distinguish her by, I am no less at a loss, as well knowing one's handsome cat is always the cat one likes best; or, if one be alive and the other dead, it is usually the latter that is the handsomest. Besides, if the point was never so clear, I hope you do not think me so ill-bred or so imprudent as to forfeit all my interest in the survivor: Oh no! I would rather seem to mistake, and imagine to be sure it must be the tabby one that had met with this sad accident. Till this affair is a little better determined, you will excuse me if I do not begin to cry: '*Tempus inane peto, requiem, spatiumque doloris.*'"

The Latin is an adaptation of Dido's lament for Aeneas, shortly before her suicide. Gray was being a smart-arse. But Walpole's grief prevailed, and ten days later, the poem was in the post.

Walpole was so pleased with it that he had the first stanza inscribed on a plaque:

> *'Twas on a lofty vase's side,*
> *Where China's gayest art had dy'd*
> *The azure flowers that blow;*
> *Demurest of the tabby kind,*
> *The pensive Selima reclin'd,*
> *Gaz'd on the lake below.*

The plaque was affixed to a pedestal on which, for many years, the blue and white china tub in which Selima had perished stood as memorial in a place of honour in Strawberry Hill's cloister.

According to Gray's version of events, Selima's death was an accident, brought about by her greed, vanity and clumsiness. Some detect misogyny in the poem. She's arraigned for having "purred applause" at her reflection, and there's that snarky line asking: "What female heart can gold despise?"

Dr Johnson, one of the poem's harshest if most literal-minded critics, is again of use. "If what glistered had been 'gold'," he wrote, "the cat would not have gone into the water; and, if she had, would not less have been drowned." Quite so.

It is difficult to speculate on the thought processes of long-dead cats. We can assume Selima liked fish. "What cat's averse to fish?" asks Gray. Given. But is that the end of it? According to Gray's biographer, Robert L Mack, the cats had been left behind while Walpole, a flighty character, moved from Arlington Street to a new house in Windsor. We have no way of knowing how Selima felt about this. Could Selima have meant it to look like an accident? Nor can we know how Zara, the tabby, felt about Selima being the "favourite"? Could Zara have meant it to look like an accident?

Gray's poem, scholars of prosody note, is in *rime couée*: "tailed rhyme".

What became of the goldfish, nobody knows. They rest in unvisited graves.

CHAPTER 10

HANDS ON:
THE BEST OF
JAY JAY

"NOW I'M GOING TO SHOW YOU WHAT A SCALPEL HANDLE IS FOR," SAYS MIKE GADD. I PICK THE ONE NEAREST ME UP, AND START TRYING TO AFFIX THE BLADE THAT I'VE SO FAR BEEN USING PINCHED BETWEEN FINGER AND THUMB. "DON'T BE SILLY," SAYS MIKE. "IT'S NOT FOR HOLDING A SCALPEL BLADE." AND WITH THAT, HE REVERSES THE SCALPEL HANDLE IN HIS OWN HAND AND DIGS ITS BLUNT, SPATULATE BACK END INTO THE ORBIT OF THE EYE IN THE SKINNED BIRD SKULL HE'S HOLDING. HE WHIPS IT DEFTLY ROUND IN A CIRCLE, AND NEATLY POPS OUT THE EYEBALL. HE TURNS THE SKULL OVER AND DOES THE OTHER.

I TRY IT on my own bird. Very satisfying. Jays' eyes come out dead easy. In death (as he earlier demonstrated by puffing one up with an injection of water) the eyes deflate like a tyre going down, the visible part collapsing in on itself. Sitting on the

workbench, mission accomplished, the eyes look exactly, but exactly, like a pair of blueberries.

Three hours ago, myself and the two other students on Mike's three-day beginners' course in bird taxidermy were each presented with a chilly, just-defrosted dead jay, feathers a little matted with blood, necks flopping around all over the shop. Now, as we stand around the big worktable, what I have on a piece of newspaper in front of me is ... a *mess*. All my own work. I haven't had so much fun in ages.

At last, I am getting some proper hands-on experience. We're in Mike's studio in Boston Spa, just about halfway between Leeds and York.

This morning, I arrived in Boston Spa bright and early after a hellish night spent in a fully automated Travelodge right next door to Leeds station. More alienating a place you could scarcely imagine. Not only did you need a keycard to open the door to your room, you needed it to open the front door, and the internal doors, and even to make the lift work. You had to swipe your credit card down a slot before the telephone worked. The sheets were plasticky and the room smelt of stale smoke and the innumerable tearful wanks of the lonely businessmen who had passed through it.

As my taxi arrived in Boston Spa, my heart lifted. It was a fierce, freezing cold, sunny day in February. A bakery was open, and I killed the half an hour I had before I was due at Mike's, for a 9 a.m. start, standing in the lee of the wall of a carpark, shivering, drinking coffee from a styrofoam cup, and chewing a long iced bun of the sort known in boys' schools as a "sticky willy". A road beside me led down a river. A little way away, in the trees, a bird said: *"Poo-tee-weet?"*

Mike is a professional taxidermist of considerable standing in the community, and he runs occasional three-day beginners' courses – three or four a year – in bird and small mammal taxidermy. His facility is the subject of admiration and, I sensed, a little envy, among taxidermists at the conference. I heard one person muttering that he was too much a businessman and not enough an artist; that he wasn't using his god-given talents for a higher purpose.

"If you want him to bang you out a ten-pound owl, bosh, that's what he'll do," someone said. Actually, I don't think even Mike, working at top speed and mate's rates, would do you an owl for a tenner. Essentially, he simply regards his exhibition pieces – painstaking, as close to perfect as human hand can aspire – differently from his day-to-day work. If you're going to make a living as a taxidermist, you can't spend two weeks on every pigeon.

His skills are quite something. He once, as an experiment, did a bird blindfold ("not pretty"). How fast can he stuff? For a bet, he took one from dead bird to mounted and posed as fast as he could. It took him 27 minutes. He's rather proud of that.

It was that facility that led me to him. It was as the 2004 conference was winding down, the time of fag-ends and goodbyes, as the many, many victors in the raffle were carting off their gallons and gallons of meths, that I cornered Dave Astley. Once again, could he recommend how I could go further?

"Mike Gadd," he said. "Mike does the best courses."

Mike has been stuffing dead animals for thirty years and he is very, very good at it. The hallway of his house throngs with foxes and owls. Lined along one wall of his studio are a pair of diving otters, a handsome badger, and a spectacular trio of huge raptors having a fight, just completed for a client, draped in a polythene dust sheet. You name it, he's peeled it and stuffed it: rhino, tiger, golden eagle, secretary bird ("look at the eyelashes on that!"), giraffe ... He has never done a moose, but is planning a trip to Canada in the hopes.

On the wall, by the garage stairs leading up to the studio, is mounted a full-size rhino's head – cast in a single "take" from the real animal. By the end of three days, I'm really starting to appreciate how difficult this stuff is.

As already mentioned, I had originally wanted to Stuff A Schnauzer (how difficult, I thought like the idiot I am, can it be?). But I soon realised that dogs are for advanced learners, and that the chapter was probably going to have to be called *How To Stuff A Songbird (Not Very Well At All)*.

Even that's going to be a struggle, and all.

Jays and partridges are, nevertheless, good birds to start on (though, bear in mind, you have to obtain them legitimately; the only birds that aren't legally protected in one way or another are feral pigeons and woodpigeons). Their fluffy feathers are forgiving of the badly-made mannequin ("Really," says Mike, "you could stuff these with a bag of nails and you'd be able to make it come out all right"); and their skins are tough enough that the amateur has a fair chance of arranging them without poking them full of holes. I asked Mike whether these techniques would be equally suitable for the parrots, cockatiels and so on that the dead pet taxidermist will be interested in mounting. He reassured me breezily that they would. Then he added, "There is a special substance you have to use when you're doing a parrot, though." "Hmnh?" "Polyfilla." Tee hee.

My fellow student, Wayne, has a freezer full of partridges and a woodcock. Mike says: "What I advise you to do with the woodcock is eat it. Woodcocks are a nightmare: they have skins like soggy tissue paper."

"Right," Mike said, at the beginning of the day, immediately after issuing us with our feathery subjects. "Where shall we start?" "Hmmn?" I suggested bloodthirstily, running my forefinger in a line down the bird's tum. "An incision?" he said. "No. How are you going to put it back together if you don't take some notes on what size and shape it is before you take the skin off?" Oh. You might as well, he points out, try to reconstruct the musculature of a human leg from a discarded leotard. Oh. Callipers came out. How far is it from the eye to the beak? What's the distance across the shoulders? How far between wingtip and the tip of the tail? This is difficult. This is fascinating.

Think of all the things you enjoyed doing at school, combine them, and you have taxidermy. "Skinning out" your specimen is an operation with all the gory fun of dissection in biology, and all the fascination of a natural history lesson. You get to see what goes on inside a bird: where the joints articulate; how surprisingly long, under all those feathers, is its neck, and how tiny its body. The musculature on the bird's back is incredibly human-looking: from one angle it resembles that famous photo of Tracey Emin crouched up naked on her front. Plus, you get to wear latex gloves and imagine you are a customs officer. It's hard to resist the temptation to give the wrists a snap as you put them on.

Then there are the Craft, Design and Technology pleasures of finding it a log to sit on. "What's this log telling you?" asks Mike, as we scrutinise the woodpile, trying to imagine where a jay would stand, if it had to, on this or that log. The choice of log to sit on is, it turns out, a semi-mystical process. I can only see logs. Mike sees mounts: birds pointing this or that way; birds in this or that posture – rooting for something on a flat, mossy bit of wood, or alert, on a thin branch. Some logs are too good, too interesting, to squander on a jay. Will it be a wall-mount, or sit on a table? Can two logs be spliced with a stick to create an interesting arrangement?

It goes further. Wherever Mike goes, he is looking for interesting logs; interesting rocks. On a walk in the forest, he might stumble across a sodding great rock, and – if he can carry it – stagger back to the car with it. Walking with a brother taxidermist and another friend, once, he recalls over coffee, the friend caught up to find the two taxidermists transfixed, just rapturous, by an interesting rock formation at the side of a river. He has been known to rappel perilously over little cliff-faces with tubs of latex to cast their involutions. He is a mine of knowledge about how you cast things; ways, even, to arrange that the lichens and discolourations on a nice rock can be lifted and transmitted on the mould onto the surface of the artificial simulacrum you're casting.

There's sawing and drilling and screwing things to other things and – if you so choose – adding in fake moss, fibreglass rocks, painted dried grass, or what you will.

Then, of course, there are the pleasures of the sculptor. You have to build the jay a replacement body, as close as possible to the exact size and shape of the original whether by carving it from some sort of styrofoam block, or, as we did, by scrunching up wood wool (the stuff they used to use to pack crockery in in tea crates) to shape in your fist, and winding it round and round with thread.

Into this, in due course, wires slipped cunningly along the bones of wing and leg will be cinched, flexed and posed. Always, you're having to think of anatomy. "Where are you going to put the wing?" asks sensei. "There?" "Think about it," he says. "Does your shoulder come out halfway down your chest?" Oh.

But, before you are ready to bring the whole thing together, you have to wash and treat the skin – a series of small chemical miracles. When you've finished skinning the bird out, you are left with a pair of wings, flesh stripped from the bones, the legs and tail still attached to the skin of the torso, and, at the top of the neck, the bare skull, bird brains tapped neatly out with a sharp rap on the edge of the bin. You rinse the skin in cold water, then wash it with Fairy Liquid to get rid of any grease. Then rinse, rinse, wring and squeeze (surprisingly resiliant, birdskin)

– and what you are left with looks completely hopeless: a few scrags of soggy feather on a wet, pitifully bald pale yellow hide. But – clever bit, this – you roll the hide in a bucket of white spirit, causing the water to flee the hide and precipitate to the bottom of the bucket. Then you spend ten minutes rolling the hide in a barrel of Sepiolite (a sandy substance sold in pet shops as "chinchilla sand"), run a cold air blower over them and, miraculously, the feathers you thought were long gone spring back into resplendent, fluffy life. That's the chemistry lesson. Later, of course, comes sewing class…

Unlike other communities of hobbyists, there doesn't seem to be a stereotype for the aspiring taxidermist. One of the people on the course with me is a farmer's daughter, raised in Lincolnshire and now living in Somerset, who works as a gardener and has always dreamed of learning to stuff animals. Her husband sent her on this course as a present. The other is a guy who, having made an early career in bare-knuckle boxing and cage-fighting,[118] works as area manager for a firm providing doormen for nightclubs. He's had enough of confronting psychos and "horrible people" night in, night out, and hopes to move to the countryside with his wife and kids and aim towards, one day, making a modest living as a professional taxidermist.

Of an evening the three of us meet up for supper in the Crown, where two of us are staying. We feast on fish and chips and talk excitedly about the day's lessons, and about our lives and backgrounds. Taxidermy produces instant bonding.

We have, I reckon, some way to go before any of us will be able to stuff a jay in twenty-seven minutes. It has taken us three days. But we all got – with a little help and supervision – what sensei calls "a result". My jay, lodged at last on its branch, has mean little eyes, skinny legs and enormous feet. I decide to call it Margaret.

I meet my friend Marcus for a drink in a pub a little way from Leeds station on the way back on Sunday night. The flimsy plastic bag protecting Margaret's modesty has blown off in the wind outside. "What the fuck?" says Marcus, when I introduce

†118
He is extremely thoughtful and pleasant. He says he transforms into somebody very much scarier, for professional purposes, at the moment when, in his car on the way to work, he puts his tie on. He always makes a point of leaving the house, the wife and kids, before he puts the tie on. The stories he tells are truly hair-raising for the habitual non-combatant. I divine – from the pristine condition of his ears, nose and head – that Wayne is not a man who has lost very many of the fights he has been in.

him to Margaret. "You're standing in a pub. With a bird. On a stick. You're not going anywhere near the bar like that. I'll get them in."

Later, three and a half pints of cider mellower, I fumble through the ticket gates at the station with Margaret held aloft. The ticket-inspector's eyes follow me all the way onto the train. Margaret sits happily on the luggage rack for the journey down to London. I feel very proud.

What I do not realise until my mother comes to stay and nearly jumps out of her skin when she catches sight of Margaret looking beadily down from the wall of my study, is that jays have a special significance in my family. They appear on my grandfather's crest, and as a child, my mother adopted a whole brood of baby jays as pets. When my mum's older brother Roderick was ten years old, he loved nothing more dearly than to roam through the woods near his house with an air-rifle, slotting squirrels. One day, he shot a mother jay by accident. Seized with remorse, he shinned up a tree and lifted down a nestful of motherless baby birds. He brought them into the house, and the siblings hand-raised them, feeding them with pipettes. These creatures grew up very tame, and lived in the house – save for the occasional excursion to the fruit cage to eat all my grandmother's beloved raspberries.

"Each one met a grisly death," my mum recalls now. The one that particularly stuck in her mind was the jay that, hopping about the place, made the mistake of hopping onto a particularly shiny loo-seat, and took a fatal header into the toilet.

Is Margaret lifelike? Hard to say. All I know is that Henry – with the instincts of a furry bird-killer hardwired into her tiny brain – pays Margaret not the blindest bit of notice. She pounces, instead, on her fluffy, dusty old nylon mouse. Some you win.

LESBIA'S SPARROW.
OR LINNET. OR COCK.

ONE OF THE FIRST AND MOST IMPORTANT DEAD PETS IN LITERARY HISTORY LIVED IN THE FIRST CENTURY BEFORE CHRIST AND BELONGED TO "LESBIA", THE GIRLFRIEND AND MUSE OF THE ROMAN POET CATULLUS. WHAT DO WE KNOW ABOUT CATULLUS? VERY LITTLE. BORN QUINTUS (OR, ACCORDING TO A RIVAL SCHOOL OF THOUGHT, GAIUS) VALERIUS CATULLUS, HE LIVED FROM AROUND 84–54 BC. HIS DAD WAS A VERONA BIGWIG AND A PAL OF JULIUS CAESAR.

WHEN HE MOVED to Rome in about 62 BC, Catullus ran with the Novi Poetae: a small gang of posh wastrels who disdained epic in favour of brisk lyrics about drinking and shagging.

Catullus's brother died around 58 BC, and Catullus spent the following two years Working For The Man in Bithynia. He came back to Rome in 54 BC, and pegged out at 30 – a broken heart? He left 116 poems.

What do we know about "Lesbia"? Even less. She was married. Catullus called her "Lesbia" – an allusion to Lesbos, the island on which the Greek poet Sappho lived – to protect her reputation. Many scholars have identified Lesbia as Clodia Metella, a wealthy older woman who was, history records, no nun.

What do we know about the dead pet? Practically bugger all.

It was a sparrow, according to some translators, and a linnet according to others. What's the difference between a sparrow and a linnet? I do not know. The matter is further complicated by widespread scholarly conjecture that Catullus wasn't really talking about a bird at all, but his own penis during an attack of brewer's droop. I do know the difference between a sparrow and a penis – and so, judging by the rest of his surviving output, did Catullus.[119]

No matter. Whether it was a sparrow or a penis, we do know that Lesbia was very fond of it, and that she was extremely put out when it died. Catullus was moved to commemorate its passing in perky mock-grandiloquent hendecasyllables:

†119
The more I think about it, actually, the less I buy the whole penis thing. Catullus's pleasingly alliterative "pipiabat" – describing the happy chirping of the bird – doesn't sound like any noise a penis makes. In many years of searching, I still haven't found one that can even say "peanuts".

Lugete, o veneres Cupidinesque,
et quantum est hominum venustiorum:
passer mortuus est meae puellae,
passer, deliciae meae puellae ...

For those whose Latin is not fluent – or smarty-pantses who can't bear to see the letters 'u' and 'v' vsed in free uariation in a Latin text, when as any fvle kno they were a single vniform letter – there exist translations. Some are good, some are bad, but none are quite so strange as my favourite, below.

A bonkers Scotsman named G. S. Davies, in the year 1912, had the scholarship to understand the Latin original, the metrical fluency to put it into iambic tetrameters ... and the vision to reinvent the voice of an ancient Roman poet as that of the tam-o-shantered "see you Jimmy" character from *Russ Abbott's Madhouse*. Enjoy.

Weep, weep, ye Loves and Cupids all
And ilka Man o' decent feelin':
My lassie's lost her wee, wee bird,
An that's a loss ye'll ken, past healin'.

The lassie lo'ed him like her een:
The darling wee thin lo'ed the ither,
And knew and nestled to her breast,
As ony bairnie to her mither.

Her bosom was his dear, dear haunt —
So dear, he cared no long to leave it;
He'd nae but gang his ain sma' jaunt,
And flutter piping back bereavit.

The wee thing's gane the shadowy road
That's never travelled back by ony:
Out on ye, Shades! Ye're greedy aye
To grab at ought that's brave and bonny.

Puir, foolish, fondling, bonnie bird,
Ye little ken what wark ye're leavin':
Ye've gar'd my lassie's een grow red,
Those bonnie een grow red wi' grievin'.

CHAPTER 11

HENRY VI

OH JESUS. IT HAS HAPPENED AGAIN. I'M STARTING TO THINK THAT I'VE JINXED MY PARENTS. THIS BOOK. I AM IN THE OFFICE. IT IS COMING UP LUNCHTIME, AND I OPEN AN EMAIL FROM MY MOTHER. LAST NIGHT NONNIE DIED IN HER ARMS.

"HURRAH!" I SHOUT, aloud. "My mum's cat's dead!"

My colleague Alex gives me a bewildered and extremely disapproving look. "Material," I say. "For the book." As I say it, I feel deeply, momentarily, ashamed.

What is this book, this trade, doing to me? There is a moment in the memoirs of the former tabloid editor Piers Morgan where he remembers how he felt when he heard Concorde had crashed leaving the runway in Paris. He felt exhilarated. Clear the first ten pages of the newspaper! Who was on board? Models! Film-stars! Famous businessmen! *Dead!*

Then someone tells him that there were no celebrities aboard: the plane had been chartered by a group of anonymous German businessmen. He curses his luck aloud. And then he catches himself, and wonders whether his line of work might have desensitised him, a little.

We are all, in newspapers, a bit like that I think. I remember with real shame my reaction to watching the collapse of the twin towers of the World Trade Center, on the TV in the Canary Wharf branch of the Corney and Barrow pub. "Yess!" I cried inwardly, exhilarated with astonishment. "Look. My god. They're actually falling down. Look at that!"

It was spectacle. It was omigodwhataSTORY! It was news.

I did not know, as I watched it – a terrible disaster that played on the TV like the most exciting Bruckheimer movie you've ever seen – what it would feed into. I didn't think of how many people were dying. I didn't think of how many more people would die as it kicked forward into the convulsion of aggressive American interventions in the Middle East that are still going on.

I didn't know, either, that I was to spend most of the following year in New York, as a correspondent for my paper – that 9/11 was to be my big running story. And that I'd be interviewing the widows and the parents of those who died; talking to firemen and volunteers who spent days and days on end, exhausted, fishing unrecognisable bodies, and parts of bodies, out of the wreckage and their time off going to the funerals of their colleagues and friends.

That made it all kind of real.

I'm a bad human being. I don't think I'm alone in that.

†120
She is right.

This, anyway, was what my Mum wrote.

†121
Her proper epitaph is from Auden's meditation on the difference between humans and animals, 'Our Hunting Fathers':
"…his mature ambition
To think no thought
  but ours
To hunger, work illegally,
And be a Nonnie Mouse."

The bad news is I have a new dead pet this morning. Little Nonnington has gone the way of all fluff. Very, very sad. Put down in my arms. I assumed you were not yet up to stuffing cats so I have asked for her to be cremated.[120]

Lots of love and hugs xxx

Hey no Nonnie.

Nonnie. The lazy, fluffy white one who did nothing all day but lounge on my little sister's bed, that being the territory she had determined was her own. So called to go with her cat companion, Mouse: Nonnie Mouse.[121]

A few days ago, Nonnie had stopped eating and started behaving very erratically. She spent long hours camped out under my sister's bed. Then, one bitterly cold afternoon, Mum and Dad came back from a night away and found her out in the garden, sitting immobile in a temperature barely above zero, with the wind howling. She refused to move. They brought her inside to try to warm her up, and took her to the vet.

The vet could find nothing wrong, so they took her away again and tried antibiotics and anti-inflammatories. She didn't improve. When she went back, they took her into hospital. She spent the night in intensive care, on a glucose drip. They took blood tests. The results were not good.

Nonnie was suffering from a chronic renal disorder – polycystic kidneys – to which her fluffy breed is particularly vulnerable. There was a possibility, the vet thought, that she might be bleeding internally, too. She was a goner. And so, she died in my mother's arms.

We are down, Mum points out, from two dogs to one, four cats to one, eight chickens to two.

The fox, and all it represents, is still on the prowl.

IT IS THE first week of March 2005. Evening is closing in and it is very, very cold indeed. Snow is falling outside in tilting fat flakes, the sort that sometimes seem strangely to warm the air.

I have been worried about Henry, lately.

First, there was the dirty protest. It was the eve of an old friend's stag party and, knowing I was going to have to drive him down to Devon the following morning, I turned in early – well before midnight. It was about half past four in the morning when the cat woke me. She looked very pleased with herself. She had decided not to use her litter tray, but instead to take a pee on the duvet underneath which her owner was trying to sleep. I threw off the duvet and slept until dawn, fitfully, in the sliver of dry bed to one side. As soon as I could face it I got up, went downstairs, threw out the old litter in her tray (had she been making a point about its condition?) and filled it with a deep layer of pristine litter. Then I went back upstairs, stripped the cover from the duvet and the sheet from the bed, and bunged them in the washing machine on a boil wash. I returned upstairs. Henry was sitting on the bare mattress beside the bare duvet. She had used the five-minute window of opportunity to return for a second pass. Crowning the duvet were three generous, well-formed brown lumps of cat shit. She was purring.

The bitch.

I bundled the duvet into a binliner, and went on the stag weekend. The following week I trekked into the centre of town and went to John Lewis to buy a new duvet. Bewildering array of options. The best and softest was made of 100 per cent hand-plucked white Siberian goose-down. I went for something cheaper. Ha ha, I said to my brother. No point in buying the expensive one. She'll only piss on it again.

Two nights later, I came home from an evening in town to find she had. The new duvet was positively marinated in cat piss. I rubbed the cat's nose in it and slung her out of the bedroom, shutting the door. I threw off the duvet and slept until dawn, fitfully, in the sliver of dry bed to one side. All night, tirelessly, she alternated mewing pitifully and scrabbling at the door with her paws to be let in.

The following morning my brother seemed to find the whole thing funny. "All that mewing and scrabbling?" he said. "That's cat language. What she was trying to say was: 'Are you going to be much longer in there? You're reading, aren't you? Hurry up. I'm dying for a cack.'"

But I was worried. Were these erratic behaviours the symptoms of some deep psychological anxiety? Or of some neurological disorder? Or was the cat simply evil? I fretted. I started to watch her obsessively for signs of a brain tumour. I saw them everywhere.

I caught her, shortly afterwards, sitting on the end of the bed, quite upright, with her tongue poking out. She was staring through me into space, one centimetre of pink tongue protruding, very bright against her black furred face. She didn't seem to recognise me at all.

"Cat?" I said. "Your tongue is sticking out. Cats don't do that."

She did not react.

I extended an index finger and gently poked her tongue. The tongue stayed where it was. The cat looked very alarming; and very silly. Fifteen seconds later, she snapped out of it, shrugged, and trotted downstairs, restored to herself.

The vet recommended some special food and a course of little pink pills for the bedwetting problem. (You have to bend the cat's head gently back until it opens its mouth to protest, then pop the pill in. Henry swallowed hers without complaint. She hasn't, touch wood, gone on the duvet since.)

But I had barely been to the vet about the bedwetting before I started to notice something else. There was something wrong with her back legs. Once she had bounded pranksomely into the air at the slightest encouragement, and had been a dedicated clothes-horse mountaineer. Lately she was spending more and more time lying down. Sometimes, it seemed involuntary. She'd be walking towards me and one of her back legs would seem to wobble. She'd let it go and sit quickly down on that hip. At other times, she'd stop walking forwards and then take three or four quick, pained steps backwards, mewing as if in discomfort, and then sitting down. I caught her struggling to jump up onto a chair.

Wild conjectures animated me. Had she bruised her hip falling from the clothes horse while I was out? Or did she have a disease of the joints? Or a spinal injury of some sort? Or – still my favourite candidate – a brain tumour; something pressing down on some crucial nerve running to the back legs. I continued to watch her obsessively. I took her back to the vet, feeling embarrassed – feeling, in fact, like a feline hypochondriac. The vet was seeing a lot of me. He was greeting my cat by her name.

The appointments would go like this. The vet would smile indulgently. I would look very embarrassed. I would pour out my fears and – while Henry bounded happily around the vet's office as if she had the back legs of a feline marathon runner – feebly enumerate the symptoms that had given rise to them, each of them sounding more neurotic and imaginary than the one before the very moment they left my mouth.

"She's not doing it now," I'd mumble. "But it's sort of like that leg goes…" And I'd do a little wobbly dance with one of my own legs. "Or perhaps it was the other leg. I'm not sure…" I'd tell him about the sticky-out tongue incident, thinking I'd see a look of alarmed recognition on his face. He'd continue to smile indulgently. I'd feel like a complete idiot. I imagined thought bubbles above his head. Those thought bubbles had something to do with lonely, neurotic pensioners, and with a mild curiosity as to why the apparently sane young man in front of him was so anxious about his apparently healthy cat.

He'd examine the cat's back legs, making them click. Then he'd go next door and do the same thing to a normal cat. He'd explain that it was possible she had a luxating patella; a wobbly kneecap condition common in dogs but, according to him, never before seen in cats. Not a brain tumour, I'd say, then? Not an incurable spinal injury? He'd be reassuring, but not reassuring enough.

He'd suggest I bring Henry back in for an X-ray. Did I have medical insurance? Yes, I'd say. I do. His indulgent smile would – barely perceptibly – broaden.

Now Henry is sitting on the sash window in my study where I am typing, looking intently out of the window. She is sitting in that particular, attent posture cats sit in that makes them from the side like a furry black ampersand. I can tell from the faint up-and-down movements of her head that she is watching the snow fall. I imagine she can feel, at least against her nose, cold breathing off the glass pane.

Perched on her branch on the wall four feet away from Henry, Margaret jay stares glassily into the room, head turned away from the snow outside.

This is the first time, I think, that Henry has seen snow. She makes a funny, barely articulated clicking sound back in her throat. Then she makes a sound almost like a hamster's squeak. What is going on in her head?

Falling faintly through the universe and faintly falling . . .

Ampersand ampersand ampersand.

THE END

A MODEST ANTHOLOGY OF GRIEF

INSCRIPTION ON BOATSWAIN'S MEMORIAL

Near this spot
Are deposited the Remains of one
Who possessed Beauty without Vanity,
Strength without Insolence,
Courage without Ferocity,
And all the Virtues of Man without his Vices.
This Praise, which would be unmeaning Flattery
If inscribed over human ashes,
Is but a just tribute to the Memory of
BOATSWAIN, a DOG
Who was born at Newfoundland, May, 1803,
And died at Newstead, Nov 18th, 1808.

When some proud son of man returns to earth,
Unknown to glory, but upheld by birth,
The sculptor's art exhausts the pomp of woe,
And storied urns record who rest below:
When all is done, upon the tomb is seen,
Not what he was, but what he should have been:
But the poor dog, in life the firmest friend,
The first to welcome, foremost to defend,
Whose honest heart is still his master's own,
Who labours, fights, lives, breathes for him alone,
Unhonour'd falls, unnoticed all his worth,
Denied in heaven the soul he held on earth:
While man, vain insect! hopes to be forgiven,
And claims himself a sole exclusive heaven.
Oh man! thou feeble tenant of an hour,
Debased by slavery, or corrupt by power,
Who knows thee well must quit thee with disgust,
Degraded mass of animated dust!
Thy love is lust, thy friendship all a cheat,
Thy smiles hypocrisy, thy words deceit!
By nature vile, ennobled but by name,
Each kindred brute might bid thee blush for shame.
Ye! who perchance behold this simple urn,
Pass on – it honours none you wish to mourn:
To mark a friend's remains these stones arise;
I never knew but one, – and here he lies.

LORD BYRON
Newstead Abbey, November 30, 1808

BOUNCE TO FOP

An heroick epistle from a dog at Twickenham to a dog at court

To thee, sweet Fop, these Lines I send,
Who, tho' no Spaniel, am a Friend.
Tho, once my Tail in wanton play,
Now frisking this, and then that way,
Chanc'd, with a Touch of just the Tip,
To hurt your Lady-lap-dog-ship;
Yet thence to think I'd bite your Head off!
Sure Bounce is one you never read of.

FOP! you can dance, and make a Leg,
Can fetch and carry, cringe and beg,
And (what's the Top of all your Tricks)
Can stoop to pick up Strings and Sticks,
We Country Dogs love nobler Sport,
And scorn the Pranks of Dogs at Court.
Fye, naughty Fop! where e'er you come
To f---t and p---ss about the Room,
To lay your Head in every Lap,
And, when they think not of you – snap!
The worst that Envy, or that Spite
E'er said of me, is, I can bite:
That sturdy Vagrants, Rogues in Rags,
Who poke at me, can make no Brags;
And that to towze such Things as flutter,
To honest Bounce is Bread and Butter.

While you, and every courtly Fop,
Fawn on the Devil for a Chop,

217

I've the Humanity to hate
A Butcher, tho' he brings me Meat;
And let me tell you, have a Nose,
(Whatever stinking Fops suppose)
That under Cloth of Gold or Tissue,
Can smell a Plaister, or an Issue.

Your pilf'ring Lord, with simple Pride,
May wear a Pick-lock at his Side;
My Master wants no Key of State,
For Bounce can keep his House and Gate.

When all such Dogs have had their Days,
As knavish Pams, and fawning Trays;
When pamper'd Cupids, bestly Veni's,
And motly, squinting Harvequini's,
Shall lick no more their Lady's Br---,
But die of Looseness, Claps, or Itch;
Fair Thames from either ecchoing Shoare
Shall hear, and dread my manly Roar.

See Bounce, like Berecynthia, crown'd
With thund'ring Offspring all around,
Beneath, beside me, and a top,
A hundred Sons! and not one Fop.

Before my Children set your Beef,
Not one true Bounce will be a Thief;
Not one without Permission feed,
(Tho' some of F---'s hungry Breed)
But whatsoe'er the Father's Race,
From me they suck a little Grace.
While your fine Whelps learn all to steal,
Bred up by Hand and Chick and Veal.

My Eldest-born resides not far,
Where shines great Strafford's glittering Star:
My second (Child of Fortune!) waits
At Burlington's Palladian Gates:
A third majestically stalks
(Happiest of Dogs!) in Cobham's Walks:
One ushers Friends to Bathurst's Door;
One fawns, at Oxford's, on the Poor.

Nobles, who Arms or Arts adorn,
Wait for my Infants yet unborn.
None but a Peer of Wit and Grace,
Can hope a Puppy of my Race.

And O! wou'd Fate the Bliss decree
To mine (a Bliss too great for me)
That two, my tallest Sons, might grace
Attending each with stately Pace,
Iulus' Side, as erst Evander's,
To keep off Flatt'rers, Spies, and Panders,
To let no noble Slave come near,
And scare Lord Fannys from his Ear:
Then might a Royal Youth, and true,
Enjoy at least a Friend — or two:
A Treasure, which, of Royal kind,
Few but Himself deserve to find.

Then Bounce ('tis all that Bounce can crave)
Shall wag her Tail within the Grave.

And tho' no Doctors, Whig, or Tory ones,
Except the Sect of Pythagoreans,
Have Immortality assign'd
To any Beast, but Dryden's Hind:

Yet Master Pope, whom Truth and Sense
Shall call their Friend some Ages hence,
Tho' now on loftier Themes he sings
Than to bestow a Word on Kings,
Has sworn by Sticks (the Poet's Oath,
And Dread of Dogs and Poets both)
Man and his Works he'll soon renounce,
And roar in Numbers worthy Bounce.

ALEXANDER POPE (1736)

DEATH OF A GOLDFISH

LAST WEEK MY pet goldfish was found floating upright in her tank. Marigold had shown no sign of illness the night before and ate her chopped mosquito larvae without complaint. No noise escaped from the kitchen where she slept and no ripple was left on the surface of the water to mark any death struggle. She was a blameless fish and died as she had lived, giving a minimum of trouble.

America, I have been told by a friend, is stuffed with books called How To Cope With Your Grief Reactions and titles in a similar vein. The stages of grief are carefully listed, with hints about how to progress through them in an approved and healthy way: first, bereavement is met by a refusal to accept it; then by a bitter wish that it had not happened; then extravagant sorrow and self-pity, possibly touched with guilt. Finally, there comes a settled acceptance, when the bereaved person is ready to return to society free of the emotional instability which might, uncorrected, lead him to antisocial attitudes and behaviour.

I find myself stuck in the guilt stage. We discussed raising a monument over Marigold's grave, but this seemed an unworthy way of coping with our grief reactions. Can storied urn or animated bust back to its mansion call the fleeting breath? Instead, we buried her with minimum fuss – no useless coffin enclosed

her breast – but this, too, seemed somehow rat-like and furtive. She lay like a warrior taking her rest with her golden scales around her, but her dignity rebuked us. There was no explicit reproach in her eye as we steadfastly gazed on the face that was dead and we bitterly thought of the morrow. The guilt was in our own hearts.

For more than six years that goldfish had lived with us and shared our fortunes, ever since my wife had won her by throwing hoops at the Mop Fair in Marlborough, Wiltshire. In all that time I had never introduced Marigold to another goldfish. Probably, in the course of the six and a half years she spent swimming backwards and forwards in her tank, she lost any memory that other fishes existed. It is true that she always had plenty to eat and was kept cold and wet in well-ventilated conditions. Her water was changed and her tank decorated with semi-precious stones – amethystine, quartz, fool's gold, agate and chalcedony. But she never knew the meaning of companionship, laughter and the love of friends – or, indeed, the pleasures of sex.

Sex. Beyond one cursory glance at where I imagined her private parts would be if she had any (she did not appear to) I never made any serious attempt to discover whether Marigold was a male or a female goldfish. I never spared a thought about how she coped with her libido, if she had any. Quite possibly, she never learned about such things, never associated any strange bodily urges which visited her with anything but indigestion. Do female goldfish have monthly troubles? Do lonely male goldfish experience nocturnal emissions and if so, how do they distinguish wet dreams from any other type of dreams in the encircling wetness?

Stricken by remorse after her death, I have taken to reading all I can find in the house on the subject of goldfish. It would have been quite easy, I learn, to decide whether she was male or female. Spawning occurs in spring and as the season approaches the female's colours grow brighter while the male may develop pin-head-sized tubercles (or shag-spots) on his gills.

This only makes me feel guiltier. The thought of Marigold blushing brightly in her prettiest colours every spring (or growing fine, manly tubercles on his gills, as the case might be) strikes me as unbearably poignant in light of the fact that nobody ever noticed:

Full many a flower is born to blush unseen
And waste its sweetness on the desert air.

I know, I know. It is all very beautiful and poetic. But I do feel we might have looked.

It may be possible to live a full and satisfactory life without any experience of sex. Many monks and nuns achieve it and quite a few secular priests, I dare say, but they at least have the consolation that they are storing up riches in Heaven. A hairy young monk at the establishment where I received my education (it did not prepare me to look after goldfishes properly) used to invite his Religious Instruction class to think of Heaven as a perpetual experience of sexual intercourse. Being a callow fifteen-year-old I took him at his word. Then I thought I understood why that pungent monk was so unswerving in his fidelity to the vows of poverty, chastity and obedience. It is only as I get older that I am less tempted by the thought of perpetual intercourse, more by Sydney Smith's notion of eating *pâté de foie gras* to the sound of trumpets. Perhaps this preference is something to do with the air at Combe Florey, where Sydney Smith lived 135 years before me.

But even if Combe Florey water has the same properties, there is no reason to suppose that goldfish like *pâté de foie gras* and every reason to think they detest the sound of trumpets. A thoughtless guest once put Marigold on an organ in my house and then played *Faith of Our Fathers* simultaneously on the dulcet, diaposon, sub-bass and vox humana. Her resulting agitation marked only the second dramatic event in her life, the first being when the cat decided to try his luck at gaff-hook fishing about a year before. On that occasion – how the guilty memories torment me now – I tended to take the cat's side. What cat's averse to fish, I argued, and what pleasures could possibly await Marigold in the years ahead which would compare to the cat's pleasure in eating her?

Next I began to reflect that Marigold was almost certainly so stupid that she never even noticed when she died, like certain chickens I have seen senselessly trying to fly after their heads have been cut off. If an animal is too stupid even to notice whether is is alive or dead there can be no sense in shedding intelligent human tears for it. Why, for that matter, should one goldfish occupy so much valuable space in a serious weekly magazine when hundreds of thousands of golfish die every week unwept, unhonoured and unsung?

But then I think of the tender sight of her little corpse. It would have been an act of unspeakable callousness to recycle that innocent thing into cat-protein. Like the Tomb of the Unknown Soldier, there must always be privileged exceptions from which everyone else can draw comfort and inspiration. Now I feel I have passed through all the stages of my grief reaction and am ready to return to normal society.

AUBERON WAUGH
From the *New Statesman*, 7th February 1975

DINAH IN HEAVEN

She did not know that she was dead,
But, when the pang was o'er,
Sat down to wait her Master's tread
Upon the Golden Floor,

With ears full-cock and anxious eye
Impatiently resigned;
But ignorant that Paradise
Did not admit her kind.

Persons with Haloes, Harps, and Wings
Assembled and reproved;
Or talked to her of Heavenly things,
But Dinah never moved.

There was one step along the Stair
That led to Heaven's Gate;
And, till she heard it, her affair
Was – she explained – to wait.

And she explained with flattened ear,
Bared lip and milky tooth —
Storming against Ithuriel's Spear
That only proved her truth!

Sudden — far down the Bridge of Ghosts
That anxious spirits clomb —
She caught that step in all the hosts,
And knew that he had come.

She left them wondering what to do,
But not a doubt had she.
Swifter than her own squeal she flew
Across the Glassy Sea;

Flushing the Cherubs every where,
And skidding as she ran,
She refuged under Peter's Chair
And waited for her man.

...

There spoke a Spirit out of the press,
Said: — "Have you any here
That saved a fool from drunkenness,
And a coward from his fear?

"That turned a soul from dark to day
When other help was vain;
That snatched it from Wanhope and made
A cur a man again?"

"Enter and look," said Peter then,
And set The Gate ajar.
"If I know aught of women and men
I trow she is not far."

"Neither by virtue, speech nor art
Nor hope of grace to win;
But godless innocence of heart
That never heard of sin:

"Neither by beauty nor belief
Nor white example shown.
Something a wanton – more a thief –
But – most of all – mine own."

"Enter and look," said Peter then,
"And send you well to speed;
But, for all that I know of women and men
Your riddle is hard to read."

Then flew Dinah from under the Chair,
Into his arms she flew –
And licked his face from chin to hair
And Peter passed them through!

RUDYARD KIPLING
From *Limits and Renewals* (1932)

THE RAINBOW BRIDGE

JUST THIS SIDE of heaven is a place called Rainbow Bridge.

When an animal dies that has been especially close to someone here, that pet goes to Rainbow Bridge.

There are meadows and hills for all of our special friends so they can run and play together.

There is plenty of food, water and sunshine, and our friends are warm and comfortable.

All the animals who had been ill and old are restored to health and vigor; those who were hurt or maimed are made whole and strong again, just as we remember them in our dreams of days and times gone by.

The animals are happy and content, except for one small thing; they each miss someone very special to them, who had to be left behind.

They all run and play together, but the day comes when one suddenly stops and looks into the distance. His bright eyes are intent; his eager body quivers. Suddenly he begins to run from the group, flying over the green grass, his legs carrying him faster and faster.

You have been spotted, and when you and your special friend finally meet, you cling together in joyous reunion, never to be parted again. The happy kisses rain upon your face; your hands again caress the beloved head, and you look once more into the trusting eyes of your pet, so long gone from your life but never absent from your heart.

Then you cross Rainbow Bridge together ...

ANON

ODE ON THE DEATH OF A FAVOURITE CAT, DROWNED IN A TUB OF GOLD-FISHES

'Twas on a lofty vase's side,
Where China's gayest art had dyed
The azure flowers that blow;
Demurest of the tabby kind,
The pensive Selima reclined,
Gazed on the lake below.

Her conscious tail her joy declared,
The fair round face, the snowy beard,

The velvet of her paws,
Her coat, that with the turtle vies,
Her ears of jet and emerald eyes,
She saw, and purred applause.

Still had she gazed but 'midst the tide
Two angel forms were seen to glide,
The Genii of the stream:
Their scaly armour's Tyrian hue
Through richest purple to the view
Betrayed a golden gleam.

The hapless nymph with wonder saw:
A whisker first and then a claw,
With many an ardent wish,
She stretched in vain to reach the prize.
What female heart can gold despise?
What cat's averse to fish?

Presumptuous maid! with looks intent
Again she stretched, again she bent,
Nor knew the gulf between.
(Malignant Fate sat by, and smiled)
The slippery verge her feet beguiled,
She tumbled headlong in.

Eight times emerging from the flood
She mewed to every wat'ry god,
Some speedy aid to send.
No dolphin came, no Nereid stirred:
Nor cruel Tom, nor Susan heard,
A favourite has no friend!

From hence, ye beauties, undeceived,
Know, one false step is ne'er retrieved,

And be with caution bold.
Not all that tempts your wandering eyes
And heedless hearts is lawful prize;
Nor all that glisters, gold.

THOMAS GRAY (1747)

ELEGY ON THE DEATH OF BINGO, OUR TRENCH DOG

Weep, weep, ye dwellers in the delved earth,
Ah, weep, ye watchers by the dismal shore
Of No Man's Land, for Bingo is no more;
He is no more, and well we knew his worth,
For whom on bully beefless days were kept
Rare bones by each according to his means,
And while the Quartermaster-Sergeant slept,
The elusive pork was rescued from the beans.
He is no more, and impudently brave
The loathly rats sit grinning on his grave.

Him mourn the grimy cooks and bombers ten,
The sentinels in lonely posts forlorn,
The fierce patrols with hands and tunics torn,
The furtive band of sanitary men.
The murmuring sound of grief along the length
Of traversed trench the startled Hun could hear;
The Captain, as he struck him off the strength,
Let fall a sad and solitary tear;
'Tis even said a batman passing by
Had seen the Sergeant-Major wipe his eye.

The fearful fervour of the feline chase
He never knew, poor dog, he never knew;
Content with optimistic zeal to woo
Reluctant rodents in this murky place,
He never played with children on clean grass
Nor dozed at ease beside the flowing embers,
Nor watched with hopeful eye the tea-cakes pass,
Nor smelt the heather smell of Scotch Septembers
For he was born amid a world at war
Although unrecking what we struggled for.

Yet who shall say that Bingo was unblest
Though all his Sprattless life was passed beneath
The roar of mortars and the whistling breath
Of grim nocturnal heavies going West?
Unmoved he heard the evening hymn of hate,
Unmoved would gaze into his master's eyes,
For all the sorrows men for men create
In search of happiness, wise dogs despise.
Finding ecstatic joy in every rag
And every smile of friendship worth a wag.

MAJOR E DE STEIN

FLUSH, OR FAUNUS

You see this dog. It was but yesterday
I mused forgetful of his presence here
Till thought on thought drew downward tear on tear;
When from the pillow, where wet-cheeked I lay,
A head as hairy as Faunus, thrust its way

Right sudden against my face, – two golden clear
Large eyes astonished mine, – a drooping ear
Did flap me on either cheek, to dry the spray!
I started first, as some Arcadian,
Amazed by goatly God in twilight grove:
But as my bearded vision closelier ran
My tears off, I knew Flush, and rose above
Surprise and sadness; thanking the true PAN,
Who, by low creatures, leads to heights of love.

ELIZABETH BARRETT-BROWNING

IF GOD HAD WANTED A GERBIL

If God had wanted a gerbil
He should have saved up like me
And gone to the shop and bought one
That's doing things properly.

If God had wanted a gerbil
Then I think it awfully mean
To have made me drop mine and kill it
When I fed it and kept it so clean.

If God had wanted a gerbil
He should have taken its cage and straw
No, I won't have another gerbil
Just in case God wants some more.

ANON

From THE LAST WILL AND TESTAMENT OF SILVERDENE EMBLEM O'NEILL

"I have little in the way of material things to leave. Dogs are wiser than men. They do not set great store upon things. They do not waste their days hoarding property. They do not ruin their sleep worrying about how to keep the objects they have, and to obtain the objects they have not. There is nothing of value I have to bequeath except my love and my faith . . . if I should list all those who have loved me it would force my Master to write a book. Perhaps it is vain of me to boast when I am so near death, which returns all beasts and vanities to dust, but I have always been an extremely lovable dog.

"I ask my Master and Mistress to remember me always, but not to grieve for me too long. It is painful for me to think that even in death I should cause them pain. Let them remember that while no dog has ever had a happier life (and this I owe to their love and care for me) now that I have grown blind and deaf and lame . . . my pride has sunk to a sick, bewildered humiliation. I feel life is taunting me with having over lingered my welcome. It is time I said good-bye, before I become too sick a burden on myself and on those who love me. It will be sorrow to leave them, but not sorrow to die. Dogs do not fear death as men do. We accept it as part of life, not as something alien and terrible which destroys life. What may come after death, who knows? I would like to believe with those of my fellow Dalmatians who are devout Mohammedans, that there is a Paradise where one is always young and full-bladdered; where all the day one dillies and dallies with an amorous multitude of houris . . .

"I am afraid this is too much for even such a good dog as I am to expect. But peace, at least, is certain. Peace and long rest for weary old heart and head and limbs, an eternal sleep in the earth I have loved so well. Perhaps, after all, this is best."

EUGENE O'NEILL December 17th, 1932

PET SEMATARY

*(The prohibitive expense of obtaining permission to reproduce
the lyrics of this moving song forces me to reimagine them.)*

From under the shelter of rotten planks,
Age-old trolls, and the leaders of armed militias,
Emerge from the earth, completely silent,
The pong of death is completely horrible,
It's dark, and it's extremely parky out,
No one minds, or even has a clue what's going on.

I'd rather not be buried in an animal graveyard,
I'd on the whole rather stay dead,
I'd rather not be buried in an animal graveyard,
I'd on the whole rather stay dead,

Tag along with Victor to the sanctuary.
I'm not having a nightmare, and I can't run away even
    though I'd like to.
Flat teeth and sharp teeth. The clunk of skeletons.
Ghosts are complaining among the graves.
And at night-time, when the moon is shining,
Somebody's blubbing. This is a rum business.

I'd rather not be buried in an animal graveyard,
I'd on the whole rather stay dead,
I'd rather not be buried in an animal graveyard,
I'd on the whole rather stay dead,

There's a full moon. It isn't windy any more.
I'm still cold, though.
Victor is decomposing, but he seems cheerful.

Skeletons boogie. Drat.
At night-time, when the foxes are shouting,
Listen carefully and you can hear me yell.

I'd rather not be buried in an animal graveyard,
I'd on the whole rather stay dead,
I'd rather not be buried in an animal graveyard,
I'd on the whole rather stay dead.

THE RAMONES

THE CANDLE CEREMONY

WE GATHER TOGETHER TO HONOR AND REMEMBER OUR PETS

TONIGHT, MONDAY, WE join hands, hearts and souls across the land as one large extended family to pray for our sick and dying pets and to pay tribute to our furbabies who have gone ahead to Rainbow Bridge.

Someday, we will meet them again, with hugs, tears and kisses, as we walk together, in eternity, to our new home.

Until that blessed day, we honor these precious souls and remember them with the warm glow of flickering candles, sending a message of love, light and healing, and the faith to believe in miracles.

PRAYER

God, Creator of all living things, we ask that as we light our candles, the healing warmth of love will flow into the brokenhearted who are tending their ailing pets. Give to them Your strength and comfort.

We also pray that the soft glow of light will part the clouds of grief and sorrow to surround our furbabies at the Bridge.

May excitement *reign supreme* as wagging tails, ecstatic purrs and flapping feathers feel our gentle touch once again.

May they know the gratitude we hold in our hearts for their faithfulness and gift of unconditional love as they are forever remembered.

We are temporarily separated for only a short while.

The silver cord that connects us through time and space can never be broken.

Amen.

FIRST CANDLE: *Personal Furbaby*

(Anything you wish to say)

I will not look back for there is sorrow.

I will not look for today for there is longing.

I will look forward for there is our tomorrow.

SECOND CANDLE: *Furbabies Of Friends And Family*

(Read the names of those who are ill or have gone on before us as a tribute to them and their loving parents.)

As we all meet here, our Bridgekids will be meeting all newcomers, easing their way.

THIRD CANDLE: *For Acknowledgment And Peace*

In honor of all the homeless, forgotten, abandoned, abused animals.

For the nameless furchildren who gave their lives for others, for research and as a result of humankind's inhumanity.

May the Higher Powers that be forgive the cruelty.

We light this candle for them.

As our lights shine brightly through the galaxy, may the angels smile upon us, and know that for a brief moment, we have put aside worldly differences to bond as one.

CLOSING

I have sent you on a journey to a land free from pain, not because I did not love you, but because I loved you too much to force you to stay.

(Moment of Silence)

"Blessed are they that mourn, for they will be comforted."
Love, light and healing to all. *Amen*.

> The candles being lit tonight;
> Cast a soft and welcome flame.
> And draw our loved ones to the light,
> As we call to them by name.
> Imagine spirits taking flight,
> For a moment our souls entwine.
> Say not Good Night, but in some
> Brighter Time
> Bid them all —
> Good Morning.

THE FURRY
& THE
FEATHERED
& THE FALLEN

IN 1943 MARIA DICKIN, the founder of the veterinary charity PDSA (People's Dispensary for Sick Animals), inaugurated the world's first military decoration for animal valour on the battlefield: the Dickin Medal, known as "the animals' VC".

Suspended from a green, brown and blue ribbon, the Dickin Medal is a large bronze disc inscribed with a laurel wreath and the mottoes "For Gallantry" and "We Also Serve".

It would not comfortably fit on a pigeon.

ITS FIRST WINNER was Winkie the Pigeon.

Winkie, two, from Dundee, Scotland, was decorated for having saved the entire crew of a Beaufort bomber from a watery grave. It was a chilly evening in February, 1942, and the bomber had been forced to ditch in the North Sea. Escaping from her cage when the plane broke up, plucky Winkie set off for home. With only two hours of daylight left, Winkie flew like the wind.

When she arrived at her loft, her perspicacious owner George Ross was able to deduce from the oil on the exhausted pigeon's feathers that something was wrong. A call to the Royal Homing Pigeon Service confirmed his suspicions.

He calculated she must have flown somewhere between 120 and 140 miles through the night. A search party – which had been combing an area of the Norwegian coast miles from the actual crash site – was hastily redeployed. The crew was found, bobbing in a dinghy, just where Winkie had predicted. All safe.

They showed their gratitude by giving a banquet in Winkie's honour. Winkie sat at the table. Winkie was subsequently stuffed, and sits alongside her medal in the McManus Museum in Dundee.

BETWEEN 1943 AND 1949, the Dickin Medal was awarded 54 times: to 32 pigeons, 18 dogs, 3 horses and a cat.

Though the pigeons, arguably, had the sharp end of the Second World War – the average carrier pigeon had only a one in eight chance of ever seeing home again – Mary of Exeter, and G I Joe served with particular distinction. Brave British pigeon Mary served for five years of the Second World War, during which time she was shot at, savaged by hawks, and brought down in a bombing raid. G I Joe, who served with the US Army Signal Corps, had a role peculiarly appropriate to his country's military history. It was only by making a 20-mile flight in 20 minutes and delivering an urgent message that he was able to prevent 100 allied soldiers from being bombed by their own planes.

Many of the dogs were cited for their perseverance in rescuing human air-raid victims from the rubble of the Blitz or from burning buildings. A special nod must

go to Beauty, a wire-haired terrier whose compassion as a rescue dog extended even to a traditional foe. She risked life and limb to rescue a cat trapped beneath a pile of rubble.

Two anti-terrorist boxer dogs, Punch and Judy, joined the roll of honour in 1946: "These dogs saved the lives of two British officers in Israel by attacking an armed terrorist who was stealing upon them unawares and thus warning them of their danger. Punch sustained four bullet wounds and Judy a long graze down her back."

Top for derring-do was Rob, a collie who stopped working as a sheepdog in order to join the SAS. He made over twenty parachute drops behind enemy lines in North Africa and Italy and, according to the historians of the Dickin Medal, many of the operations in which he was involved remain classified.

Oh. The cat. Not traditionally very disciplined, cats. Tend to bail out on you in times of trouble. Not so Simon, the "Captain's cat" aboard HMS *Amethyst*. In April 1949, en route to Nanking, Chinese Communist forces attacked *Amethyst* as she made her way up the Yangtse River. Several sailors, including the captain, were killed, and the crippled ship spent 100 days trapped in the river. So impressed was Commander Kerrans with Simon's spunk in the face of the enemy, and his determination to deter rats from eating the surviving crew, that as the ship finally fled for home, he cabled ahead to Blighty to recommend the moggy for a medal.

IN 2000, THE Dickin Medal was revived and awarded posthumously to Gander, a Newfoundland dog that saved the lives of Canadian infantrymen during the battle of Lye Mun on Hong Kong Island in December 1941. The mascot of the Royal Rifles of Canada, one of the regiments sent to defend Hong Kong against the Japanese invasion, Gander, who had been awarded the honorary rank of Sergeant, fell at Lye Mun when he took a grenade intended for a group of wounded riflemen.

Since then, five further Dickin medals have been awarded. During the conflict in Bosnia-Herzegovina, a German shepherd called Sam showed exceptional bravery – first apprehending a fleeing gunman and later holding off a rioting crowd outside

a compound in Drvar where a number of Bosnian Serbs had taken shelter.

Salty and Roselle, two guide dogs who led their owners down more than 70 floors to escape the burning World Trade Center, were officially recognised after September 11th; as was Appollo, a German shepherd chosen by ballot as a representative of the 300 search and rescue dogs who served in the rubble of the Twin Towers.

The most recent Dickin dedicatee was Buster, a six-year-old springer spaniel who served as a bomb dog in Southern Iraq. In early 2003, he unearthed a stash of insurgent goodies in the city of Safwan including "AK47 assault rifles, a pistol, six primed grenades, grenade fuses, ammunition in magazines, loose ammunition and large quantities of cash, drugs and propaganda material". At a ceremony at the Imperial War Museum in London in December 2003, Buster was presented with his medal by Princess Alexandra. The ceremony was conducted in the presence of Miss Jenny Seagrove.

THE 60 WINNERS of the Dickin Medal – both living and dead; both named and, in the case of so many of those brave pigeons, nameless – were further honoured when, in November 2004, Princess Anne unveiled a permanent £1 million Portland stone memorial to all the animals who have fallen in man's wars in Brook Gate, Park Lane, London.

The curved bas-relief, by the sculptor David Backhouse, includes bronze images of all the animals who served; from dogs and horses and pigeons to bears, monkeys, mules, and – looking dignified in its eternal rest – the glow-worm.

It bears the same legend as the Dickin medal: "For Gallantry ... We Also Serve".

Speaking at the time, Jilly Cooper put it better than I ever could have. "Countless millions of innocent animals served and died terrible deaths beside our British and Commonwealth armies during the 20th Century," she said. "They had no idea why they had been drawn into our conflicts and acted solely out of loyalty and love."

At the unveiling ceremony, a flock of racing pigeons was released. Unlike those they were there to remember, they all came safely home.